READING RESEARCH

Advances in Theory and Practice

Volume 6

READING RESEARCH

Advances in Theory and Practice

Volume 6

MEREDYTH DANEMAN

Erindale College
University of Toronto
Mississauga, Ontario, Canada

G. E. MACKINNON
T. GARY WALLER

Department of Psychology
Faculty of Arts
University of Waterloo
Waterloo, Ontario, Canada

ACADEMIC PRESS, INC.
Harcourt Brace Jovanovich, Publishers

San Diego   New York   Berkeley   Boston
London   Sydney   Tokyo   Toronto

ACADEMIC PRESS, INC.
1250 Sixth Avenue
San Diego, California 92101

United Kingdom Edition published by
ACADEMIC PRESS INC. (LONDON) LTD.
24-28 Oval Road, London NW1 7DX

ISBN   0-12-572306-7   (alk. paper)

ISSN   0191-0914
This publication is not a periodical and is not
subject to copying under CONTU guidelines.

PRINTED IN THE UNITED STATES OF AMERICA
88 89 90 91   9 8 7 6 5 4 3 2 1

CONTENTS

INTRODUCTION

Meredyth Daneman

ON-LINE COMPREHENSION PROCESSES
AND EYE MOVEMENTS DURING READING
Keith Rayner and Susan A. Duffy

COMPONENT PROCESSES IN READING COMPREHENSION
Karl Haberlandt

VERBAL EFFICIENCY IN READING ABILITY
Charles A. Perfetti

WORD KNOWLEDGE AND READING SKILL
Meredyth Daneman

INFERENCES IN READING COMPREHENSION
Murray Singer

CONTRIBUTORS

Numbers in parentheses indicate the pages on which the authors' contributions begin.

MEREDYTH DANEMAN (1, 145), *Erindale College, University of Toronto, Mississauga, Ontario L51 1C6, Canada*

SUSAN A. DUFFY (13), *Department of Psychology, Amherst College, Amherst, Massachusetts 01002*

KARL HABERLANDT (67), *Department of Psychology, Trinity College, Hartford, Connecticut 06106*

CHARLES A. PERFETTI (109), *Learning Research and Development Center, University of Pittsburgh, Pittsburgh, Pennsylvania 15260*

KEITH RAYNER (13), *Department of Psychology, University of Massachusetts, Amherst, Massachusetts 01003*

MURRAY SINGER (177), *Department of Psychology, University of Manitoba, Winnipeg, Manitoba R3T 2N2, Canada*

PREFACE

The articles in the present volume focus on reading comprehension. Our intent with this volume is not to provide extensive, broad coverage of the field of reading comprehension; rather, it is to provide in depth a sample of current theoretical and methodological trends in a continually expanding field. Our hope is that the volume will be useful to those actively engaged in research on reading as well as to consumers of reading research.

The book begins with a chapter by Daneman, which provides an overview and critical commentary on the issues addressed in the rest of the book. Chapters then follow by Rayner and Duffy and by Haberlandt, who attempt to study text comprehension on-line as it occurs. These researchers provide data that are critical for the construction of realistic models of reading comprehension. Individual differences in reading comprehension are the focus of the next two chapters by Perfetti and by Daneman. Perfetti accounts for individual differences using Verbal Efficiency Theory, and Daneman discusses the long recognized but poorly understood relationship between vocabulary size and reading ability. The final chapter by Singer reviews critically, in light of current models of text comprehension, what is known about the higher level inferential processes that occur in reading.

M. DANEMAN
T. GARY WALLER
G. E. MACKINNON

INTRODUCTION

MEREDYTH DANEMAN

Erindale College
University of Toronto
Mississaugua, Ontario L5L 1C6, Canada

Usually, our use of the word *read* implies comprehension. It would be redundant if not outright rude to say to a friend, "Here's a book you might like to read and comprehend." Of course, if she replied "No thanks. I've been trying to read that book for weeks already but I haven't understood a single word of it yet," her use of the word *read* would be quite acceptable even though, in this case, it clearly does not imply comprehension. The word *read,* like any other word in the language, can take on different meanings according to the context in which it is used. What this short exchange serves to illustrate, though, is that there are two conceptually distinct but highly interrelated aspects to reading: (1) decoding the visual print and (2) comprehending the message it represents. These two aspects are behaviorally distinguishable, too; we probably all know of children who can produce errorless recitations of long strings of words from print and yet know nothing about what any of the words mean. Some researchers and authors (e.g., Crowder, 1982) have even tried to keep comprehension outside of the scope of reading research on the grounds that the psychology of reading has no particular claim on comprehension because the mechanisms underlying reading comprehension are identical to those underlying oral language comprehension. Empirical justification for this position comes from finding that reading comprehension ability and listening comprehension ability are highly correlated, particularly in adult populations (Daneman & Carpenter, 1980; Jackson & McClelland, 1979; Palmer, MacLeod, Hunt & Davidson, 1985; Sticht & James, 1984). Nonetheless, nobody would disagree that comprehension is the single most important goal of reading, and ensuring that students can comprehend a written message once they have decoded it is the single most important goal for reading instructors. If tests of language comprehension predict reading ability better than do tests of

1

visual word processing (Jackson & McClelland, 1979; Palmer *et al.*, 1985),
then reading instruction programs should be geared toward developing
general language comprehension skills and not simply word decoding
ones. In other words, to preclude comprehension from a study of reading
would be to invite theories of reading that are incomplete and of no
practical relevance.

Theoretical and empirical interest in reading comprehension is a rather
recent phenomenon; in fact, there was little systematic research on reading comprehension before the 1960s, with books of the time not even
mentioning the phrase "reading comprehension," let alone giving it much
treatment (e.g., Anderson & Dearborn, 1952; Woodworth, 1938). In contrast, topics such as word recognition and eye movements had whole
chapters devoted to them; after all, they had been systematically investigated since the inception of experimental psychology, either as vehicles
for studying traditional psychological processes (e.g., Cattell, 1888) or as
areas of psychological interest in their own right (e.g., Dearborn, 1906;
Huey, 1908). Comprehension was not considered important by researchers at the beginning of this century because, to them, reading usually
meant oral reading and comprehension of a given text was simply assumed if a reader's "pronunciation was correct and natural" (Venezky,
1984, p. 13). The importance of comprehension became more salient with
the advent of the testing movement because its goal was to assess comprehension ability. The testing movement gave rise to a plethora of tests
of reading comprehension—early tests by Thorndike and Gates, and later
tests like the Davis Reading Test, the Metropolitan Reading Test, and the
Nelson–Denny Test, to name but a few. While many of these tests proved
useful for quantifying reading comprehension ability and predicting performance in academic and other settings, they remained largely atheoreti-
cal. It was not until the reemergence of cognitive psychology after World
War II (cf. Venezky, 1984) that reading comprehension became a target of
theoretical investigation. As a result of developments in the disciplines of
human factors research, computer science, and linguistics, there was a
shift in psychology from a behaviorist to an information-processing or
cognitive orientation. The shift has had a significant impact on the study
of many complex cognitive processes including reading comprehension.
Reading is no longer seen as a passive and automatic by-product of having
cracked the letter–sound code. Meaning is no longer assumed to reside in
the text alone. In the new conceptualization, the reader actively constructs meaning based on the text and what he or she already knows. The
research goal is no longer simply to *quantify* individual differences in
reading comprehension tasks. The goal is to attempt to *explain* individual
and group reading comprehension performance in terms of the architec-

ture and processes of the human information-processing system. Constructs from computer science (such as knowledge representations, buffers and working memory, and parallel, serial, and interactive processes) as well as constructs from linguistics (such as discourse structures, integration, and inferencing) have become part and parcel of the theoretically oriented field of reading comprehension research.

Our intent with this volume is not to provide extensive and intensive coverage of the vast field of reading comprehension; that would be impossible. Rather, it is to provide a sample of current theoretical developments and methodological trends as related by some prominent researchers in the field.

Because comprehension is the goal or end product of reading, it can be affected by all of its component processes, ranging from the lower level processes that recognize the printed words and encode contextually appropriate meanings for them to the higher level processes that assemble and integrate the underlying propositions and relate them to previously acquired knowledge. Many of these processes are explored in the present volume. The volume contains articles dealing with comprehension processes as revealed by readers' eye movements (Rayner & Duffy), the component processes of reading comprehension as revealed in the way readers distribute processing time across the text (Haberlandt), a global theory of reading ability (Perfetti), a theory of how word knowledge is related to reading ability (Daneman), and a description of the role of inferences in reading comprehension (Singer).

Despite the great diversity of topics, there are some common themes to be found in the approaches and contents of these articles. For example, the work by Rayner and Duffy and by Haberlandt both make use of on-line measures of reading comprehension. Rayner and Duffy provide a comprehensive review of what eye-movement data can and have revealed about the reading comprehension processes. Of course, their approach depends on the availability of highly specialized eye-tracking technology. However, there is a simpler and more economical way to collect on-line reading time data that resemble the quality of eye-fixation duration data. By displaying text one word at a time on a computer terminal and having the reader control each word's exposure duration by pressing a button for the next word, Haberlandt shows how interbutton latencies can also be used to infer the component processes of reading comprehension. The articles by Rayner and Duffy and by Haberlandt are representative of a growing belief in the importance of using on-line measures to model the comprehension processes rather than relying solely on postcomprehension memory measures which confound comprehension processes with memorial processes such as forgetting, retrieval, and reconstruction.

While the contributions by Rayner and Duffy and by Haberlandt share methodological approaches, those by Perfetti and Daneman share conceptual concerns. Both focus on individual differences in reading comprehension ability, and both propose processing resource explanations for these differences. Finally, all four of these articles are alike in their concern with documenting some of the component processes of comprehension and how they interact. Rayner and Duffy examine the way in which eye-movement data reflect lexical, semantic, and syntactic processes. Haberlandt compiles a list of word-, sentence-, and text-level processes and documents their effects on reading comprehension. Perfetti subdivides reading comprehension into two major components: local text processing and text modeling. Both he and Daneman focus on local lexical processes in their articles in addition to emphasizing how lexical processes are related to the higher level comprehension processes. While Singer acknowledges the complexity and range of processes involved in comprehension, his contribution differs from the others in that it deals exclusively with the higher level inferential processes. Inferences play a crucial role in text comprehension, and Singer gives a taste of just how many different kinds of inferences there can be.

Of course, each contribution has many unique elements. In order to introduce some of these and convey the essence of each, I have singled out what I believe to be the key question each article addresses. I raise each question in turn and then discuss briefly how it is tackled in each article.

1. *Do eye-movement data reflect the on-line comprehension processes during reading; if so, what do they reveal?*

The study of the relationship between eye-movement patterns and reading comprehension has a long history. Early reading researchers noted that poor readers make more and longer fixations as well as many more regressions, than good readers (Buswell, 1937). However, the correlation between eye-movement behavior and reading skill has not always been interpreted to mean that poor eye-movement control is a manifestation of underlying cognitive and linguistic problems. Indeed, some researchers argued the exact opposite—that is, poor eye movement control is the source of poor reading comprehension. Based on this reasoning, attempts were made to improve the reading comprehension performance of poor readers by training them to make the same patterns of eye movements as good readers, namely, shorter fixations and fewer regressive fixations. Although some researchers still propose that poor eye-movement control is the source of reading problems (Nodine & Lang, 1971; Nodine & Simmons, 1974), most researchers now believe that poor eye-movement control is simply a reflection of the reading problems (Carpenter & Daneman, 1981; Just & Carpenter, 1980; Rayner, 1978). This conclusion is based on evidence that the oculomotor training studies were sometimes able to alter readers' eye movements, but never to improve their comprehension performance (Tinker, 1958), and from observations that poor readers' immature eye movements did not generalize to non-reading scanning tasks like picture scanning (Stanley, 1978).

While eye movements are only indices of the underlying comprehension processes, they have proved to be very useful indices. This is the conclusion Rayner and Duffy reach after reviewing a large body of research that has used eye-movement data to make inferences about the comprehension processes. Most of the research they describe uses the individual word as its unit of analysis for comprehension. As Rayner and Duffy so convincingly demonstrate, the amount of time a reader spends looking at a particular word is a reflection not only of the time it takes to acquire the visual information necessary to identify the word, but also of the time to access the meaning for the word and integrate it with prior information in the text. They estimate that the visual encoding process occurs during the first 50 msec of an eye fixation, with the remainder of the fixation devoted to lexical access, syntactic parsing, and semantic integration. Programming the location of the next fixation is executed simultaneously with the perceptual and cognitive processes. On some fixations the word immediately to the right of the fixated word is identified during the same fixation, but most often it is only previewed in part. Rayner and Duffy describe in detail how preview effects and contextual constraints influence the amount of time a reader will spend processing a word. More challenging, of course, to researchers of eye movements are the comprehension processes that cannot be localized to a specific word in the text but tend to be spread over a larger region of the sentence. These include the processes involved in antecedent search and syntactic parsing. Antecedent search is the process of establishing an antecedent or referent for an anaphoric noun phrase such as *the sailor* or *he*. If a reader encounters a noun phrase such as *the sailor* or *he* during the course of reading a sentence, a search of the earlier text for some mention of a sailor or some referent for *he* may be initiated. Syntactic parsing is the process of assigning a structural representation to a sentence. Rayner and Duffy review research on both antecedent search and syntactic parsing. Recent studies on syntactic parsing have been particularly encouraging as they have shown that eye-movement data are reasonably sensitive to syntactic processes and can be used effectively to distinguish between rival theories of syntactic parsing. Studies of how readers process structurally ambiguous sentences have provided support for "late-closure" and "minimal-attachment" parsing strategies. According to the late-closure strategy, readers cope with temporary ambiguities by pursuing just a single analysis, an analysis that favors attaching incoming words to the clause or phrase currently being constructed rather than starting a new clause. Take, for example, *Since Jay always jogs a mile* (Frazier & Rayner, 1982); readers will tend to analyze the ambiguous phrase *a mile* as the direct object of the verb *jogs,* not as the subject of the clause to follow. Consequently, if the example is, *Since Jay always jogs a mile seems like a short distance to him,* they will have to revise their initial analysis; if it is, *Since Jay always jogs a mile this seems like a short distance to him,* they will not have to revise it. The additional computational complexity involved in revising the former or early-closure structure shows up in longer eye fixation duration on the disambiguating region and more regressive fixations to the ambiguous region. According to the minimal-closure strategy, there is a bias toward postulating the minimal number of structural nodes. In the example, *The city council argued the mayor's position* (Frazier & Rayner, 1982), the ambiguous noun phrase *the mayor's position* will be interpreted as the simple direct object of the verb *argue,* as in, *The city council argued the mayor's position forcefully,* rather than as the subject of a sentential complement, as in, *The city council argued the mayor's position was incorrect,* since the former analysis requires the postulation of fewer syntactic nodes. Again, Rayner and Duffy show how the syntactic bias is revealed in the sequence and duration of a reader's eye fixations. All in all, Rayner and Duffy show that eye-movement data can be used productively to monitor the comprehension processes as they occur. As such, eye-movement data provide an invaluable window to the mind.

2. *What are some of the component processes of reading, and how do they affect reading-time behavior?*

As we have seen, the eye-tracking methodology allows for monitoring comprehension processes during the act of reading rather than for making inferences about comprehension after the fact on the basis of memory measures like recognition, recall, and question answering. There is the additional advantage that the task approximates normal reading rather closely, in that readers can proceed through text at their own rate and no unnatural secondary task needs to be introduced. While the "moving-window" paradigm used by Haberlandt does not involve the monitoring of eye movements, it shares many of the naturalistic, on-line advantages of the eye-movement paradigm and has been shown to produce reading-time data with many of the characteristics of eye-fixation-time data (Just, Carpenter, & Woolley, 1982). In this paradigm, a reader presses a button to see each successive word in a text, and the previous word is removed as each new one appears. The new word appears in the same location as it would in normal text, and word-length information about the upcoming word is available in peripheral vision. Since reading times for individual words are collected, effects can be located to specific regions of the text. Haberlandt uses the moving-window paradigm in conjunction with multiple regression, another technique popularized by Just and Carpenter (1980), to study the component processes of reading comprehension. The research is based on the following logic. Component processes occur in real time. However, even the time on a single word may reflect an aggregate of processes. Accordingly, the first step is to identify text or experimental variables assumed to affect the different processes; then, the independent contributions of the variables to reading time on a given word or text unit can be assessed with the use of multiple-regression techniques. Haberlandt investigates the spatial and temporal characteristics of an impressively large number of component processes and briefly discusses many more. Included among the processes he investigates are word-level processes (such as word encoding and lexical access, which are sensitive to word length and word frequency, respectively), sentence-level processes (such as sentence modeling, which is sensitive to a sentence's propositional and syntactic structure), and text-level processes (such as continuity monitoring, model refinement, and knowledge application, which are sensitive to word repetition, sentence position, and text familiarity, respectively). The list of component processes is not exhaustive, and the way in which the component processes interact is only treated in part. Nevertheless, Haberlandt's framework can be used by researchers to generate additional processes and new text variables for investigating them.

3. *What accounts for individual differences in general reading comprehension ability?*

Readers differ greatly in how well they can comprehend text. Any theory of reading comprehension would be incomplete if it did not consider the mechanisms that account for these differences. While the previous two contributions deal almost exclusively with general models of reading comprehension, Perfetti deals directly with the issue of individual differences by trying to provide a theory of reading ability, a theory of why some readers are better than others at comprehending text. While Perfetti's theory, which he calls *verbal efficiency theory,* is described elsewhere (e.g., Perfetti, 1985), here we are treated to a lucid and detailed description of the theory—its structure, its assumptions, and its practical implications. Verbal efficiency theory focuses on the resource costs of different components of reading. The central tenet of the theory is that individual differences in reading comprehension are produced by individual differences in the efficient operation of local processes, particularly the lexical processes. When lexical processing is efficient, its resource costs are low, and so more resources can be allocated to the demanding higher level processes that assemble and integrate propositions; the net result is qualitatively superior comprehension. Perfetti's theory challenges the commonly held position that individual differences in reading comprehension ability can be attributed to schemata or knowledge differences.

4. *What accounts for the high correlation between vocabulary knowledge and reading comprehension ability?*

Numerous theories have been proposed for the long-recognized but poorly understood finding that vocabulary size is the single best predictor of reading comprehension and overall intelligence. Daneman discusses some of the major theories, focusing on the learning-from-context theory, a theory which takes into consideration how individuals acquire word knowledge in the first place (Sternberg & Powell, 1983). According to this theory, vocabulary is primarily acquired by inferring the meanings of words from the verbal contexts in which they are encountered. Consequently, the extent of an individual's current vocabulary knowledge is a reflection of the net products of his or her ability to learn from context. It is this ability to acquire knowledge from verbal contexts, so the theory goes, that may be the mechanism underlying the high intercorrelations among tests as diverse in content and form as those tapping vocabulary knowledge, reading comprehension, and overall intelligence. However, if learning from context is to play an explanatory role in a theory of verbal intelligence in general, and reading comprehension in particular, we need to account for why individual differences in the ability to learn from verbal context exist. Daneman attempts to do this by appealing to individual differences in the processing and storage capacity of working memory, the explanatory construct in her more general model of reading comprehension ability (Daneman & Carpenter, 1980). There are both similarities and differences in the way Daneman and Perfetti treat working memory capacity. Moreover, as is the case with Perfetti's theory, evidence for Daneman's theory is largely correlational. More research is needed to explore exactly how and when working memory capacity influences the processes involved in comprehending vocabulary and text.

5. *What are the text and reader characteristics that influence the computation of inferences during reading comprehension?*

Developing a coherent representation of a text does not only involve comprehending and integrating the propositions conveyed explicitly in the text; it also includes filling in the many missing but implied propositions. The reader makes inferences about the missing propositions by referring to his or her knowledge about the world and how it works. While the previous articles allude to the importance of knowledge-based inferences in comprehension, Singer explores this topic in detail. Singer reviews the literature on inferences and documents some of the text and reader variables that affect inference processing. A text's coherence requirements, thematic value, and interest value will influence the inferences accompanying comprehension; a reader's background knowledge and goals for reading will do so, too. As Singer points out, the way in which inferences are processed and represented can be fully understood only with reference to general theories of reading comprehension. Singer discusses inferences in the context of coherence graph theory (Kintsch & van Dijk, 1978) as well as several other script and schema theories (e.g., Rumelhart & Ortony, 1976; Schank & Abelson, 1977). The problem of inference is enormous in scope; it brings the study of reasoning, problem solving, knowledge acquisition, and knowledge representation into the domain of reading research.

Although all five articles in this volume are concerned with theoretical issues, namely, identifying and explaining the processes and structures underlying reading comprehension performance, it is legitimate to ask what, if any, practical implications can be derived from the theory. Only Perfetti broaches the topic explicitly, and he does so by stressing the problems inherent in extrapolating from theory to practice. Given that his verbal efficiency theory is a theory of skilled performance at reading, one might think that it speaks directly to practical issues of reading instruction and remediation. Perfetti, however, reminds us that a theory of skilled performance is not the same as a theory of skill acquisition, and he argues that an independent theory of skill acquisition is needed to make the bridge to instruction. William James (1901) was dubious about psychology's relevance for practical issues of instruction: "You make a great, a very great mistake, if you think that psychology, being the science of mind's laws, is something from which you can deduce definite programmes and schemes and methods of instruction for immediate schoolroom use. Psychology is a science, and teaching is an art, and sciences never generate arts directly out of themselves" (pp. 7–8). I think James was correct in his observation that the link between theory and instruction is not a direct one. However, I am less pessimistic about psychology's ability to forge the link. Like Perfetti, I believe that the gap is not so much a result of science on the one side and art on the other, but rather is a result of basic science on the one side and practical work on the other, with no linking science between the two. In his presidential address to the American Psychological Association in 1899, John Dewey (1900) recognized the need for a linking science between psychological theory and practical work: "Do we not lay a special linking science everywhere else between the theory and practical work? We have engineering between physics and the practical workingmen in the mills; we have a scientific medicine between the natural science and the physician'' (p. 110). Reading research is particularly in need of a linking science—a science that takes constructs from basic research, such as working memory capacity, efficiency at local processes, acquiring vocabulary from context, and inferencing, and systematically explores the implications of these constructs for the teaching of reading and for the diagnosis and remediation of reading difficulties.

REFERENCES

Anderson, I. H. & Dearborn, W. F. (1952). *The psychology of teaching reading*. New York: Ronald Press.

Buswell, G. T. (1937). *How adults read*. Chicago: Chicago University Press.

Carpenter, P. A., & Daneman, M. (1981). Lexical retrieval and error recovery in reading: A model based on eye fixations. *Journal of Verbal Learning and Verbal Behavior,* **20,** 137–160.

Cattell, J. M. (1888). The psychological laboratory at Leipzig. *Mind,* **15,** 373–380.

Crowder, R. G. (1982). *The psychology of reading*. New York: Oxford University Press.

Daneman, M., & Carpenter, P. A. (1980). Individual differences in working memory and reading. *Journal of Verbal Learning and Verbal Behavior,* **19,** 450–466.

Dearborn, F. B. (1906). The psychology of reading: An experimental study of the reading pulses and movements of the eye. *Archives of Philosophy, Psychology and Scientific Methods,* **4,** (4).

Dewey, J. (1900). Psychology and social practice. *The Psychological Review,* **7,** 105–124.

Frazier, L., & Rayner, K. (1982). Making and correcting errors during sentence comprehension: Eye movements in the analysis of structurally ambiguous sentences. *Cognitive Psychology,* **14,** 178–210.

Huey, E. B. (1908). *The psychology and pedagogy of reading*. New York: MacMillan. (Republished: Cambridge, MA: MIT Press, 1968.)

Jackson, M. D., & McClelland, J. L. (1979). Processing determinants of reading speed. *Journal of Experimental Psychology: General,* **108,** 151–181.

James, W. (1901). *Talks to teachers on psychology*. New York: Holt.

Just, M. A., & Carpenter, P. A. (1980). A theory of reading: From eye fixations to comprehension. *Psychological Review,* **87,** 329–354.

Just, M. A., Carpenter, P. A., & Woolley, J. D. (1982). Paradigms and processes in reading comprehension. *Journal of Experimental Psychology: General,* **111,** 228–238.

Kintsch, W., & van Dijk, T. A. (1978). Toward a model of discourse comprehension and production, *Psychological Review,* **85,** 363–394.

Nodine, C. F., & Lang, N. J. (1971). The development of visual scanning strategies for differentiating words. *Developmental Psychology,* **5,** 221–232.

Nodine, C. F., & Simmons, F. G. (1974). Processing distinctive features in the differentiation of letterlike symbols. *Journal of Experimental Psychology,* **103,** 21–28.

Palmer, J., MacCleod, C. M., Hunt, E., & Davidson, J. E. (1985). Information processing correlates of reading. *Journal of Memory and Language,* **24,** 59–88.

Perfetti, C. A. (1985). *Reading ability*. New York: Oxford University Press.

Rayner, K. (1978). Eye movement in reading and information processing. *Psychological Bulletin,* **85,** 618–660.

Rumelhart, D. E., & Ortony, A. (1976). The representation of knowledge in memory. In R. Anderson, R. Spiro, & W. Montague (Eds.), *Schooling and the acquisition of knowledge*. Hillsdale, NJ: Erlbaum.

Schank, R. C., & Abelson, R. P. (1977). *Scripts, plans, goals, and understanding: An inquiry into human knowledge structures*. Hillsdale, NJ: Erlbaum.

Stanley, G. (1978). Eye movements in dyslexic children. In G. Stanley & K. W. Walsh (Eds.), *Brain impairment: Proceedings of the 1977 brain impairment workshop*. Victoria: Dominion Press.

Sternberg, R. J., & Powell, J. S. (1983). Comprehending verbal comprehension. *American Psychologist,* **38,** 878–893.

Sticht, T. G., & James, J. H. (1984). Listening and reading. In P. D. Pearson, R. Barr, M. L. Kamil, & P. Mosenthal (Eds.), *Handbook of reading research*. New York: Longman.

Tinker, M. A. (1958). Recent studies of eye movements in reading. *Psychological Bulletin,* **55,** 215–231.

Venezky, R. L. (1984). This history of reading research. In P. D. Pearson, R. Barr, M. L. Kamil, & P. Mosenthal (Eds.), *Handbook of reading research*. New York: Longman.

Woodworth, R. S. (1938). *Experimental psychology*. New York: Holt.

ON-LINE COMPREHENSION PROCESSES AND EYE MOVEMENTS DURING READING

KEITH RAYNER* and SUSAN A. DUFFY†

Department of Psychology
University of Massachusetts
Amherst, Massachusetts 01003
and
† Department of Psychology
Amherst College
Amherst, Massachusetts 01002

I. INTRODUCTION

Silent skilled reading is a very private process with few observable indications of the cognitive activities that occur at any point in time. Most techniques that have been used to measure reading comprehension have not relied on on-line measures but have utilized techniques or paradigms that measure the product of reading (i.e., what the reader can remember from the text). However, a complete model of the reading process will have to specify comprehension processes as they occur on line. Recently, a fair amount of evidence has been accumulating to indicate that the amount of time that a reader looks at a particular word or portion of the text provides a good reflection of the cognitive processes associated with comprehending that word or region of text. In this article, we will review some of the evidence concerning the use of eye-movement data as a reflection of on-line comprehension processes during reading. In particular, we will review evidence with respect to the comprehension of words in text by examining studies dealing with (1) word recognition and lexical access in reading, (2) the effect of context on word recognition, (3) antecedent search processes, and (4) syntactic parsing during reading. However, prior to doing so, we will review two questions that are central to any attempt to use eye-movement records to infer comprehension processes.

13

II. PERCEPTUAL ISSUES

The use of eye-movement data to study reading comprehension raises many interesting questions. The two which we have judged to be central to the claim that the behavior of the eyes can be used as a window to the language comprehension process deal with the nature of the perceptual span and the eye–mind span. Each of these issues will be discussed, and then we will review research on the four areas described in Section I.

A. The Perceptual Span

As a person reads a passage of text, a series of eye movements are made. Between the movements (called *saccades*), which average 7–8 character spaces, the reader fixates for about 200–250 msec. It is during the *fixation* that new information is brought into the processing system. About 10–20% of the time, the reader makes an eye movement back to a region that has already been read. These *regressions* are typically quite short, 2–5 character spaces, but can, at times, be to previous lines of text. While the values we have cited represent averages, they are often considered stable indices of the eye-movement pattern during reading. In reality, however, there is considerable variability not only between readers but also within any given reader (Rayner, 1978). In addition, the difficulty of the text and the level of comprehension expected of the reader can affect some or all of these factors. A primary goal for researchers interested in using eye movements to monitor the reading process has been to account for this variability.

The perceptual-span issue is essentially the question of how much information a reader can see and use during a single fixation. If readers can process a number of words on each fixation (as our subjective impressions might suggest), then eye-movement data would not be particularly useful as a measure of on-line processing. However, if readers only process the word (or two) closest to their point of fixation, then the amount of time that a word is looked at might be a good reflection of the cognitive processes associated with understanding that word. Indeed, a great deal of recent research (see Rayner, 1984) indicates that different types of information can be acquired at various distances from the fixation point. Information that is used for word identification seems to be acquired from the word currently fixated (and sometimes the word to the right of fixation); more gross types of information (used for word identification on a subsequent fixation or for determining where to look next) appear to be acquired further to the right of fixation than the region of word identification. Thus, it is probably appropriate to talk about different types of perceptual spans (Rayner & McConkie, 1977). That is, the total perceptual-span region can be differentiated from the perceptual-span region for word identification in that the total span region is larger than the word-identification span.

Research to determine the total perceptual-span region has utilized a technique introduced by McConkie and Rayner (1975) in which eye movements are recorded and display changes are made on a cathode-ray tube (CRT) from which the subject is reading that are contingent upon the subject's eye position. In the prototypical "moving-window" experiment, a version of mutilated text (in which every letter from the original text is replaced by another letter) is initially displayed on the CRT. However, when the reader fixates on the text, the display is immediately modified by the replacement of letters within a certain region around the fixation point with corresponding letters from the original text. This creates an experimentally defined *window* region of normal text for the reader to see on that fixation. When the reader makes an eye movement, the text in the window area returns to its unreadable form and a new window of normal text is created at the location of the next fixation. Thus, wherever the reader looks, there is normal text to read. Moreover, the experimenter can determine the size and location of that region with respect to the reader's fixation point. While the moving-window technique has been very useful in determining the total perceptual-span region, a more subtle technique introduced by Rayner (1975), in which only a single display change is made (as the reader's eye crosses a boundary location), has also been used to determine the perceptual-span region for word identification.

Figure 1 (taken from Rayner, 1984) represents the general findings from the perceptual-span research and shows five successive fixations on a line of text. The region between the solid vertical lines represents the total perceptual-span region. The area between the vertical line to the left of fixation and the dotted vertical line to the right of fixation represents the region in which word identification occurs. Rayner (1984) has also argued that there are regions in which beginning letter and letter feature information is obtained and that word-length information can be obtained farthest from fixation of the various types of information that have been investigated. We shall return to the implications of the results of various studies indictating that partial word information is obtained parafoveally later when we discuss word recognition in more detail. For our present purposes, however, the important point to be gleaned from Fig. 1 is that the area of word identification is limited to a region extending from the beginning of the currently fixated word (but no more than 3–4 characters to the left of fixation) to roughly 6–8 character spaces to the right of fixation. In

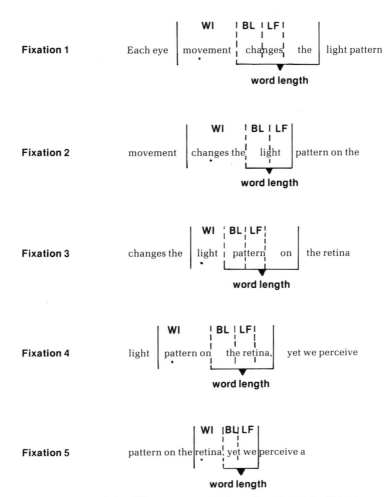

Fig. 1. An example of the different types of information obtained within the perceptual span on five successive fixations. The dot marks the location of fixation. WI, Word identification; BL, beginning letters; LF, letter features. Reproduced from Rayner, 1984, with permission from the Attention and Performance Organization.

fact, to state it more precisely, readers seem to be identifying the currently fixated word on most fixations and, on a smaller percentage of fixations, the currently fixated word and one word to the right of that are identified (and on an even smaller percentage of fixations, two words to the right, if all three words are very short).

The conclusion that the perceptual span for word identification is relatively small is very important for using fixation times of the eyes as a reflection of language processing. Evidence for such a conclusion has been obtained from a number of different studies.

The mean number of words identified in one fixation and the range of that number can be estimated from data reported by Rayner, Well, Pollatsek, and Bertera (1982). Rayner *et al.* used the moving-window paradigm and presented subjects text in which only the fixated word (and all words to the left of fixation) was visible on each fixation (with letters to the right replaced by *X*s). This "word-by-word" condition was compared to other conditions in which the currently fixated word plus 1, 2, or 3 words was presented to the right of the currently fixated word. Table I shows the results of that experiment. When no window was presented (so that the entire line of text was available), reading rate was 348 words per minute (wpm). When subjects were presented only the fixated word, reading was slowed to 61% of normal. When the fixated word and the word to its right were both available on each fixation, reading rate was 90% of normal. When the second and third words to the right of fixation were also available, reading rate was 97% of normal and did not differ significantly from the normal condition. We can estimate the mean number of words identified per fixation by counting the total number of fixations made in reading a given text and dividing that total by the number of words in the text. Such an analysis yields a mean of 1.13 words identified per fixation. Since reading rate reaches the normal rate when 2 words to the right of fixation are available, we can also infer that the number of words identified per fixation rarely exceeds 3.

TABLE I

Estimated Frequency of Fixation Pattern and Probability with Which Words Different Distances from Fixation are Identified[a]

Hogaboam (1983)		McConkie & Hogaboam (1985)			Rayner *et al.* (1982)	
Saccade distance[b]	Word identified	Relative frequency[c]	Reported word	probability	Reading rate (wpm)	Word available
0	—	.09 (.13)	$n - 1$	.10	—	—
1	n	.38 (.53)	n	.39	212	n
2	$n + 1$	.21 (.30)	$n + 1$	.28	309	$n + 1$
3	$n + 2$	.03 (.04)	$n + 2$	.10	339	$n + 2$
4	$n + 37$	.001 (.002)	$n + 3$	.05	339	$n + 3$

[a] n, Fixated word; $n - 1$, word to left of fixation; $n + 1$, word to right of fixation.

[b] Saccade distance measured in words for forward fixations preceded by a forward fixation.

[c] Relative frequency is based on forward fixations preceded by forward fixations, forward fixations preceded or followed by a regression. Values in parentheses are relative frequencies based only on forward fixation preceded by a forward fixation.

Work by Hogaboam (1983) and McConkie and Hogaboam (1985) further supports these estimates. Hogaboam (1983) examined a large corpus of data and delineated various types of eye-movement patterns in the text.[1] He reported that the most commonly occurring pattern was for the eye to fixate on word n and for the next saccade to take the eyes to word $n + 1$. The second single most common pattern was a forward movement from word n to word $n + 2$ (thus skipping $n + 1$). On 2.4% of the saccades, the eye moved from word n to word $n + 3$ (skipping over two words), and on one-tenth of 1% of the saccades the eyes skipped three or more words. Hogaboam's analysis of eye-movement patterns is also consistent with an experiment reported by McConkie and Hogaboam (1985), in which readers read text and, at a predetermined point, the text was masked and the subject had to report the last word read. Word n (the fixated word) was reported roughly 40% of the time, and word $n + 1$ was reported about 30% of the time. Word $n - 1$ (the word left of the fixated word) and word $n + 2$ were both reported approximately 10% of the time. Table I presents data from Hogaboam (1983) and McConkie and Hogaboam (1985). From their work, we can conclude that the word to the right of fixation is identified on roughly 30% of the fixations, and the word two to the right of fixation is identified less than 10% of the time. Note that the studies by Hogaboam and by McConkie and Hogaboam provide highly consistent results in that a saccade distance of two in Table I (from Hogaboam, 1983) means that word $n + 1$ was skipped (implying that it had been identified prior to the saccade). The results of McConkie and Hogaboam (1985) provide converging evidence in providing the frequency with which the word to the right of fixation was identified using the masking technique.

We would like to make the point that our estimates of the frequency with which words to the right of the fixated word are identified without a direct fixation varies with several factors. First, the likelihood of fixating a word varies with the length of the word. Rayner and McConkie (1976) reported that the probability of fixating a word increased as word length increased and that words six letters long received a forward fixation 72% of the time. Longer words received fixations most of the time. Carpenter and Just (1983) reported that content words were fixated 83% of the time

---

[1] Hogaboam's (1983) data presented in his Table 18.1 were for (1) forward fixations preceded by forward fixations, (2) forward fixations followed by regressive fixations, and (3) forward fixations preceded by regressions. Added together, these different patterns sum to 59.5% of all fixations. Hogaboam states that the remaining fixations fall into a rather large number of different kinds of patterns, each occurring fairly infrequently, but collectively accounting for a large proportion of the data. In Table I, we have determined the relative frequency of different patterns of word skipping on the basis of the three main categories, since we are uncertain what the remaining patterns may be (blinks and regressions followed by regressions are two obvious patterns).

while function words (which tend to be shorter) were fixated only 38% of the time. In recent experiments that we have conducted in which the target phrase contained the function word *the* followed by a noun (ranging in length between five and nine letters) we found that the noun was fixated 84% of the time, and that *the* was fixated only 19% of the time.

Second, the length of the currently fixated word affects the likelihood of fixating the next word. Rayner (1979) reported that the probability is relatively low that one of two short words (words four characters or less) appearing in succession will be fixated (the probability being less than .5 that one of the pair of two- and three-letter words will be fixated). However, as either the word prior to or after the short word increases in word length, so also does the probability that one of the words will be fixated.

Third, the proximity of the preceding fixation to a target word affects the likelihood of directly fixating that word. For example, when a three-letter word is followed by a target word (5 to 10 characters long), the target word is fixated 95% of the time when the immediately preceding fixation falls before the three-letter word. If the immediately preceding fixation falls on the three-letter word, the target word is fixated only 69% of the time (see Rayner, 1979, for details).

Evidence concerning the perceptual-span region for word identification has been obtained via both correlational and empirical means. The evidence that we have presented to this point has been primarily correlational. We now consider more empirical evidence.

In a study dealing with the perceptual span and the types of parafoveal information obtained during a fixation, Rayner (1975) inserted nonwords in text and examined how close to fixation the nonword letter strings had to be to produce any disruption in the eye-movement pattern. In essence, the results indicated that unless the reader was fixated with three characters of the first letter of the nonword, there was no disruption in the pattern of fixations preceding the nonword. If the reader fixated between three and one characters from the beginning of the nonword, the duration of that fixation was increased by 50 msec or so. However, if the reader fixated directly on the nonword, fixation duration increased by 200–250 msec. Certainly, this result is highly consistent with the results we have discussed up to this point.

The nonwords in Rayner's experiment were initially presented in the text, but changed to a contextually appropriate word when the reader's eye movement crossed an invisible boundary location near the target word.[2] By varying the visual characteristics of the relationship between the initially displayed nonword and the target word (presented after the

---

[2] Since the boundary location was sometimes the third letter in the target word, subjects could fixate directly on a nonword.

display change), Rayner attempted to determine how far to the right of fixation readers obtain information about the lexical properties of words. This was done by comparing fixation time on a target word (for example, *chest*) when either the identical word (*chest*), a visually similar word (*chart*), or a visually similar nonword (*chovt*) was initially presented in the target location. Rayner found that if the reader's eye was seven or more characters from the beginning of the target word on the fixation prior to crossing the boundary, there were no differences between the three conditions for the fixation duration on the target word. However, if the reader's eye was six or fewer characters from the beginning of the word, there were differences between the conditions. If the reader had been fixated between four and six character spaces from the beginning of the target word in the identical condition, they fixated on the target word for 211 msec. However, if a visually similar word (*chart*) had initially been displayed in the target location and changed to *chest* during the saccade, readers fixated for 242 msec on the target; if a visually similar nonword (*chovt*) had initially been displayed and changed to *chest* during the saccade, they fixated for 279 msec on the target. If readers fixated three to one characters from the beginning of the target word, fixation duration on the target word was 212 msec in the identical condition, 208 msec in the visually similar word condition, and 245 msec in the visually similar nonword condition. With respect to the fact that there was no difference between the two word conditions when the reader was fixated only one to three characters to the left of the target word, Rayner pointed out that when a saccade was begun from that particular area, it generally landed at the end of, or just to the right of the target word. In such cases, the reader had apparently reached an interpretation of the word (in the example, *chart*) and since that interpretation fit into the sentence frame, the reader devoted attention to the next portion of the text and failed to perceive the change.

The results of Rayner's experiment are quite consistent with the arguments that we have made earlier in this section. The lack of a difference between the two word conditions when readers were fixated close to the beginning of the target word indicates that subjects had identified the initially displayed word on the fixation prior to crossing the boundary location. Thus, not only do word length factors influence whether or not the word to the right of fixation is identified, but also fixation location influences whether or not the word to the right of fixation will be identified.

The fact that there were differences in fixation duration when the target word replaced a visually similar word if the reader was fixated less than six characters from the target location does not necessarily mean that readers had identified the initally presented word. One of two possibilities exists. First, it could be that on some fixations the word was indeed identified. Then, when the eye landed on that word, the discrepancy between the information obtained on fixation n and that obtained on fixation $n + 1$ (namely, that they were two different words) when it was in foveal vision would lead to reprocessing time. If the parafoveal word was identified, say, 30% of the time, we would expect an increase in fixation duration of roughly 50 msec due to the inconsistency and associated reprocessing time. Temporal factors, which we shall discuss in more detail in the next section, would seem to dictate such a level of reprocessing as well as account for the fact that sometimes subjects will fixate on a word that has already been identified. The second possibility is that the information obtained from the parafoveal word was at a visual rather than a lexical level and that subjects detected the inconsistency at this visual level (in which words are not yet identified). Clearly, only gross information about visual form was obtained beyond 6 characters from the beginning of the word. That is, there were no differences between the 3 conditions we have been discussing here in terms of fixation duration on the target word when the eye was more than 6 character spaces from the beginning of the word and the next saccade landed on the target word. However, if nonwords differing in visual characteristics (such as *ebouf* or *chyft*) were initially presented and then changed to the target word (*chest*), there were large increases in fixation duration on the target word. This effect held when the eye had been between 6 and 12 characters from the beginning of the target word on the prior fixation (and the ensuing saccade landed on the target). Finally, we would like to point out that recent research by Balota, Pallatsek, and Rayner (1985; see also Pollatsek, Rayner, & Balota, 1986) is very consistent with Rayner's (1975) findings.

In summary, we would like to argue that there is good evidence that the perceptual-span region for word identification is quite limited. We suggest that, on most fixations, readers identify the word that is directly fixated. About 30% of the time, the word to the right of the fixated word is also identified. On such fixations, readers will skip over the identified word to the right of fixation. Consistent with our argument, it is important to note that when a word is skipped, the duration of the fixation preceding the skip is inflated (Pollatsek *et al.*, 1986). Also, the frequency of a skipped word predicts the duration of the preceding fixation, not the one following it (Hogaboam, 1983). In Section III,C,1, we will discuss the relationship between word frequency and fixation duration more explicitly. Our point here is that on roughly 30% of the fixations, the word to the right of fixation is identified along with the directly fixated word. However, the majority of such identifications can be accounted for by word length factors (a short word to the right of fixation) or by fixation location factors (fixated near the end of the currently fixated word). Thus, it appears safe to conclude that subjects are primarily identifying the currently fixated word when dealing with content words.

B. The Eye–Mind Span

A second critical issue with respect to using eye fixation times as a reflection of on-line language comprehension concerns the extent to which the eye and the mind are tightly yoked in reading. If there is a sufficient lag between when a word is initially fixated and when the cogitive processes associated with understanding that word are initiated (so that, for example, the eyes have moved away from the word before the cognitive processes are well underway), then eye fixation times would not be a good measure of moment-to-moment processes. When we read aloud, our eye is ahead of our voice so that if the lights in the room are turned off, we are able to vocalize another word or two. Is there a similar lag between the eye and the mind with respect to silent reading?

Some simple facts about oculomotor reaction times have led some to suggest that there must be an eye–mind span in silent reading with the brain processing a given word only after the eye has moved on to a new location. If a subject is asked to look at a fixation cross continually, so that when the cross moves, the subject moves his or her eyes to the next location, the average latency of the eye movement will be in the range of 150–250 msec.[3] Of course, such a value is about the same as the average fixation in reading and has led some to conclude that since so much time is taken up programming the next saccade, the processing of the contents of any given fixation must be decoupled from the cognitive processes associated with understanding that particular word (or words). Such models (Bouma & deVoogd, 1974) have generally assumed that memory buffers hold the contents of a number of fixations and that cognitive processes are carried out on the information in the buffer rather than directly on the fixated text.

Recently, there has been a great deal of evidence to suggest that the duration of a fixation represents a good indiction of the cognitive processes associated with processing a given fixated word. Indeed, much of the evidence we cited in the previous section is consistent with the argu-

---

[3] The latency for a saccade can vary dramatically depending upon a number of factors, and average latencies may sometimes be as high as 400 msec. However, in latency tasks that most closely approximate reading, the latency is in the range we have stated.

ment that fixation times reflect cognitive processes, and much of the data we will subsequently review is also consistent with that view. However, one could argue that all such evidence is somewhat circumstantial because information viewed on a given fixation has *not* been shown to unambiguously affect the duration of that particular fixation. In the remainder of this section we will discuss experiments that have directly investigated the issue.

One major motivating force behind models stressing memory buffers is the assumption that there is not sufficient time during a fixation to process the text as well as program an eye movement contingent upon that processing. Since it has been argued that the minimal eye-movement latency is 150–175 msec (see Rayner, Slowiaczek, Clifton, & Bertera, 1983, for such evidence) and the average fixation in reading is about 200–250 msec, proponents of buffer-control models feel that it would be unfeasible to program eye movements based only on the information analyzed in the first 50–75 msec of each fixation. However, Rayner, Inhoff, Morrison, Slowiaczek, and Bertera (1981) presented a visual mask a certain amount of time after the beginning of each fixation and found that if the mask was delayed 50 msec or longer, reading was not appreciably hampered. Thus, it is possible that much of the visual information necessary for reading can be acquired during the first 50 msec of a fixation, leaving the remainder of the fixation period for programming the next eye movement and for higher level linguistic processing.

In order to further investigate the control of fixation duration in reading, Rayner and Pollatsek (1981) presented a visual mask at the end of each saccade, thereby delaying the onset of the text. The rationale in the experiment was that if fixation duration is dependent upon information encoded on the current fixation, then delaying the onset of the text should increase fixation duration by an amount proportional to the text delay. In the experiments, the text delay ranged between 25 and 300 msec. Rayner and Pollatsek found evidence to indicate that as text delay increased, fixation duration increased in a roughly linear fashion. However, such a conclusion emerged only after anticipatory saccades (eye movements that began prior to the offset of the mask) were removed from the data. Morrison (1984) replicated the Rayner and Pollatsek results and examined the characteristics of the anticipatory saccades in greater detail. He proposed a model to account for eye-movement control in reading which is consistent with the points we have raised here. The general conclusion to be reached from the work of Rayner and Pollatsek (1981) and Morrison (1984) is that most fixation durations are determined by the processing associated with the fixated words. However, a small percentage of the time, two consecutive saccades are programmed for execution. On those occasions, the preprogrammed fixation duration will be independent of the actual word fixated (see Morrison, 1984, for a discussion). It is also the case, as we shall discuss in a Section IV,D,1, that there are spill-over effects in which the processing associated with a given word spills over into the next fixation.

Prior to leaving this section of the chapter, we wish to make some distinctions between different measures of processing time associated with how long the eyes remain in a given location in the text. There is currently some debate over the most appropriate measure of processing time to be inferred from eye-movement data (see Blanchard, 1985; Inhoff, 1984; Just & Carpenter, 1980; McConkie, Hogaboam, Wolverton, Zola, & Lucas, 1979; Rayner & Pollatsek, 1987). We shall distinguish between fixation duration, gaze duration, and total viewing time.[4] When we refer to fixation duration, we shall generally be referring to the duration of the first fixation on a word. When we refer to gaze duration, we shall refer to a measure that has been advocated by Just and Carpenter (1980) in which all fixations occurring on a given target word prior to any eye movement out of that target word are summed as a measure of processing time for that word. Total viewing duration involves summing all fixations on a target word (including regressions). For most words in text, there will only be a single fixation on the word. In such cases, it is absolutely clear what to use as a measure of looking time on the word. However, for words that receive more than one fixation, it is desirable to compute the first fixation duration and the gaze duration. Inhoff (1984) has argued that first fixation duration is primarily sensitive to initial processing operations (like lexical access), whereas gaze duration reflects lexical access as well as cognitive operations which occur later in processing. However, both measures are likely to reflect processes occurring fairly early in a fixation since the decision of how long to remain in the first fixation and where to move next must be made during that fixation. Hence, we will assume that both measures reflect similar types of processes, though more work on the issue is clearly needed.

We would also like to point out that there are differences in how gaze duration is computed. For example, if a word does not receive a fixation,

---

[4] Prior to 1980, when Just and Carpenter made a clear theoretical statement concerning gaze duration, there was not much attention paid to the most appropriate measure for determining looking time. The distinctions outlined in the text have become much more clear due to Just and Carpenter (1980), Inhoff (1984), and Blanchard (1985). In the past, fixations on adjacent letters may have been added together, particularly if one of the durations was relatively short. Other studies may have summed the fixations on a word and divided by the number of fixations to obtain the average fixation duration. It is now clear that for research on on-line language processing, the most sensible measures are the first fixation duration and gaze duration.

Just and Carpenter (1980) assigned a score of zero to that word. Our approach would be to not include that particular trial in computing a processing time or to determine a region of encoding (based upon work from our laboratory on the perceptual span described earlier) and to compute gazes for a target word within its encoding region. For example, when readers do not fixate directly on a target word, the encoding fixation might be defined as the fixation closest to the beginning of target word (but no more than six character spaces from the beginning of a word).[5] In reality, such decisions are based upon the individual researchers' theoretical persuasions, characteristics of the eye-movement recording system, and the nature of given experiments.

C. Summary of Perceptual Span and Eye–Mind Issues

We have reviewed work dealing with two critical issues concerning the use of eye-movement data as on-line measures of reading comprehension. First, we reviewed work on the perceptual span and concluded that readers' word-identification processes are limited to words falling in the center of vision. We then reviewed research demonstrating that encoding processes during an eye fixation occur very early in a fixation and that processing of information presented on a given fixation is reflected in the duration of the current fixation or gaze. The results of such studies lead us to be optimistic about using eye-movement data as a reflection of cognitive processes associated with on-line reading comprehension processes.

III. WORD RECOGNITION AND LEXICAL ACCESS

In understanding how words are identified or recognized during reading, there are two fundamental processes to focus on: *encoding processes* and *lexical access*. By encoding processes, we refer to those processes which acquire the visual information necessary to identify a word. By lexical access, we refer to those processes which locate the word and its meaning in the lexicon. Of course, these processes are identical to those that have been studied for some time by researchers in traditional word-recognition experiments in which isolated words are presented tachistoscopically, often under impoverished conditions. That is, in a great many

---

[5] Since the probability of fixating on a word increases as word length increases (Rayner & McConkie, 1976), researchers can increase the probability that target words will be fixated by using target words that are five or more letters long. Of course, sometimes the researcher will be interested not only in fixation times on a word, but also in the probability of a fixation on the target word (Ehrlich & Rayner, 1981; Pollatsek *et al.*, 1986).

such experiments, words are presented for very brief durations (often under 50 msec) and followed by some type of masking pattern. While the results of such experiments may give us valuable cues as to how words are processed in reading, it is possible to be fairly skeptical that such research very accurately mimics the process of reading in which (1) the word is always available and (2) there is parafoveal preview of the word. This latter consideration is generally not taken into account in most experiments on word recognition. The fact that there is parafoveal preview of words in reading has important implications for both word-encoding processes and lexical access. We turn now to a discussion of each of these stages of word recognition, as well as a discussion of parafoveal preview effects.

A. Word Encoding

We have already pointed out that much of the visual information necessary for reading can be acquired during the first 50 msec of a fixation. This is not to say that such information is always utilized at the outset of a fixation. Indeed, Blanchard, McConkie, Zola, and Wolverton (1984) have presented data to suggest that readers utilize visual information for word encoding at crucial points throughout a fixation and that the crucial period can occur at different times on different fixations. During selected fixations, they briefly masked the text (either 50, 80, or 120 msec into the fixation), and when it reappeared the word fixated on was different than it was prior to the onset of the mask. Subjects sometimes reported seeing the first presented word, sometimes the second presented word, and sometimes both. However, it should be pointed out that the paradigm used by Blanchard *et al.* (1984) is quite different from that used by Rayner *et al.* (1981); in the latter experiment, when a word was masked it was masked for the remainder of the fixation. This is a much different situation than one in which two different words are presented in the same location during a fixation. Accordingly, we will argue that on the majority of fixations, the visual encoding of the fixated word occurs during the first 50 msec. Such an estimate not only agrees with the Rayner *et al.* (1981) results, but is also consistent with estimates from studies using the *rapid serial visual presentation* (RSVP) reading task in which words are presented at very fast rates in the same spatial location (see Rayner & Pollatsek, 1981).

One critical issue is what happens when two words are encoded on a fixation. There are two possibilities. First, both words may be encoded during the initial 50 msec of the fixation. Second, the first word may be initially encoded while the second word (the one to the right of fixation) is encoded later in the fixation. For a variety of reasons, we find the second alternative considerably more attractive than the first. We prefer a model of eye-movement control during reading (cf. Morrison, 1984; Pollatsek & Rayner, 1982; Rayner & Pollatsek, 1981) in which visual information from the foveal word is encoded very quickly and information obtained parafoveally is used to determine the location of the next fixation. Thus, two processes occur simultaneously. For the fixated word, lexical access processes are underway to obtain the meaning of that word while, at the same time, the eye-movement control system is determining the location of the next fixation. We will further assume that lexical access processes are generally completed prior to the initiation of the next eye movement. This assumption seems reasonable since the average minimal motor reaction time for an eye movement is at least 150–175 msec, and there is a good amount of data to indicate that word characteristics influence fixation time on a word. Thus, attention will often shift to the next word prior to the actual saccade. On many fixations, the reader will not be able to identify the next word and preliminary processing of the beginning letters of the word will take place. However, on some fixations the reader will identify the next word prior to the eye movement. If identification of the word occurs sufficiently early in the fixation, the planned saccade will be cancelled and the reader will reprogram the saccade to skip over that word. If the identification of the word to the right of fixation occurs fairly late during fixation *n,* the reader will make a saccade to that word followed with a rather short latency by a saccade to the word after that. These short-latency fixations would thus not reflect processing associated with the fixated word (since it was identified on the prior fixation). In fact, during such fixations the reader would be processing the next word to the right. Morrison (1984) has described in detail the characteristics of a model in which the encoding of the fixated word and the programming of the next eye movement are carried out in parallel. Our purpose here has been to briefly sketch out the relationship between encoding processes and eye-movement control.

In summary, we have argued that encoding of the visual information necessary for reading occurs during the first 50 msec of a fixation. The reader spends the remainder of the fixation carrying out processes associated with lexical access, syntactic parsing, and perhaps higher level semantic integration. Simultaneously, the eye-movement control system is computing the location of the next fixation. At some point in the fixation, attention shifts to the next word to the right of the fixated word. On some fixations, this word is also identified during the current fixation and we have briefly described two possible eye-movement patterns which result when the next word is identified. However, on most fixations the word to the right of fixation is not identified and the reader obtains only partial (or preview) information from that word. We turn now to the implications of preview effects on word identification in reading.

B. Preview Effects

A great deal of research on preview effects during word recognition has demonstrated that information about the beginning of a word is facilitative in naming a word. In such experiments (Rayner, McConkie, & Ehrlich, 1978; Rayner, McConkie, & Zola, 1980; McClelland & O'Regan, 1981; Balota & Rayner, 1983), subjects are asked to fixate on a target cross and a word or a letter string is presented in parafoveal vision. The subject's task is to make an eye movement to the location of the stimulus and name the word presented there as quickly as possible. During the saccade, the initially presented word or letter string is replaced by the word that the subject must name. The distance that the initial string is presented from fixation is varied as is the relationship between the first and second stimulus. The results from these experiments indicated that increasing the similarity of the parafoveal stimulus to the target word decreased the time taken to name it. In particular, if the first two or three letters in the initial parafoveal string and the target word were identical, facilitation occurred. Furthermore, this facilitation depended on how far into the parafovea the stimulus occurred. That is, there was more facilitation at 1° than at 3° and more at 3° than at 5°. Thus, these results indicate that subjects can use partial parafoveal word information to aid in their recognition of the word after a saccade has been made that brings that word into the fovea.

Results consistent with these findings have also been obtained in reading experiments. In particular, Rayner *et al.* (1982) varied the amount of information available to the right of fixation using the moving-window technique. On each fixation, either only the fixated word was available (with all words to the left of fixation also available) or the fixated word plus one, two, or three letters from the word to the right of the fixated word were available. Rayner *et al.* found that when the fixated word plus the first three letters were available (and the remaining letters from the next word replaced by visually similar letters) reading speed did not differ from a condition in which the entire word to the right of fixation was available on each fixation. Thus, it is clear that, in reading as well as the word recognition experiments dealing with preview effects, the beginning letters of the upcoming word facilitate performance.

What about the beginning letters is facilitative? On the basis of the results obtained in the experiments dealing with the effects of preview on word recognition, Rayner *et al.* (1980) argued that there is some type of preliminary letter identification for the beginning letters of words. The preliminary letter identification apparently involves an abstract code rather than a strictly visual code since changes in the case of the letters from fixation to fixation has no effect on reading performance (McConkie & Zola, 1979). As we pointed out earlier, on some fixations the reader identifies the word to the right of the fixated word. However, on most fixations temporal factors, acuity limitations, and lateral masking prevent the identification of the word to the right of fixation. On such fixations, the reader may be able to identify only the first few letters of the next word. Suppose the reader is fixated seven character spaces to the left of the beginning of the word *changes* (as in Fixation 1 in Fig. 1). The reader may be able to unambiguously identify the first letter (c) and make some preliminary identification of the next few letters. The letters b and h share many features in common, as do the letters c and a. It seems likely that after the reader has identified the c, knowledge of orthography would rule out b and c as possible second and third letters. This would allow preliminary identification of the letters h and a on fixation n. Alternatively, it may be the case that the threshold for letter identification is not reached until fixation $n + 1$. Thus, preliminary letter identification for the parafoveal word begins, but is incomplete. Information based partly on visual features and partly on orthographic rules begins accumulating for the beginning letters of the parafoveal word, but identification does not take place until after the eye movement. According to this alternative, the preliminary letter-identification process leads to information accruing differentially for various possibilities. Both alternatives are consistent with a model in which (1) an internal representation of a word is activated when evidence for the word exists, (2) feature information from parafoveal vision contributes some activation, and (3) identification of the word occurs when the activation reaches some threshold level. According to such a model, partial word information obtained on fixation n could facilitate reading in two ways. It could contribute activation sufficient to result in an identification, or it could merely increase activation (or "prime" the word) so that the threshold is more readily reached when additional information is obtained on fixation $n + 1$. We shall argue that the former (identification) will occur with a highly constraining context and the later (visual priming) in the more typical low contextual constraint situation. We will return to these points again when we discuss contextual effects on word recognition.

C. Lexical Access

A number of factors specific to the word itself are likely to affect the ease with which that word and its meaning are accessed in the lexicon. Below we discuss a series of studies investigating the effect of two kinds of factors on lexical access: the frequency of the word (and of its initial letter sequence) and the complexity of the word's meaning representation on the lexicon.

1. Frequency

There have been a number of recent demonstrations that readers look at low-frequency words for longer times than high-frequency words (Rayner, 1977; Just & Carpenter, 1980; Inhoff, 1984). Inhoff and Rayner (1986) used the moving-window technique and had subjects read sentences such as

(1)   The heavy rain damaged the crops.

(2)   The heavy hail damaged the crops.

The word *rain* is a high-frequency target word while the word *hail* is a low-frequency target word. Other than the target word, the remainder of the sentence frame was identical and word length and predictability were controlled for the target word. Inhoff and Rayner found that when subjects had available only the fixated word and no information to the right of fixation (with all words to the left of fixation available), first fixation durations on high- and low-frequency words did not differ. Gaze durations on low-frequency words were, however, longer than on high-frequency words. When parafoveal information was available (the next word or two available on each fixation), first fixation durations and gaze durations were decreased by a larger amount on the high-frequency words than on the low-frequency words.

Inhoff and Rayner's results are important because they indicate that parafoveal information can be used more effectively when a high-frequency word is to the right of fixation. More importantly in the present context, the results demonstrate a clear effect of word frequency on fixation times. Kliegl, Olson, and Davidson (1982) had earlier argued that the finding that low-frequency words are fixated for longer periods of time may have been artifactual since low-frequency words are, on the average, longer than high-frequency words. Thus, longer words would result in a higher probability of more than one fixation on the word, thereby inflating the gaze-duration measure. However, in the study by Inhoff and Rayner (1986) word length was precisely controlled, thus clearly indicating that low-frequency words take longer to process.

We (Rayner & Duffy, 1986) have also obtained results consistent with those reported by Inhoff and Rayner. We used sentences like (1) and (2) and compared fixation times on high- and low-frequency word pairs (*music–waltz, church–mosque, vehicle–gondola*). The average high-frequency word in our experiment had a Kucera–Francis (Kucera and Francis, 1967) frequency count of 122, and the low-frequency word had an

TABLE II

First Fixation Duration (msec) and Gaze Duration (msec) on a Target Word as a Function of Word Type[a]

Target word type	First fixation	Gaze duration
High frequency	225	243
Low frequency	262	330
Ambiguous, equibiased	237	275
Unambiguous control	229	258
Ambiguous, nonequibiased	227	260
Unambiguous control	230	263
Factive	252	289
Nonfactive	250	308
Causative	247	307
Noncausative	254	294
Negative	257	308
Nonnegative	252	299

[a] Data are from Rayner and Duffy (1986).

average count of 5. As seen in Table II, subjects looked considerably longer at the low-frequency target words. In summary, there is clear evidence that word frequency yields differential fixation times on words. It was also the case that the fixation following a low-frequency word was inflated, suggesting that difficulties processing the word spilled over into the next fixation. We should point out that although word frequency does affect fixation durations, there are a number of different mechanisms which might account for this effect. For example, frequent words might be accessed more quickly in the lexicon; alternatively, once accessed they might be more easily integrated into the meaning of the sentence.

Lima and Inhoff (1985) investigated a second kind of frequency effect, the frequency of the initial three letters (the initial trigram) of the word. Their original goal was to test a particular hypothesis of lexical access based on word–initial letter sequence, namely, that ease of lexical access increases whenever the size of the set of potential word candidates is particularly limited by beginning letter information. In their experiment, subjects read sentences of the form

(3)   The weary dwarf hated his job.
(4)   The weary clown hated his job.

The word *dwarf* shares its initial trigram *dwa* with few other words while the initial trigram of *clown* appears in many words. Words of these two types were matched for mean length and frequency. The prediction that Lima and Inhoff tested was that a word like *dwarf* should receive less viewing time than one like *clown* because the former has an initial sequence delineating a much smaller set of word alternatives than the latter. Such a position is compatible with the cohort model proposed by Marslen-Wilson and Welsh (1978) for speech perception, except that it remains neutral with respect to whether the letters in a word are processed serially, from left to right, or in parallel, with an attentional bias favoring the word-initial letters. A second prediction of the cohort model was that parafoveal availability of a target word should reduce subsequent foveal viewing time to a greater degree if a target word begins with letter sequences that are infrequent than if it begins with more familiar letters. The logic here was that if a word's beginning few letters are crucial to lexical access, and if the detailed letter information obtainable from the word to the right of fixation is largely confined to its first three letters, then it is conceivable that much of the information necessary to identify a word is obtainable while the word is still in the parafovea. In two experiments, the moving-window technique was used so that in one condition the subject had no parafoveal preview of the target word while in two other conditions there was a parafoveal preview. In contrast to the prediction of the cohort model, words with infrequent beginnings received significantly longer fixations than words with frequent beginnings. Moreover, a comparison of fixation times in viewing conditions with and without parafoveal letter information showed that the amount of decrease in target fixation time due to prior parafoveal availability was the same for both types of target words. Lima and Inhoff concluded that it is the familiarity of word-initial letter sequences that facilitates word identification; readers have a greater amount of exposure to these letter sequences, leading to more efficient identification of words containing them.

2. Lexical Complexity

Words differ in the complexity of their meaning representation. For example, an ambiguous word like *punch* can be considered complex because it has two different meanings to be represented compared with an unambiguous word like *cider*. A negative verb like *doubt* is complex because of the negative element, which is not part of the representation of its positive counterpart, *believe*. One can easily generate arguments why the complexity of a word's representation might increase the processing required for lexical access. Cutler (1983) has recently tested this claim using a phoneme-monitoring task and found no effect of lexical complexity. Since there is some question about exactly what the phoneme-monitoring task measures (Newman & Dell, 1978; Mehler, Segui, & Carey, 1978) and because we were interested in the extent to which lexical complexity might affect fixation times, we (Rayner & Duffy, 1986) have conducted a similar experiment using fixation time as the dependent variable. We will now discuss the results for ambiguous words and for lexically complex verbs.

3. Lexical Ambiguity

Current evidence (Swinney, 1979; Seidenberg, Tanenhaus, Leiman, & Bienkowski, 1982) strongly suggests that the irrelevant meanings of an ambiguous word are momentarily available even when context makes it clear which meaning is appropriate. To determine if readers look longer at ambiguous words, we asked subjects to read a set of sentences such as
(5)   He saw the boxer was barking at the cat.
(6)   He saw the puppy was barking at the cat.
The sentence frames were identical except for the target word. The target word was either an ambiguous noun or an unambiguous control noun. Two kinds of ambiguous nouns were used, those for which both meanings were fairly likely (equibiased, such as *coach, pitcher,* and *palm*) and those for which one meaning was very unlikely (nonequibiased, such as *boxer, cabinet,* and *band.*) The ambiguous word and its matched control were equated for length and word frequency. The control word always corresponded to the less likely meaning of the ambiguous word. Our primary finding (see Table II) was an interaction between ambiguity and bias. Gaze durations were significantly longer on equibiased ambiguous words than on their matched controls; there was no difference between the nonequibiased ambiguous words and their controls. We did, however, find considerably longer looking times in the disambiguating region of the sentence for the nonequibiased ambiguous condition.

Our results suggest that readers were initially accessing two meanings for the equibiased ambiguous words, but not for the nonequibiased. Processing on the target word was more time consuming when two meanings were involved. There are at least two possible reasons for this additional time. First, accessing two meanings in the lexicon may take longer than accessing one. Second, once the two meanings are accessed, the process of integrating the current word meaning with the preceding sentence context may be more difficult because two meanings must be considered.

4. Verb Complexity

Rayner (1977) reported that the main verb in declarative sentences received longer fixation times than the subject noun or the object noun (see also Holmes & O'Regan, 1981). Why are verbs looked at for longer amounts of time than nouns? Rayner speculated that it is because the verb serves the function of specifying the relations between the noun phrases in the sentence. Thus, longer looking times for verbs in simple active sentences may be accounted for by the notion that when a reader reaches the main verb, the relationship between the subject noun and the verb can be specified. Unless the reader is able to understand the relationship specified by the verb, the sentence is meaningless. Wanat (1971) recorded eye movements while subjects read left- and right-embedded sentences. He also reported that inspection times tend to be greatest in the area of the main verb of the sentence. The results of the experiments by Rayner and by Wanat imply that the verb is very important in processing the sentence. The general finding that verbs receive longer looking times than nouns could be due to integration processes as Rayner suggested. However, it could also be the case that certain lexical properties of verbs entail longer processing times. Accordingly, we examined a number of characteristics of verbs that could make them complex.

Cutler (1983) argued that lexical presuppositions are an inseparable part of the definition of words. For example, a factive verb presupposes that its sentence complement expresses a true proposition. This presupposition should be stored with factive verbs in the mental lexicon, and when such a verb is encountered in a sentence, the presupposition should be retrieved as part of the verb's meaning. Accessing this complex representation might be expected to be more time consuming than accessing the representation of a verb with no presuppositions. We tested this claim by comparing fixation times on factive vs. nonfactive verbs, using sentences such as [7] and [8]. The nonfactive verbs are in parentheses.

[7]   The girl noticed (insisted) that the cake was moldy.

[8]   The maid forgot (implied) that the sailor had left.

There were no significant differences between factive and nonfactive verbs in either initial fixation duration or gaze duration (see Table II). Inhoff (1985) reported a similar finding.

Some linguists have argued that the meanings of some words are represented in the lexicon in terms of the meaning of other words. For example, the causative verbs *kill* and *convince* might be expressed as *to cause to die* and *to cause to believe*. Thus, the actual representation for a sentence such as

(9)   The farmer killed a chicken.

might be the structure containing two propositions shown in sentence (10).

(10)   The farmer caused (the chicken to die).

Accessing the verb's complex meaning and integrating it into the full sentence representation might result in increased processing time on causative verbs compared with noncausative verbs. We examined first fixation duration and gaze duration on causative and noncausative verbs (in parentheses) in sentences such as (11) and (12):

(11)   The policeman frightened (encountered) the little girl.

(12)   Paul never convinced (understood) the new president.

We equated the causative and noncausative verbs for word length and word frequency and found, as seen in Table II, no differences in fixation times.

Finally, we examined fixation times associated with negative verbs. Negation is known to result in increased reaction times in a number of psycholinguistic tasks. As was the case with decomposable causatives, the claim has been made that the lexical representation of negative verbs is a complex one containing the negative element and a nonnegative verb. For example, *dislike* means *not to like,* and *doubt* means *not to believe.* Thus, the lexical representation for negative verbs is more complex than their nonnegative counterparts. This complexity of representation might be expected to cause increased processing difficulty for negative verbs. We tested this claim by examining fixation times for negative and nonnegative verbs. We again equated word length and word frequency and asked subjects to read sentences like (13) and (14). The nonnegative verbs are in parentheses.

(13)   The teacher despised (rewarded) the unhappy child.

(14)   The fireman ignored (advised) the town council.

Again, we found no differences in fixation times on the verb as evidenced in Table II.

In summary, there appears to be good evidence that fixation times are influenced by word frequency and by ambiguity when both meanings of a word are likely. Verb complexity appears to have no effect on fixation times. The implication is thus that the retrieval of a complex lexical representation (e.g., one characterized by factivity, negation, or decomposition) is no more difficult than retrieval of a simple one.

IV. CONTEXTUAL EFFECTS ON WORD RECOGNITION

We have so far discussed how preview effects and lexical access influence how long a reader will look at a given word. There have recently been a number of demonstrations that contextual constraints can also strongly influence how long a reader looks at a target word in text. While it is clear that context can affect how long a reader looks at a word, it is less clear what mechanisms account for this finding. We will review work on context effects and then discuss alternative conceptions concerning the mechanisms involved.

A. Context Effects

Zola (1984; see also, McConkie & Zola, 1981) was the first to use eye-movement data to examine the effects of context on word perception. Subjects were asked to read short passages of text while their eye movements were recorded. Each passage had two versions differing only by a single adjective, which either highly constrained or predicted the immediately following noun, or was neutral with respect to it. For example, subjects read a passage about the movie industry. One of the sentences in the passage read as follows:

(15)   Movie theatres must have buttered popcorn to serve their patrons. When subjects were given the passages up through the word *buttered* in a modified cloze task, they responded with the word *popcorn* 83% of the time. On the other hand, when *buttered* was replaced by the word *adequate,* subjects chose *popcorn* as the completion only 8% of the time. In the experiment, subjects read passages with the constraining and neutral adjective. In some conditions, Zola systematically introduced spelling errors in the critical noun so that the *c* in *popcorn,* for example, was replaced with either an *e* or a *t.* He found that the probability of fixating on the target noun was not influenced by the type of adjective or by whether or not there was a misspelling; readers fixated 97% of the time on the target in all conditions. The mean fixation duration and total time spent fixating the target noun were significantly longer in the cases in which there was a misspelling. In cases in which there was not a misspelling, the average fixation duration on the critical noun was 221 msec in the high-constraint condition and 237 msec in the low-constraint condition. The total viewing time (the sum of forward fixations and regressions to the target) was 290 and 313 msec in the high- and low-constraint conditions, respectively.

Zola concluded that the reader encounters all of the visual detail that is available in the text, and the finding that the misspellings influenced fixation duration even in the middle of seven-letter words is consistent with his conclusion. He also concluded that while context did decrease the fixation duration on the target word, the savings were slight.

Zola's experiment is important because the study represented the first attempt to use eye-movement data to measure local context effects on word perception during silent reading. However, the target word in Zola's experiment was constrained only as a result of the immediately preceding word. Ehrlich and Rayner (1981) argued that the effect of context in connected discourse is more likely to be built up and maintained over time than open to constant and immediate changes. Accordingly, in their experiment, Ehrlich and Rayner examined fixation times on target words

TABLE III

Passages from the Experiments of Ehrlich and Rayner (1981)[a]

High constraint (Experiment 1)
He saw the black fin slice through the water and the image of sharks' teeth came quickly to his mind. He turned quickly toward the shore and swam for his life. The coast guard had warned that someone had seen a *shark* off the north shore of the island. As usual, not everyone listened to the warning.

Low constraint (Experiment 2)
The young couple were delighted by the special attention they were getting. The zookeeper explained that the life span of a *shark* is much longer than those of other animals they had talked about. The scientists decided that this man would make a great ally.

High constraint (Experiment 2)
It is often said that dead men tell no tales. But, Fred was very nervous as he put his shovel into the ground where he knew the makeshift grave was. He soon uncovered the skeletal remains and cleared the dirt away. He reached down and picked up one of the *bones* and quickly threw it aside realizing that it was not what he was searching for.

[a] Constraint refers to the predictability of target (italicized) word in the context (the target word is italicized in the examples, but not in the experiments).

(for example, *shark* in Table III) that were highly constrained by the context in one passage but not in another. Half of the time, the spelling of the target word was altered by replacing one of its letters with another letter, thus creating a different word (in this case *shark* became *sharp*). The respelling produced a word which was anomalous in the context of the passage. Table IV presents the fixation-duration data as well as the probability of fixating on the target word as a function of contextual

TABLE IV

Fixation Duration (msec) on a Target Word as a Function of Contextual Constraint and Whether or Not There Was a Respelling[a]

	High Constraint	Low Constraint
Fixation duration		
Normal	221 (.51)	254 (.62)
Respelling	313 (.56)	324 (.79)
Total viewing time		
Normal	248 (.54)	305 (.71)
Respelling	476 (.73)	541 (.87)

[a] Values in parentheses indicate the probability of fixating the target word. Data are from Ehrlich and Rayner (1981).

constraint. As the table shows, there were highly reliable effects of contextual constraint and the presence of a spelling change in the target word.

In a second experiment, Ehrlich and Rayner prepared passages that were also highly constraining for a particular word. However, either the predicted word (for example, the word *bones* in the third paragraph of Table III), or a word that both differed from the target word by a minimally confusable letter in the middle-letter position (*boxes*) and did not result in an anomalous reading of the sentence was used as the target. This latter word, while not being semantically inappropriate, was not consistent with nor predicted by the context. The data from this experiment are presented in Table V. The probability of fixating the target word on forward (left-to-right) saccades did not differ between the two conditions. However, when regressive eye movements were considered, there was a higher probability of fixating on the target word when it was not constrained by the context. Fixation durations on the target were shorter when the predictable word was present in the passage than when the neutral word was used.

The experiments by Zola and by Ehrlich and Rayner demonstrated that fixation time is reduced on a word that is highly predictable from prior context. Ehrlich and Rayner obtained larger differences than did Zola, but the target word in his experiment was constrained only by the immediately preceding word. Three other studies are also relevant with respect to contextual influences on word perception.

Inhoff (1984) asked subjects to read short excerpts taken from *Alice in Wonderland*. Certain critical words in the passage had been rated as being either predictable or unpredictable from the prior context. These target words also varied in word frequency. Inhoff reasoned that high-frequency

TABLE V

Probability of Fixating on the Target Word and Fixation Duration (msec) as a Function of Whether the Target Word Was Predictable or Unpredictable[a]

	Probability of fixating[b]	Fixation duration[c]
Predictable	.68 (.72)	228 (269)
Unpredictable	.68 (.82)	283 (429)

[a] Data are from Ehrlich and Rayner (1981).

[b] Values in parentheses for the probability of fixating include regressions.

[c] Values in parentheses for fixation duration indicate total reading time for target word.

words that were consistent with the thematic context should be read relatively easily. On the other hand, words that were unexpected and infrequent should require more effort for processing. In order to better identify the source of possible processing difficulties, Inhoff used an experimental condition in which a small visual mask (covering only the letter in the center of fixation) moved in synchrony with the eye. Presumably, this mask interfered with initial word identification but had little effect on integration of the words into the sentence or passage. As mentioned previously, he found effects of word frequency. More importantly, he found that unusual items took longer to read than words more likely within the context. The difference was even greater when there was a mask covering part of the target word.

Carpenter and Daneman (1981) had subjects read aloud passages while their eye fixations were monitored. Each passage contained a homograph, such as *bass* in the passage shown in Table VI. In the experiment, prior context was intended to prime (or be consistent with) one meaning of the homograph. Thus, in the example shown in Table VI, the context primed the music interpretation of *bass*. The contexts varied in how strongly they primed one meaning. Carpenter and Daneman found that gaze duration was considerably shorter on the target words when the context more strongly primed the interpretation selected by the subject (as indicated by the subject's pronounciation of the target word).

The preceding studies of context effects varied the overall predictability or consistency of a target word in context. Carroll and Slowiaczek (1986) investigated a related type of context effect, specifically, the effect of the proximity of a priming word which was a semantic associate of the target word. For example, the subject might read

(16) The salesman said that the cloth was actually cotton which had been dyed.

TABLE VI

Sample Passage from Carpenter and Daneman (1981) for the Inconsistent Condition in Which *Bass Guitarists* Is Inconsistent with the Context[a]

The young man turned his back on the rock concert stage and looked across the resort lake. Tomorrow was the annual one-day fishing contest and fishermen would invade the place. Some of the best bass guitarists in the country would come to this spot. The usual routine of fishing resort would be disrupted by the festivities.

(Alternative penultimate sentence: Some of the best bass catchers in the country would come to this spot.)

[a] When the alternative penultimate sentence replaced the *bass guitarists* sentence, context was consistent with and primed *bass catchers*.

The target word is *cotton,* and the related prime word is *cloth,* the category of which *cotton* is an exemplar. In their first experiment Carroll and Slowiaczek varied the strength of the relationship by varying the typicality of the exemplar (*cotton* v. *canvas*), the distance between prime and target, and the presence vs absence of a prime (e.g., *cloth* was replaced by *stuff* in the neutral condition). The semantic associate might be expected to influence fixation time on the target word either by facilitating lexical access or by aiding in postaccess integration, or both. Both hypotheses predict a priming effect and a typicality effect in the prime present condition, but no typicality effect in the unprimed condition. Results are displayed in Table VII. Gaze durations were shorter on the target noun when it was typical (even in the unprimed condition) and when it was primed. There was no effect of distance. The typicality effect was as large in the unprimed condition as in the primed condition, although much of the unprimed typicality effect seems to be due to the shorter gaze duration in the high typical–distant cell.

Carroll and Slowiaczek argued that the priming effect is due to the presence of a semantic associate earlier in the sentence. As indicated earlier, this effect may be due to facilitation of lexical access or of postaccess integration. Carroll and Slowiaczek suggested that the typicality effect is due to the facilitation of the postaccess integration stage by the whole sentence context. Even in the absence of a prime, the typical exemplar probably fit better into the sequence context than did the atypical exemplar.

In another experiment Carroll and Slowiaczek investigated whether the effect of the semantic prime is modified by clausal structure. Contexts

TABLE VII

Gaze Duration (msec) on the Target Noun as a Function of Exemplar Typicality, Distance between Prime and Target, and Presence of Prime[a]

	Exemplar typicality	
Distance	High	Low
Short		
Primed	224	246
Unprimed	265	276
Long		
Primed	228	244
Unprimed	238	276

[a] Data are from Carroll and Slowiaczek (1986).

TABLE VIII

Sample Materials from Carroll and Slowiaczek (1986)[a]

	Across-clause condition
Associative prime:	Although the pilot was unable to brake, the plane on the icy runway rolled to a stop.
Nonassociative prime:	Although the captain was unable to brake, the plane on the icy runway rolled to a stop.
Neutral prime:	Although the fellow was unable to brake, the plane on the icy runway rolled to a stop.
Control:	Everyone watched nervously out of the window. The plane on the icy runway rolled to a stop.
	Within-clause condition
Associative prime:	Although the pilot was unable to brake the plane on the iey runway, it rolled to a stop.
Nonassociative prime:	Although the captain was unable to brake the plane on the icy runway, it rolled to a stop.
Neutral prime:	Although the fellow was unable to brake the plane on the icy runway, it rolled to a stop.

[a] Target word is *plane*.

were created in which a semantic associate primed a target noun either within a clause or across a clause boundary. Three types of primes were used: a semantic associate, a nonassociate at the same level of specificity as the associate, or a general, neutral term. Examples are given in Table VIII. Results are in Table IX. Gaze durations on the target words were shorter when preceded by a semantic associate. In addition, this priming effect was significantly larger in the within-clause condition. This interaction suggests that some of the priming effect may be due to a stage of processing which follows syntactic parsing. Thus, it is consistent with the

TABLE IX

Gaze Durations (msec) on Target Noun as a Function of Prime Type and Clause Condition[a,b]

	Type of prime		
	Associative	Nonassociative	Neutral
Across	237	255	245
Within clause	219	246	267

[a] Control = 242.

[b] Data are from Carroll and Slowiaczek (1986).

hypothesis that at least some of the effect is due to a postaccess integration process.

All of the studies that we have described in this section have documented clear effects of context on fixation time on a target word that is (1) predictable from the context, or (2) highly consistent with the prior context, or (3) highly related to a specific word in the prior content. Many of the experiments also reported lower probabilities of fixating on highly constrained words. The general set of results can be taken as evidence that there is some type of reduced processing for constrained target words or added processing for unexpected words. Experiments such as those described in this section have an advantage over many prior experiments dealing with context effects since the subjects were actually engaged in the ongoing task of reading for meaning (and not making lexical decisions, pushing buttons, or naming words). They also suffer, however, in that there are no clear and obvious baseline conditions (such as a row of Xs or an unrelated word as are typically used in other paradigms) against which to assess patterns of facilitation and interference. As in many types of research, there are thus tradeoffs associated with the particular paradigms used. Nevertheless, despite this limitation there are three possible mechanisms that can be used to account for the general pattern of results. The three explanations for the context effects on eye-movement behavior deal with (1) visual priming, (2) semantic priming, and (3) text integration. We have alluded to each of these mechanisms earlier and now specifically turn to explanations associated with each of them.

B. Visual Priming

We assume that, in isolation, word recognition requires the analysis of a certain amount of visual information acquired while the word is directly fixated. In normal reading some of that visual information can be acquired during a parafoveal preview, thus lowering the amount of visual information analyzed on direct fixation. Recently, McClelland and O'Regan (1981) have proposed a modified logogen (word detector) model in which parafoveal information is used more effectively in the presence of a constraining context. The model assumes that logogens accumulate activation from a number of sources of information, including contextual inputs and parafoveal visual sensory inputs. To influence performance, a logogen must accumulate sufficient activation to reach its threshold. McClelland and O'Regan specifically suggested that a single source of parafoveal information would not produce a sufficient amount of activation to influence performance; although parafoveal visual information will produce activation, this activation will occur for a number of visually similar logogens, and these activated logogens will mutually inhibit each other such that no logogen passes its threshold. In the same manner, a single source of contextual constraint would produce activation for a number of related logogens via priming processes, which ultimately would have the impact of mutually inhibiting each other to produce little net effect of contextual facilitation. However, if contextual constraint is coupled with parafoveal visual information, a single logogen may receive sufficient activation from both sources to pass its threshold. This type of model can account for the general findings reported earlier, that highly constrained contexts resulted in reduced fixation durations when the target word was directly fixated. The model can also explain why the target word was fixated less frequently in the high-constraint condition than in the low-constraint condition of Ehrlich and Rayner's first experiment. If the reader were fixated to the left of the beginning of the target word, the visual information picked up from the target would be the same regardless of experimental condition. However, since parafoveal information can be used more effectively in the high-constraint condition, the visual information acquired nonfoveally may be sufficient to convince the processing system that the word has been identified. The combination of the contextual information and the visual information would lead the reader to skip over the target word more frequently in the high-constraint condition. In Ehrlich and Rayner's (1981) second experiment, the quality of the information picked up from parafoveal vision is again relatively similar whether the predicted or the nonpredicted word is present in the paragraph. For a given context, there should be no difference in forward fixations to the target. However, when the target is fixated, the contextual constraints should have an effect, as was shown by longer fixation durations for the nonpredicted word. A similar account can also explain why Zola (1984) found no differences in the probability of fixating the target word, but did find fixation duration differences.

While the account that we have given is consistent with the results reported by Ehrlich and Rayner (1981), it is the case in their experiment that while contextual constraints were varied, parafoveal information was held constant. Thus, exactly how parafoveal information and contextual constraint interact is indeterminant from their experiment. To examine more precisely how these two sources of information may interact in reading, Balota *et al.* (1985) asked subjects to read sentences like

(19) Since the wedding was today, the baker rushed the wedding cake
    (pies) to the reception.

The target word *cake* is highly predicted by the prior context. On the other hand, the word *pies* is not predicted by the prior context but is an acceptable word in that context. Balota *et al.* (1985) used the boundary technique introduced by Rayner (1975) such that when a reader's eye movement crossed a boundary location in the text, the stimulus presented initially in the target location was replaced by either a predicted word or an acceptable, but low-predictable word. The initially presented stimulus in the target location varied in systematic ways with respect to the target word. Thus, it could be identical to the target word, visually similar to the target word (*cahr* initially presented with *cake* as the target word), identical to the alternative word for that context (*pies–cake*), similar to the alternative word (*picz-cake*), or visually dissimilar and sematically unrelated (*bomb-cake*). The major results from the study are shown in Table X.

There are a number of important implications from these results. First, the data indicate that informative visual information in parafoveal vision is utilized more effectively under conditions of high-contextual constraint. Gaze duration on the target word was the shortest when the parafoveal information was visually similar across saccades and the target word was predictable from prior context. Second, there was not a large effect of contextual constraint on first fixation duration. If we examine the first fixation duration on the target word in the control condition in which the target word does not change (so that *cake* or *pies* in our example is presented throughout the trial), we find the duration is 4 msec shorter in the high-predictable than the low-predictable condition. However, there was a large effect of contextual constraint upon gaze duration when the parafoveal information was visually similar. It is tempting to conclude that context has little effect at the beginning of a fixation, but has a significant influence later in processing. However, it should be emphasized that gaze duration is a fairly immediate response since the decision to make a second fixation on a word must be made well within 200 msec or

TABLE X

Fixation Duration (msec) with Gaze Duration (msec) Presented in Parentheses for the Ten Conditions in the Balota *et al.* (1985) study [a,b]

	Ident	VS	SR	VD	AN
High predictable	223 (232)	218 (248)	232 (280)	236 (280)	240 (292)
Low predictable	227 (264)	232 (263)	258 (287)	242 (277)	240 (290)

[a] VS, Visually similar (*cahr*); SR, semantically related (*pies*); VD, visually different (*picz*); AN, anomalous (*bomb*).

[b] In the high-predictable condition, the target following the display change was always the predictable word (*cake* in our example) and the low-predictable word (*pies*) was always the target in the remaining conditions. Apart from the Ident condition, the other conditions represent the stimulus presented in the target location prior to the display change.

so from starting the first fixation on that word. Third, it is difficult to know if the pattern of results reflects facilitation for the predictable–visually similar condition or interference for the other conditions. The problem here, of course, is the baseline condition issue we discussed previously. However, whether one ascribes to the facilitation or inhibition explanations the clear conclusion which arises is pretty much the same (see Balota *et al.*, for a discussion of facilitation versus interference).

In summary, the results by Balota *et al.* (1985) provide clear evidence that parafoveal visual information can be more effectively used under conditions of high-contextual constraint. Thus, more effective use of parafoveal vision in the presence of high context will lead to a reduced threshold for word identification. The crucial issue is how frequently words are highly predictable from context. In fact, with normal text, readers are not very good at predicting the next word even when they are given unlimited amounts of time to do so (McConkie & Rayner, 1976; Gough, Alford & Holley-Wilcox, 1981). Thus, only a small percentage of the words we read in text are highly predictable from and constrained by the prior context. For words that are of low-contextual constraint (as most words in text are), readers do not appear to be able to use parafoveal information as effectively (Balota *et al.*, 1985; McConkie, Zola, Blanchard, & Wolverton, 1982). In such cases, we would argue that readers simply engage in preliminary letter identification of the next word as we outlined earlier.

C. Semantic Priming

Under the preceding account, context interacted with parafoveal preview to raise the activation level of a logogen above threshold. A semantic priming account of context effects would claim that a highly constraining context alone would raise the activation level of related words, thus facilitating their recognition. For example, in Zola's experiment when the highly constraining adjective is encountered, perhaps by a process of spreading activation, all concepts or semantically related words may be activated in memory so that when the target word is encountered, less processing time is needed on the word. Thus, to use the example that we used previously, when *buttered* is encountered, a number of related concepts such as *toast, corn,* and *popcorn* are all activated. When the reader fixates on *popcorn*, which is the most likely candidate and, hence, most strongly primed, less processing of the visual information would be necessary. On the other hand, when *adequate* is encountered, certain concepts may be activated, but *popcorn* will not be activated as strongly as in the prior case and so longer processing would be required for the target word.

The results reported by Carroll and Slowiaczek (1986) and by Carpenter and Daneman (1981) could also be explained by semantic priming. Carroll and Slowiaczek argued that the effect of the semantic associate was due to semantic priming. Thus, in the example that we used previously, when the reader encounters the word *cloth,* activation processes would quickly lead to the associated concepts *cotton* or *canvas* which would require less processing time when directly fixated. On the other hand, the neutral word *stuff* has no strong semantic relationship to the target words. In Carpenter and Daneman's experiment, the stronger contexts contained several semantic associates of one interpretation of the homograph. For example, in Table VI, the words *lake, fishing,* and *fishermen* may all serve to prime the fish interpretation of *bass.*

It is thus the case that a semantic priming account can also explain why there are decreased fixation times on certain target words constrained by context. The major issue with respect to a semantic priming account of the data is how far back in text can influences of semantic associations be reasonably expected to extend. Certainly, if a work like *buttered* precedes a word like *popcorn,* one can expect priming effects. Also, if the words *doctor* and *nurse* occur in close proximity in the text one might expect priming effects. But, if the word *doctor* occurs followed ten lines later by *nurse,* should we expect priming effects across such a great distance? It seems unlikely given both the rapid decay of activation and the number of concepts which would be activated by intervening words. To date, there is little evidence with respect to the effect of distance on priming effects in a discourse situation (see Foss, 1982).

At this point, it appears possible to account for context effects via priming mechanisms. We would like to make a distinction between *forward priming* and *backward priming*. Forward priming can occur via context manipulations and resulting activation of semantically associated words. It may also occur by the effective use of information in parafoveal vision, as we suggested earlier. The critical factor in forward priming is that information obtained on the current fixation (or prior fixations) primes an upcoming word. An alternative type of priming advocated by some (Underwood, 1980, 1981) can be referred to as backward priming. In this situation, information picked up from words not yet clearly perceived (in parafoveal vision) is assumed to influence the processing of the currently fixated word. In essence, the argument is that readers do some type of semantic preprocessing of words not yet fixated and that preprocessing affects the duration of a fixation on a semantically related word. With respect to this argument, it is the case that there are logical arguments against such a possibility (see Rayner, 1978, 1984), and a great deal of evidence from tachistoscopic experiments (Inhoff & Rayner, 1980; Inhoff, 1982; Paap & Newsome, 1981; Stanovich & West, 1983; Rayner *et al.*, 1980) indicates that information picked up in parafoveal vision does not influence the processing of the currently fixated word. Furthermore, a recent experiment by Rayner, Balota, and Pollatsek (1986) clearly demonstrated that semantic preprocessing of words does not occur in reading.

Both visual priming and semantic priming accounts of contextual effects on fixation times associated with a given word localize the effects at the lexical access stage of processing. The final explanation of context effects localizes the effects at a postlexical stage.

D. Text Integration

A text-integration account of context effects would suggest that target words that are highly constrained by the context are looked at for shorter durations because the reader has less trouble integrating their meanings into a semantic representation of the discourse. Thus, context exerts its effect after the lexicon has been accessed and the meaning of the word arrived at. In the Ehrlich and Rayner (1981) experiment, for example, fixation duration on the constrained target word may have been decreased because it was easier to fit the meaning of the target word into the text representation than it was to fit the nonpredictable target word into the representation. In the Carroll and Slowiaczek (1986) experiment, the effects of typicality that they observed in their first experiment could be due to text-integration processes. Perhaps the target words fit the typical sentence contexts better even in the neutral condition when no semantic associate was present.

A number of processes are likely to be involved in integrating a target word with the rest of the sentence and text. One process which has received a great deal of attention is the search for the antecedent for a definite noun or pronoun. We now discuss a set of experiments designed to investigate this particular integration process.

Antecedent Search

Antecedent search is the process of establishing an antecedent for an anaphoric noun phrase. For example, if the reader encounters *the bird* in the course of reading a sentence, a search of the earlier text for some mention of a bird may be initiated. The process of establishing an antecedent may also entail drawing an inference about some earlier information. A number of reading time experiments have shown that these processes necessary to establishing an antecedent can be time consuming (Clark &

Sengul, 1979; Haviland & Clark, 1974; Lesgold, Roth, & Curtis, 1979).
The question which eye-movement data can address is that of where this
extra time is being spent in reading the sentence.

The research on context effects we discussed previously focused on
investigating how context affects gaze duration on a particular target
word. The research on postlexical antecedent search processes has an
additional focus: Is the process completed while the reader is fixated on
the target word (thus, the whole process is reflected in the gaze duration
on the target word) or does the reader typically move the eyes on to
subsequent words while completing the search (thus, at least some of the
antecedent search times should be reflected in fixation times on words
following the target word)? Just and Carpenter (1980) have claimed that
processing through the completion of antecedent search is carried out
immediately while the reader is fixated on the target word. While the
immediacy claim may be reasonable for various encoding and lexical-
access processes, it seems equally reasonable that certain postlexical
processes might be initiated while the reader fixates the target word, but
might not be completed before the eyes move on. Thus, processing for a
given target word may "spill over" into the next few words. The experiments we now turn to investigate this claim.

Ehrlich and Rayner (1983) monitored eye fixations for subjects reading
paragraphs which contained the target pronoun *he* or *she*. The antecedent
for the pronoun appeared either one word back (at the end of the preced-

TABLE XI

**Sample of Material from Ehrlich and Rayner (1983) Showing the
Three Levels of Distance[a]**

Near

A group of people who shared an interest in photography had recently started writing a
newsletter of their activities. In fact, in one room Mark was mailing a copy of the paper to
Susan. *She* was very involved in photography and spent every weekend taking pictures.

Intermediate

A group of people who shared an interest in photography had recently started writing a
newsletter of their activities. In fact, in one room Mark was mailing a copy of the paper to
Susan. *He* was very involved in photography and spent every weekend taking pictures.

Far

A group of people who shared an interest in photography had recently started writing a
newsletter of their activities. Mark wrote most of the copy but the other members did a lot of
work as well. In fact, in one room Cathy was mailing a copy of the paper to Susan. *He* was
very involved in photography and spent every weekend taking pictures.

[a] The target pronoun is italicized.

TABLE XII

Fixation Duration (msec) as a Function of the Distance between the Pronoun and Its Antecedent[a]

Distance	Prior	Pronoun	One after	Two after	$\bar{x}$
Near	224	248	224	207	226
Intermediate	230	253	234	206	231
Far	220	242	269	296	257
$\bar{x}$	225	248	243	236	238

[a] Data are from Ehrlich and Rayner (1983, Experiment 2).

ing sentence), one line back, or at least three lines back in the text. An example text is given in Table XI. Prior research suggests that antecedent search time increases with the distance of the antecedent (Clark & Sengul, 1979). The immediacy assumption predicts that this increased time will show up on the pronoun when first encountered. The results are displayed in Table XII. Mean times are given for the fixation on the pronoun, the fixation preceding the pronoun, and the first and second fixation following the pronoun. While fixation times on the pronoun were longer than the times on the preceding fixation, pronoun fixation times did not differ depending on distance. A distance effect did not appear until one and two fixations following the pronoun. Ehrlich and Rayner concluded that antecedent search processes were not always completed while the reader fixated the pronoun. Antecedent search may be initiated while the reader is fixating the pronoun, but it may not be completed until one or two fixations following the pronoun.[6]

It is of some interest to know whether the pattern of results for pronouns would also hold more generally for nouns requiring antecedents. It may be that pronouns are special lexical items which elicit a strategy of delaying antecedent search until more information is available. In con-

[6] Since this article was originally written, some controversy has arisen concerning the extent to which pronoun processing and anaphoric reference processes are evident immediately when pronouns are fixated (and on the one or two fixations following pronoun encoding as reported by Ehrlich and Rayner). While Vonk (1984) has reported results very similar to those reported by Ehrlich and Rayner, Blanchard (1987) and Carroll and Slowiaczek (1987) have been unable to find systematic differences in fixation times in the region of a pronoun. There is some indication (Clifton & Ferreira, 1987) that mental distance (i.e., whether or not there is a topic change in the discourse) rather than physical distance (i.e., the number of intervening words between referent and pronoun) is an important variable, but more research is probably needed.

TABLE XIII

Sample Texts in Which the Target Word is *Bird;* Its Antecedent Varies in Typicality and Distance

Close high and low typical

Fred stepped carefully onto his front porch. An unexpected snowstorm had hit the night before. Drifts covered the yard. The snow had drifted onto the porch. In fact Fred had worried that it might pile up against the front door. Fred found a [robin/goose] huddled under a porch chair. The *bird* was in a protected spot. Fred could tell that it was cold but still alive.

Distant high and low typical

Fred stepped carefully onto his front porch. An unexpected snowstorm had hit the night before. Drifts covered the yard. Fred found a [robin/goose] huddled under a porch chair. The snow had drifted onto the porch. In fact Fred had worried that it might pile up against the front door. The *bird* was in a protected spot. Fred could tell that is was cold but still alive.

trast, nouns typically have more semantic content, presumably making the immediate search for an antecedent much easier. An experiment that we have recently carried out investigated antecedent search processes using nouns as targets rather than pronouns. An example text is given in Table XIII. The target noun was always a category name (e.g., *bird*); the antecedent was always an exemplar of the category (e.g., *robin*). As in the Ehrlich and Rayner (1983) study, the distance between antecedent and target noun was varied. In addition, the typicality of the exemplar used as antecedent was varied (e.g., *robin* vs *goose*). Research of Garrod and Sanford (1977) has shown that antecedent search time is increased when the antecedent is atypical.

Table XIV displays the gaze durations on the target noun itself as well

TABLE XIV

Gaze Durations (msec) on Target Word and on Region following Target Word (msec per character) as a Function of Typicality and Distance of Antecedent

	Distance	
Typicality	Close	Distant
On target nouns		
High	249	273
Low	284	273
On rest of line		
High	25	26
Low	28	28

as the time spent on the rest of the line following the target noun. Turning first to the time spent on the rest of the line, readers were reliably slower when the exemplar was atypical. While the means also displayed a modest distance effect, this was not reliable in the statistical analyses. We attribute this pattern to the completion of antecedent search processes after the eyes have moved beyond the target noun itself. We suspect that the distant–low mean is lower than expected because frequently subjects gave up the antecedent search before finding the antecedent. In general, the spill-over pattern was consistent with that of the pronoun study. The experimental factors also affected the gaze durations on the noun itself. Gaze durations on the close–high typical target were shorter than those on the target words in the other three conditions. This effect may be due to priming of the category name by the recent mention of a typical category member.

Finally, an experiment by Just and Carpenter (1978) investigated inferential processes in antecedent search. Subjects read texts each containing a critical sentence pair such as

(20) The millionaire (was murdered/died) on a dark and stormy night. The killer left no clues for the police to trace.

The second member of the pair contained a target noun phrase whose antecedent could be inferred from the verb in the first sentence. In one condition the inference was direct (e.g., *murder* entails an agent—*killer*). In the other condition the inference was indirect (e.g., *die* does not entail a *killer*). The inference of an antecedent should be more difficult in the indirect condition, and this difficulty should be reflected in increased reading time. Two kinds of reading tasks were used, a normal reading task and a task in which the subject had to judge each sentence for consistency with the earlier information presented. Since the latter task produced more reliable data, our discussion focuses on the results of this task.

As predicted, subjects spent more time reading the target sentence in the indirect condition. More specifically, an additional 65 msec were spent fixating the target word; an additional 24 and 44 msec were spent on the first and second words following the target word, respectively. Just and Carpenter argue that the effects are due to integration processes which are more time consuming for the indirect condition. Semantic priming might also account for at least some of the effect on the target noun itself. This account would claim that *killer* is faster in the direct condition because encoding is facilitated by the recent occurrence of a semantically related word (*murdered*). The pattern of fixations on the words following the target suggests that some integrative processing from the target spills over to affect fixation times on the next few words.

The research on antecedent search suggests that this particular integration process is not generally completed before the reader moves the eyes

TABLE XV

Passages from the Experiments of Schustack *et al.* (1987)[a]

Distant prior mention

Greg was decorating his new room, and he especially wanted to cover the cracks in the walls. He had been to an art gallery and had bought a picture that he thought was bright and cheery. It was important to him that the room feel comfortable and inviting. He *hung* the *picture* on the wall that had the biggest crack.

(Alternative last sentence: He *put* the *picture* on the wall . . . .)

Recent prior mention

Greg was decorating his new room, and he especially wanted to cover the cracks in the walls. It was important to him that the room feel comfortable and inviting. He had been to an art gallery and had bought a picture that he thought was bright and cheery. He *hung* the *picture* on the wall that had the biggest crack.

(Alternative last sentence: He *put* the *picture* on the wall . . . .)

---

[a] The target word and the verb are italicized in the examples, but were not in the experiments.

beyond the target word. Thus, gaze durations on the target word do not always reflect the total time needed to complete processing on the word. Given the finding of spill-over effects, it is reasonable to ask whether gaze durations on the target word reflect the difficulty of antecedent search at all. For Ehrlich and Rayner's pronoun study, the answer seems to be no; fixation time on the pronouns themselves did not differ with differences in antecedent distance. In both the study we carried out and the Just and Carpenter study, gaze duration on the target word did vary with antecedent search difficulty, but in both cases the effects could also be explained by a semantic priming account.

A series of studies by Schustack, Ehrlich and Rayner (1987) attempted to isolate priming effects and postlexical access integration effects on a target noun. The varied the difficulty of antecedent search by varying the distance between the target noun and its previous mention in the passage. They also varied the predictability of the target noun by varying the restrictiveness of the verb immediately preceding the target noun. Table

TABLE XVI

Gaze Duration (msec) and Probability of Fixation on a Target Word (in Parentheses) in the Schustack *et al.* (1987) study

	Near	Far
General verb	215 (.80)	236 (.87)
Restrictive verb	202 (.70)	220 (.75)

XV gives examples of the passages used, and Table XVI presents the results from the experiment. Schustack *et al.* (1987) found that both the probability of fixating on the target and fixation duration on the target were reduced when the target was preceded by a restrictive verb and when the target had been recently mentioned in the passage. In a subsequent experiment, they used the same texts in a naming task (eye movements were not monitored). Subjects controlled the word-by-word presentation of the text. When the target word was presented, it was preceded by asterisks to indicate that a naming response was required. Schustack *et al.* (1987) argued that the naming task requires lexical access but not antecedent search, while the reading task requires both. Thus, effects which are common to both the reading and naming tasks should be due to the priming of lexical access; effects which appear only in the reading task must result from postaccess integrative processes (e.g., antecedent search). As in the reading task, there was an effect of verb type, with faster naming times occurring when the target word was preceded by a restrictive verb. In contrast to the reading task, however, there was no effect of distance. Given their assumptions about the processes required by the two tasks, Schustack *et al.* (1987) concluded that the effect of verb type in the reading task results from the priming of lexical access; the distance effect results from antecedent search processes.

In summary, the evidence so far suggests that antecedent search processes may be initiated while the target word is directly fixated, but such processes may not be completed until the eyes have moved one or two fixations beyond the target. Thus, while fixation time on the target may reflect some antecedent search, fixation time on the following words may also be elevated due to antecedent search. The degree to which fixation time on the target word reflects antecedent search may depend on the type of word it is. In the Ehrlich and Rayner (1983) study, pronouns showed no increased fixation time with increasing distance of antecedent; in contrast, Schustack *et al.* (1987) did find such an increase for nouns.

V. SYNTACTIC PARSING

As outlined in Section IV, antecedent search is one process whose effect is not necessarily localized on a specific target word in text, but rather is spread across a specific region of text containing several words. This is in contrast to the processes involved in word recognition. The processes involved in syntactic parsing are a second set of processes whose effects are most reasonably localized to a region of a sentence rather than to a specific word. We will now discuss a set of experiments in which eye-movement data were collected to study syntactic parsing. In these experiments, the fixation patterns in a prespecified region of a sentence were examined for evidence of parsing difficulty.

In the past, researchers interested in the immediate and on-line effects of syntax have struggled with cumbersome techniques. Syntactic analysis cannot be separated from sentence processing (as can single word effects), nor can it be simply related to end-of-sentence measures as is possible with more general comprehension questions. The more interesting questions about sentence structure concern how it is realized moment by moment and how (and when) recovery is made from inappropriate parsing and subsequent misinterpretation.

A number of recent studies have revealed that eye-movement data are reasonably sensitive to syntactic considerations. We have already pointed out that a number of studies have reported that the main verb in simple sentences received longer fixations than did nouns. It has also been demonstrated that certain types of syntactic structures result in more and longer fixation durations (Klein & Kurkowski, 1974; Wanat, 1971; Holmes & O'Regan, 1981). For example, Wanat (1971) found more and longer fixations in left-embedded sentences than in corresponding right-embedded sentences. For example, sentence (21) is a left-embedded sentence while sentence (22) is a right-embedded sentence.

(21) On the picnic the girls that Bill teased saw the child.

(22) The girls saw the child that Bill teased on the picnic.

Since there was no difference in the number of regressions and durations of regressions, he was able to isolate the difficulty with the left-embedded sentences to particular regions. Recently, Holmes and O'Regan (1981) found differences in fixation durations and eye-movement patterns when native French readers read subject and object relative clause sentences in French. The crucial syntactic form which French makes possible is the transposed-object relative clause which has a surface form almost identical to the subject relative clause, but in meaning is merely a variation on the object relative clause. When the first pass through the relative clause was examined, Holmes and O'Regan found that the pattern of fixations for the transposed-object relative clause was more similar to that of the subject relative than that of the object relative. On the other hand, the overall probability of regressing to a constituent was primarily determined by the underlying deep structure. Subject relatives were read with fewer regressions than either type of object relative. Holmes and O'Regan also pointed out that differences in the starting point for the regressive sequences between the two types of object relatives suggest a particular combination of deep- and surface-structure properties in determining when the eye makes a regression.

Structurally ambiguous sentences have traditionally proven to be one of the most useful types of stimuli for researchers interested in syntactic processing. The earliest study using such stimuli while eye movements were recorded was reported by Mehler, Bever, and Carey (1967). They had subjects read sentences such as

(23) They gave her dog candies.

(24) Visiting relatives can be a nuisance.

Such sentences were embedded in contexts appropriate for two different readings. Mehler *et al.* reported that readers tend to fixate the beginnings of surface-structure constituents. That is, subjects tended to fixate more often on the word *dog* when it was interpreted as the beginning of the noun phrase *dog candies* than when it was interpreted as the head of the noun phrase *her dog*. While this study is important because it represented a first attempt to relate patterns of eye movements to syntactic structure, there are a number of problems associated with it that make interpretation difficult (see Rayner, 1978; Frazier, 1983; and Rayner & Carroll, 1984, for extended discussions of the study). First, forward fixations were not measured separately from regressive fixations; Frazier (1983) pointed out that readers may initially compute a contextually inappropriate reading of a noun phrase and realize the need to revise it when they reach information which specifies the correct interpretation. These readers may then regress to the beginning of the ambiguous phrase leading to the observed correlation of fixations and structure. Indeed, research by Frazier and Rayner (1982) and by Kennedy and Murray (1984) has demonstrated that when readers misanalyze a phrase, they frequently regress to the ambiguous region when disambiguating information is encountered. A second problem with the study is that fixation-duration data were not reported. Third, O'Regan (1975) was unable to replicate the result. Finally, Rayner (1978) and Frazier (1983) pointed out that the correlation between structure and fixation location is conceptually problematic since it is not clear how readers could determine either the position or the number of left brackets (beginnings of constituents) before they had performed an analysis of the structural consequences of the words that they had not yet fixated. That is, the general rule of fixating the first half of the immediate constituent implies that the reader can made this determination on the basis of extra-foveal information. If this level of identification can be made from words in parafoveal vision (and our review of the perceptual-span research described in Section II, A strongly indicates that it cannot), it is difficult to see why a reader would then fixate on a region that has already been interpreted.

A number of studies recently conducted in our laboratory have examined eye-movement patterns as subjects read structurally ambiguous sentences. Frazier and Rayner (1982) suggested that the reader initially parses a sentence according to a few simple strategic preferences based on the limitations of short-term memory. Such an approach avoids the problems encountered by Mehler *et al.* (1967) of needing to postulate that the reader knows what is coming before the visual system could have taken in that information. In addition, these strategic preferences allow rather clear predictions of where the reader will detect an error during the first analysis of a sentence and what would be necessary to correct the original inappropriate analysis. Two general parsing strategies, late closure and minimal attachment (described in detail by Frazier, 1978), were investigated by Frazier and Rayner. According to the late-closure strategy, the reader should attach, whenever possible, incoming words to the clause or phrase currently being constructed (i.e., to the lowest possible nonterminal node dominating the last item analyzed). According to minimal attachment, the reader should prefer an analysis leading to the simplest structural description of the sentence consistent with the well-formedness of the language (technically, incoming material should be attached to the phrase structure being constructed using the fewest possible nodes).

Frazier and Rayner asked subjects to read sentences such as
(25) While Mary was mending the sock fell of her lap.
(26) While Mary was mending the sock it fell off her lap.
Sentence (25) can lead to a misreading if *the sock* is interpreted as the direct object of *was mending*. Sentence (26) leads to no such misreading. Reading performance for garden-path sentences such as (25) was compared with sentences such as (26) to study a subject's recovery from erroneous parsing. Frazier and Rayner found that the first fixation in the disambiguating region of the garden-path sentence was longer than normal. In studying the reanalysis processes involved in recovering from parsing errors, the pattern of regressions and fixation times indicated that the subject generally does not move backwards step by step through the sentence until the source of the error has been discovered, nor does the reader return to the beginning of the sentence to start again. Rather, the confused reader apparently uses whatever information is available at the time the error is detected to restructure the sentence appropriately. The kinds of decisions made by the reader can be predicted by the parsing strategies mentioned earlier. Thus, it is possible to explain differences among ambiguous sentences in difficulty of reanalysis. Kennedy and Murray (1984) and Rayner and Frazier (1987) have reported results which are very consistent with the Frazier and Rayner study, with the exception that Kennedy and Murray found that subjects backtracked through the sentence more frequently than did subjects in the original study.

In another study, Rayner, Carlson, and Frazier (1983) used eye-movement data to explore the various contributions of syntactic, pragmatic, and semantic information in sentence comprehension. In their first experiment, subjects read sentences which were temporarily ambiguous from the perspective of a left-to-right parser and which varied in pragmatic plausibility and structural preference, such as

(27) Susan said that the florist sent the flowers was very pleased with herself.

(28) Susan said that the performer sent the flowers was very pleased with herself.

(29) Susan said that the performer who was sent flowers was very pleased with herself.

(30) Susan said that the performer sent the flowers and was very pleased with herself.

Given the choice of reading the string *the florist sent the flowers* in 27 as a simple active clause or as a type of relative clause (the reduced relative, meaning the florist who was sent the flowers), people tend to prefer the simple active alternative. The preference for the reduced relative reading of sentence (28) was slightly greater than 50%, indicating that pragmatic information about whether performers get or send flowers influences the reading of such strings. Reading time was analyzed for different passes (initial reading and second pass or regressions) through the sentence as well as for different segments of the sentence. The results indicated that the initial analysis of the sentence followed structural preferences, not pragmatic preferences.

In a second experiment, Rayner *et al.* used sentences such as

(31) The spy saw the cop with the binoculars, but the cop didn't see him.

(32) The spy saw the cop with the pistol, but the cop didn't see him.

Sentence (31) is ambiguous with respect to the person holding the binoculars, while sentence (32) leaves little doubt that the cop had the pistol. The minimal-attachment strategy described earlier suggests that the instrumental reading of *with the binoculars* (putting them in the hands of the spy) should be preferred. Of course, if this is true, the parser should also initially prefer the instrumental reading of sentence (32), making *the pistol* a viewing instrument even though this reading is somewhat bizarre. While the ultimate reading of the sentence was consistent with pragmatic considerations of real-world plausibility, the eye-movement data indicated that a conflict between pragmatic and structural preferences leads to longer reading times and some need for reanalysis.

Ferreira and Clifton (1986) embedded sentences like those used by Rayner *et al.* in contexts that were either neutral or biased the reader to one interpretation or the other. They found results consistent with those reported by Rayner *et al.* even in biasing contexts. Apparently, the reader's initial choice of a syntactic representation of an input string is quite independent of contextual and pragmatic information. These results suggest that the parsing strategies investigated by Frazier and Rayner (1982) and by Rayner and Frazier (1987) are rather autonomous and that readers generally attach words to the clause or phrase either currently being processed (late closure) or leading to the simplest structural description (minimal attachment).

In general, the results of the studies described to this point suggest that the syntactic parser initially and immediately computes just a single syntactic analysis which can be rapidly altered if and when additional information sources are consulted. Eye-movement data have been particularly useful in distinguishing between various hypotheses concerning how temporarily ambiguous strings are parsed because the experimenter can examine a temporal record as the reader encounters such sentences. There is, however, some recent evidence to indicate that, on occasion, the parser delays in assigning an analysis to an ambiguous string until it receives disambiguating information dictating the correct analysis. In particular, Frazier and Rayner (1987) reported three experiments in which subjects read sentences such as

(33) I know that the desert trains young people to be especially tough.
(34) I know that the desert trains are especially tough on young people.
(35) I know that this desert trains young people to be especially tough.
(36) I know that these desert trains are especially tough on young people.

In sentences (35) and (36), the ambiguous string (in terms of syntactic category) *desert trains* is disambiguated by preceding material. In sentences (33) and (34) the disambiguating material follows the ambiguous string, and so when it is encountered the reader cannot determine whether *desert* is an adjective or a noun or if *trains* is a noun or a verb. Frazier and Rayner (1987) found that readers took longer to read the ambiguous string when it had been disambiguated by preceding information and that subjects took longer to read the remainder of the sentence when the disambiguating information followed the string. On the basis of a number of analyses, Frazier and Rayner (1987) concluded that in the case of categorical ambiguities the processor follows a strategy of delaying a structural analysis until more information is provided. As mentioned, this result differs somewhat from the view proposed by Frazier and Rayner (1982) and by Rayner *et al.* (1983) in which the evidence suggested that, for already categorized items, the language processor immediately initiates its attempt to integrate the current word into a constituent structure representation of the sentence. Frazier and Rayner (1987) argued that the general distinction between circumstances where the processor follows a strategy of immediately committing itself to the first available syntactic analysis on an input and circumstances where it delays selection of a single analysis is the distinction between representations that must be computed by rule (e.g., syntactic structures) and representations that are already prestored in memory (e.g., representations of words or "lexical items").

VI. SUMMARY

In this article, we have attempted to document our optimism for using eye-movement data as a means of studying comprehension processes. In much of the research we described, the unit of analysis for comprehension that we have been interested in has been the individual word. We have seen that certain characteristics of words, sentences, and text lead to reductions (or increases) in the amount of time that a reader looks at a particular target word. We take these variations in fixation time on preselected target words as being indicative of the ease (or difficulty) that a reader has in comprehending that particular word. In addition to examining fixation times on individual target words, we have also used eye-movement patterns as a means of studying the effects of syntax upon comprehension processes. Here, the general strategy has been to have readers read sentences containing temporary structural ambiguities and to examine the eye-movement record when garden-path effects occur. The pattern of eye movements has been particularly informative in determining (1) the point at which readers realize that they have misparsed the sentence and (2) how they attempt to recover from the inappropriate analysis to reparse the sentence for appropriate comprehension.

In earlier research eras, attempts to study reading comprehension and language processes via eye movements were largely unsuccessful (see Blumenthal, 1970). The research undertaken from 1900 to 1920 failed to reveal any interesting facts about language processing during reading. However, recent work in linguistics and psychology has led to a description of language more compatible with mentalistic processing models than was the case in the earlier period. Likewise, the description of the memory system underlying our knowledge of words and concepts gives us hope of separating the effects of word identification, sentence structure, and higher level inference processes. The view of language comprehension as the output of a system composed of processing components allows us to look at the independent contribution of various processing modules as well as their interrelationships and the processes coordinating their activity.

The studies that we have reviewed here lead us to believe that eye-movement data can be used to study moment-to-moment processing of language. The primary characteristic of most of the work reviewed is that we have been able to identify in advance specific locations in the text where processing should be more difficult (or easier) depending upon contextual constraints, syntactic structures, or semantic relations. In effect, this research has indicated that the processing load is reflected in the pattern of the eye movements and, particularly, the duration of the fixations. The advantage of the method is that the data can be collected on line as the subject reads the text; it is not necessary to draw inferences about comprehension processes using data from end-of-sentence tasks or using global measures such as total reading time where one is not sure which part of the sentence actually led to changes in reading time. Subjects can read at their own pace, secondary tasks need not be employed, and the situation is relatively normal.

This is not to say that other techniques are not valuable for studying reading comprehension or that even the basic groundwork has yet been fully laid for using eye movements to study reading comprehension. As has been pointed out elsewhere (Rayner & Carroll, 1984) there are a number of unanswered questions concerning mapping the pattern of eye movements onto a textual stimulus which must be described at several levels corresponding to levels of a processing system of great complexity. For example, although fixation time on certain target words can be shown to decrease as a function of specific manipulations, it generally cannot be determined if the major reason is due to semantic (and/or visual) priming operating at the lexical-access stage or due to post-lexical-access text-integration processes. Likewise, it is not certain what relationship exists between multiple and single fixations on a word. Are two 200 msec fixations equal to one 400 msec fixation? The answers to these and many other questions can only be ascertained through careful and well-designed research.

Finally, it is the case that eye-movement data, like all other types of data used by cognitive psychologists, do not necessarily yield consistent results from one study to another. We noted that results of studies dealing with eye movements and pronoun processing (Blanchard, 1987; Carroll & Slowiaczek, 1987; Ehrlich & Rayner, 1983; Vonk, 1984) have not been very consistent. Likewise, studies dealing with clausal and sentence wrap-up (Blanchard, 1985; Carrithers & Bever, 1984; Just & Carpenter, 1980) have yielded inconsistent results. Sentence wrap-up occurs at the end of a sentence and involves the reader tying together various aspects of a sentence and integrating it with the rest of the discourse. Studies dealing with this topic have confounded particular lexical items with the end of the sentence. In our lab, we have carried out some studies in which the same words occurred at the end of a sentence (or clause) in one condition, while in another they occurred at nonterminal locations in the sentence. We have found longer fixation times on target words when they ended a sentence (or clause) than when they did not. Some inconsistent results may thus be due to characteristics of any particular study and the methods used in the study. However, it may also be the case that the effects of some discourse-level (or higher order) processes are not confined to single fixations in the eye-movement record, but rather are smeared over a number of fixations. We have had the experience of producing what seemed like perfectly good passages to examine a certain type of comprehension process, only to find no obvious or immediate effect in the eye-fixation times. In such cases, the overall reading times generally reveal the processing complexity. We suggest that one goal of research using eye movements to study comprehension processes ought to be the delineation of conditions under which individual fixation times do and do not reflect higher level processing.

Our purpose here has not been to assert that the problems are simple or even that the basic parameters controlling the reading system are well defined. Research on eye-movement control and the perceptual span in reading has provided some relatively clear information concerning how much information can effectively be used during an eye fixation, and this research has naturally led us to investigate language processing. As we have documented here, recent research using eye-movement data to investigate language processing during reading has been successful, and we suspect that answers to many questions about the reading processes will be unveiled by examining in greater detail the spatial and temporal record left by the eye during the reading of text.

ACKNOWLEDGMENTS

Preparation of this contribution was supported by Grants HD12727 and HD17246 from the National Institute of Child Health and Human Development, and Grant BNS-8510177 from the National Science Foundation to the first author. The second author was supported by a postdoctoral fellowship from the National Institute of Mental Health. We thank Chuck Clifton, Meredyth Daneman, and Lyn Frazier for their comments on an earlier draft.

REFERENCES

Balota, D. A., Pollatsek, A., & Rayner, K. (1985). The interaction of contextual constraints and parafoveal visual information in reading. *Cognitive Psychology, 17,* 364–390.
Balota, D. A., & Rayner, K. (1983). Parafoveal visual information and semantic contextual constraints. *Journal of Experimental Psychology: Human Perception and Performance, 9,* 726–738.

Blanchard, H. E. (1985). A comparison of some processing time measures based on eye movements. *Acta Psychologica,* **58,** 1–15.

Blanchard, H. E. (1987). Pronoun processing during fixations: Effects on the time course of information utilization. *Bulletin of the Psychonomic Society,* **25,** 171–174.

Blanchard, H. E., McConkie, G. W., Zola, D., & Wolverton, G. W. (1984). Time course of visual information utilization during fixations in reading. *Journal of Experimental Psychology: Human Perception and Performance,* **10,** 75–89.

Blumenthal, A. L. (1970). *Language and psychology.* New York: Wiley.

Bouma, H., & de Voogd, A. H. (1974). On the control of eye saccades in reading. *Vision Research,* **14,** 273–284.

Carpenter, P. A., & Daneman, M. (1981). Lexical retrieval and error recovery in reading: A model based on eye fixations. *Journal of Verbal Learning and Verbal Behavior,* **20,** 138–160.

Carpenter, P. A., & Just, M. A. (1983). What your eyes do while your mind is reading. In K. Rayner (Ed.), *Eye movements in reading: Perceptual and language processes.* New York: Academic Press.

Carrithers, C., & Bever, T. G. (1984). Eye-movement patterns confirm theories of language comprehension. *Cognitive Science,* **8,** 157–172.

Carroll, P., & Slowiaczek, M. L. (1986). Constraints on semantic priming in reading: A fixation time analysis. *Memory & Cognition,* **14,** 509–522.

Carroll, P., & Slowiaczek, M. L. (1987). Modes and modules: Multiple pathways to the language processor. In J. Garfield (Ed.), *Modularity in knowledge representation and natural language processing.* Cambridge, MA: MIT Press.

Clark, H., & Sengul, C. (1979). In search of referents for nouns and pronouns. *Memory & Cognition,* **7,** 35–41.

Clifton, C., & Ferreira, F. (1987). Discourse structure and anaphora: Some experimental results. In M. Coltheart (Ed.), *Attention and performance 12.* London: Erlbaum.

Cutler, A. (1983). Lexical complexity and sentence processing. In G. B. Flores d'Arcais and R. J. Jarvella (Eds.), *The processes of language understanding.* New York: Wiley.

Ehrlich, S. F., & Rayner, K. (1981). Contextual effects on word perception and eye movements during reading. *Journal of Verbal Learning and Verbal Behavior,* **20,** 641–655.

Ehrlich, K., & Rayner, K. (1983). Pronoun assignment and semantic integration during reading: Eye movements and immediacy of processing. *Journal of Verbal Learning and Verbal Behavior,* **22,** 75–87.

Ferreira, F., & Clifton, C. (1986). The independence of syntactic processing. *Journal of Memory and Language,* **25,** 348–368.

Foss, D. J. (1982). A discourse on semantic priming. *Cognitive Psychology,* **14,** 590–607.

Frazier, L. (1978). *On comprehending sentences: Syntactic parsing strategies.* Unpublished doctoral dissertation, University of Connecticut. (Available from the University of Indiana Linguistics Club, 310 Lindley Hall, University of Indiana, Bloomington, IN).

Frazier, L. (1983). Processing sentence structure. In K. Rayner (Ed.), *Eye movements in reading: Perceptual and language processes.* New York: Academic Press.

Frazier, L., & Rayner, K. (1982). Making and correcting errors during sentence comprehension: Eye movements in the analysis of structurally ambiguous sentences. *Cognitive Psychology,* **14,** 178–210.

Frazier, L., & Rayner, K. (1987). Resolution of syntactic category ambiguities: Eye movements in parsing lexically ambiguous sentences. *Journal of Memory and Language,* **26,** 505–526.

Garrod, S., & Sanford, A. (1977). Interpreting anaphoric relations: The integration of semantic information while reading. *Journal of Verbal Learning and Verbal Behavior,* **16,** 77–90.

Gough, P. B., Alford, J. A., Jr., & Holley-Wilcox, P. (1981). Words and contexts. In O. L. Tzeng & H. Singer (Eds.), *Perception of print: Reading research in experimental psychology.* Hillsdale, NJ: Erlbaum.

Haviland, S., & Clark, H. (1974). What's new? Acquiring new information as a process in comprehension. *Journal of Verbal Learning and Verbal Behavior, 13,* 512–521.

Hogaboam, T. W. (1983). Reading patterns in eye movement data. In K. Rayner (Ed.), *Eye movements in reading: Perceptual and language processes.* New York: Academic Press.

Holmes, V. M., & O'Regan, J. K. (1981). Eye fixation patterns during the reading of relative-clause sentences. *Journal of Verbal Learning and Verbal Behavior, 20,* 417–430.

Inhoff, A. W. (1982). Parafoveal word perception: A further case against semantic preprocessing. *Journal of Experimental Psychology: Human Perception and Performance, 8,* 137–145.

Inhoff, A. W. (1984). Two stages of word processing during eye fixations in the reading of prose. *Journal of Verbal Learning and Verbal Behavior, 23,* 612–624.

Inhoff, A. W. (1985). The effect of factivity on lexical retrieval and post-lexical processing during eye fixations in reading. *Journal of Psycholinguistic Research, 14,* 45–56.

Inhoff, A. W., & Rayner, K. (1980). Parafoveal word perception: A case against semantic preprocessing. *Perception & Psychophysics, 27,* 457–464.

Inhoff, A. W., & Rayner, K. (1986). Parafoveal word processing during eye fixations in reading: Effects of word frequency. *Perception & Psychophysics, 40,* 431–439.

Just, M. A., & Carpenter, P. A. (1978). Inference processes during reading: Reflections from eye fixations. In J. W. Sanders, D. F. Fisher, & R. A. Monty (Eds.), *Eye movements and the higher psychological functions.* Hillsdale, NJ: Erlbaum.

Just, M. A., & Carpenter, P. A. (1980). A theory of reading: From eye fixations to comprehension. *Psychological Review, 87,* 329–354.

Kennedy, A., & Murray, W. S. (1984). Inspection times for words in syntactically ambiguous sentences under three presentation conditions. *Journal of Experimental Psychology: Human Perception and Performance, 10,* 833–849.

Klein, G. A., & Kurkowski, F. (1974). Effect of task demands on relationship between eye movements and sentence complexity. *Perceptual and Motor Skills, 39,* 463–466.

Kliegl, R., Olson, R. K., & Davidson, B. J. (1982). Regression analysis as a tool for studying reading processes: Comment on Just and Carpenter's eye fixation theory. *Memory & Cognition, 13,* 107–111.

Kucera, H., & Francis, W. (1967). *Computational analysis of present-day American English.* Providence, RI: Brown University Press.

Lesgold, A., Roth, S., & Curtis, M. (1979). Foregrounding effects in discourse comprehension. *Journal of Verbal Learning and Verbal Behavior, 18,* 291–308.

Lima, S. D., & Inhoff, A. W. (1985). Lexical access during eye fixations in reading: Effects of word-initial letter sequence. *Journal of Experimental Psychology: Human Perception and Performance, 11,* 272–285.

Marslen-Wilson, W. D., & Welsh, A. (1978). Processing interactions and lexical access during word recognition in continuous speech. *Cognitive Psychology, 10,* 29–63.

McClelland, J. L., & O'Regan, J. K. (1981). Expectations increase the benefit derived from parafoveal visual information in reading words aloud. *Journal of Experimental Psychology: Human Perception and Performance, 7,* 634–644.

McConkie, G. W., & Hogaboam, T. W. (1985). Eye position and word identification during reading. In R. Groner, G. W. McConkie, & C. Menz (eds.), *Eye movements and human information processing.* Amsterdam: North-Holland Publ.

McConkie, G. W., Hogaboam, T. W., Wolverton, G. S., Zola, D., & Lucas, P. A. (1979).

Toward the use of eye movements in the study of language processing. *Discourse Processes, 2,* 157–177.

McConkie, G. W., & Rayner, K. (1975). The span of the effective stimulus during a fixation in reading. *Perception & Psychophysics, 17,* 578–586.

McConkie, G. W., & Rayner, K. (1976). Identifying the span of the effective stimulus in reading: Literature review and theories of reading. In H. Singer & R. B. Ruddell (Eds.), *Theoretical models and processes of reading.* Newark, DE: International Reading Association.

McConkie, G. W., & Zola, D. (1979). Is visual information integrated across successive fixations in reading? *Perception & Psychophysics, 25,* 221–224.

McConkie, G. W., & Zola, D. (1981). Language constraints and the functional stimulus in reading. In A. M. Lesgold & C. A. Perfetti (Eds.), *Interactive processes in reading.* Hillsdale, NJ: Erlbaum.

McConkie, G. W., Zola, D., Blanchard, H. E., & Wolverton, G. S. (1982). Perceiving words during reading: Lack of facilitation from prior peripheral exposure. *Perception & Psychophysics, 32,* 271–281.

Mehler, J., Bever, T. G., & Carey, P. (1967). What we look at when we read. *Perception & Psychophysics, 2,* 213–218.

Mehler, J., Segui, J., & Carey, P. (1978). Tails of words: Monitoring ambiguity. *Journal of Verbal Learning and Verbal Behavior, 17,* 29–35.

Morrison, R. E. (1984). Manipulation of stimulus onset delay in reading: Evidence for parallel programming of saccades. *Journal of Experimental Psychology: Human Perception and Performance, 10,* 667–682.

Newman, J. E., & Dell, G. S. (1978). The phonological nature of phoneme-monitoring: A critique of some ambiguity studies. *Journal of Verbal Learning and Verbal Behavior, 17,* 359–374.

O'Regan, J. K. (1975). *Structural and contextual constraints on eye movements in reading.* Unpublished doctoral dissertation, University of Cambridge.

Paap, K. R., & Newsome, S. L. (1981). Parafoveal information is not sufficient to produce semantic or visual priming. *Perception & Psychophysics, 29,* 457–466.

Pollatsek, A., & Rayner, K. (1982). Eye movement control in reading: The role of word boundaries. *Journal of Experimental Psychology: Human Perception and Performance, 8,* 817–833.

Pollatsek, A., Rayner, K., & Balota, D. A. (1986). Inferences about eye movement control from the perceptual span in reading. *Perception & Psychophysics, 40,* 123–130.

Rayner, K. (1975). The perceptual span and peripheral cues in reading. *Cognitive Psychology, 7,* 65–81.

Rayner, K. (1977). Visual attention in reading: Eye movements reflect cognitive processes. *Memory & Cognition, 4,* 443–448.

Rayner, K. (1978). Eye movements in reading and information processing. *Psychological Bulletin, 85,* 618–660.

Rayner, K. (1979). Eye guidance in reading: Fixation locations within words. *Perception, 8,* 21–30.

Rayner, K. (1983). The perceptual span and eye movement control during reading. In K. Rayner (Ed.), *Eye movements in reading: Perceptual and language processes.* New York: Academic Press.

Rayner, K. (1984). Visual selection in reading, picture perception, and visual search: A tutorial review. In H. Bouma & D. W. Bouwhuis (Eds.), *Attention and Performance 10: Control of language processes.* Hillsdale, NJ: Erlbaum.

Rayner, K., Balota, D. A., & Pollatsek, A. (1986). Against parafoveal semantic preprocessing during eye fixations in reading. *Canadian Journal of Psychology, 40,* 473–483.

Rayner, K., Carlson, M., & Frazier, L. (1983). The interaction of syntax and semantics during sentence processing: Eye movements in the analysis of semantically biased sentences. *Journal of Verbal Learning and Verbal Behavior, 22,* 358–374.

Rayner, K., & Carroll, P. J. (1984). Eye movements and reading comprehension. In D. E. Kieras and M. A. Just, *New methods in reading comprehension research.* Hillsdale, NJ: Erlbaum.

Rayner, K., & Duffy, S. A. (1986). Lexical complexity and fixation times in reading: Effects of word frequency, verb complexity, and lexical ambiguity. *Memory & Cognition, 14,* 191–201.

Rayner, K., & Frazier, L. (1987). Parsing temporarily ambiguous compliments. *Quarterly Journal of Experimental Psychology, 39A,* 657–673.

Rayner, K., Inhoff, A. W., Morrison, R. E., Slowiaczek, M. L., & Bertera, J. H. (1981). Masking of foveal and parafoveal vision during eye fixations in reading. *Journal of Experimental Psychology: Human Perception and Performance, 7,* 167–179.

Rayner, K., & McConkie, G. W. (1976). What guides a reader's eye movements? *Vision Research, 16,* 829–837.

Rayner, K., & McConkie, G. W. (1977). Perceptual processes in reading: The perceptual spans. In A. S. Reber & D. L. Scarborough (Eds.), *Toward a psychology of reading.* Hillsdale, NJ: Erlbaum.

Rayner, K., McConkie, G. W., & Ehrlich, S. (1978). Eye movements and integrating information across fixations. *Journal of Experimental Psychology: Human Perception and Performance, 4,* 529–544.

Rayner, K., McConkie, G. W., & Zola, D. (1980). Integrating information across eye movements. *Cognitive Psychology, 12,* 206–226.

Rayner, K., & Pollatsek, A. (1981). Eye movement control during reading: Evidence for direct control. *Quarterly Journal of Experimental Psychology, 33A,* 351–373.

Rayner, K., & Pollatsek, A. (1987). Eye movements in reading: A tutorial review. In M. Coltheart (Ed.), *Attention and performance 12.* London: Erlbaum.

Rayner, K., Slowiaczek, M. L., Clifton, C., & Bertera, J. (1983). Latency of sequential eye movements: Implications for reading. *Journal of Experimental Psychology: Human Perception and Performance, 9,* 912–922.

Rayner, K., Well, A. D., Pollatsek, A., & Bertera, J. H. (1982). The availability of useful information to the right of fixation in reading. *Perception & Psychophysics, 31,* 537–550.

Schustack, M., Ehrlich, S., & Rayner, K. (1987). The complexity of contextual facilitation in reading: Local and global influences. *Journal of Memory and Language, 26,* 322–340.

Seidenberg, M. S., Tanenhaus, M. K., Leiman, J. M., & Bienkowski, M. (1982). Automatic access of the meanings of ambiguous words in context: Some limitations of knowledge-based processing. *Cognitive Psychology, 14,* 439–537.

Stanovich, K. E., & West, R. F. (1983). On priming by a sentence context. *Journal of Experimental Psychology: General, 112,* 1–36.

Swinney, D. A. (1979). Lexical access during sentence comprehension: (Re)consideration of context effects. *Journal of Verbal Learning and Verbal Behavior, 18,* 645–659.

Underwood, G. (1980). Attention and nonselective lexical access of ambiguous words. *Canadian Journal of Psychology, 34,* 72–76.

Underwood, G. (1981). Lexical recognition of embedded unattended words: Some implications for reading processes. *Acta Psychologica, 34,* 267–283.

Vonk, W. (1984). Pronoun comprehension. In A. G. Gale & F. Johnson (Eds.), *Theoretical and applied aspects of eye movement research*. Amsterdam: North-Holland Press.

Wanat, S. (1971). *Linguistic structure and visual attention in reading*. Newark, DE: International Reading Association.

Zola, D. (1984). Redundancy and word perception during reading. *Perception & Psychophysics, 36,* 277–284.

COMPONENT PROCESSES IN READING COMPREHENSION

KARL HABERLANDT

Department of Psychology
Trinity College
Hartford, Connecticut 06106

I. INTRODUCTION

People read texts for different purposes. They want to be informed, to be entertained, to study for a test, or even to recall the text. In each of these cases, the reader extracts the gist or the meaning of the text. It is widely assumed that the reader represents the text's meaning in an emergent model which contains the principal causal and logical relations of the text and some elaborative detail (Clark & Haviland, 1977; Collins, Brown, & Larkin, 1980; Foss, 1982; Jarvella, 1979; Kieras, 1981; Kintsch & van Dijk, 1978; Perfetti & Lesgold, 1977).

Since a text is too long to be represented en bloc, the reader creates the text model successively by processing the text's smaller units, clauses and sentences, one at a time (Kintsch & van Dijk, 1978). Of course, the representation itself is abstract, consisting of semantic units such as propositions or conceptualizations (Schank & Abelson, 1977). It has been the goal of reading research to characterize the process(es) by which the reader arrives at his or her model of the text.

During the past few years, "interactive" theories of reading have been popular. These theories propose various degrees of interaction among putative subprocesses involved in reading. Some theorists assume independence of processes (e.g., Cairns, Cowart, & Jablon, 1981; Forster, 1976, 1979; Oden & Spira, 1983). Others, on the other hand, assume an interdependence of the subprocesses (Adams & Collins, 1979; Just & Carpenter, 1980; Masson & Sala, 1978; Marlsen-Wilson & Welsh, 1978; Rumelhart, 1977; Thibadeau, Just, & Carpenter, 1982).

However, for several reasons, the interactive approach has become problematic. One reason is that there exists no agreed upon list of processes which presumably interact in reading (Gough, 1983). Some investigators focus on subword processes (Massaro, 1979), some on encoding and lexical access of words (Forster, 1979; Morton, 1969), others on sentence parsing (e.g., Frazier, 1983), and still others focus on text recall (e.g., Kintsch & van Dijk, 1978). Another problem is that many of the results supporting interactive reading theories have been gathered in experimental tasks which were *not* reading situations because they involved only individual words or sentences rather than a continuous language context (Haber, 1978). Finally, the meaning of "interaction" is not even clear. For example, according to Gough (1983) interaction could merely mean that several processes contribute, perhaps independently, to a processing outcome. Alternatively, it could mean that several processes influence the same processing stage during comprehension. In the latter case the processes could be simultaneous or successive, possibly with some overlap between them (Levy, 1982; Massaro, 1979).

Because of these problems with the interactive approach, it is perhaps best to adopt a more modest framework of reading comprehension. According to this framework cognitive processes at several levels collaborate in achieving the reader's goal in reading; the word *collaborate* implies no commitment to the relationship between the processes. One of the first tasks in developing the framework of component processes is to list the processes themselves. Then the relationships between the processes, whether they are independent or interdependent, can be examined. The principal purpose of the present chapter is to propose a list, albeit not an exhaustive one, of the component processes of reading and to document their effect on reading performance. In proposing this list, I adopt a general framework of reading which, at least in its broad outline, is shared by current theories of reading comprehension. I shall summarize this framework next and the sketch a list of four levels of reading processes.

The creation of the text model involves a variety of processes such as feature and letter analysis, lexical access, and sentence parsing. Each of these processes contributes a local outcome which is retained for a brief period. Thus, feature analysis generally yields the letters needed for lexical access. Lexical access yields the meaning of a word needed for processing of a phrase or clause. Clausal processing yields semantic relationships that are presumably added to the growing text model. In somewhat simplified terms, then, the reading process may be characterized as an "extract-and-discard" operation whereby information is extracted at various levels and retained for as long as it takes to add it to the next highest level of information. The collection of all these processes constitutes reading comprehension, and their net effect is an abstract entity of information, the meaning of the text. It is widely assumed that these processes are supported by specific mental structures. For example, the raw visual stimulus is held in a temporary register until feature analysis begins (Sperling, 1960; but see Haber, 1983). The meaning of recently read words, clauses, and sentences is stored in a short-term or "scratch-pad" memory of relatively small capacity (Jarvella, 1979). The emerging text model is assumed to be created in a working memory that has a larger capacity and a longer duration than the short-term memory (Bower, 1975; Kieras, 1981; Klatzky, 1980). The word knowledge and linguistic knowledge needed to interpret a text, including the lexicon of word meanings is maintained in long-term memory.

The framework sketched here alludes to a variety of different processes. For convenience of exposition, they will be described in terms of four levels, that is, word-, sentence-, concept-, and text-level processes with each level more or less corresponding to a unit of text. Word-level processes pertain to features of an individual word, such as its length, its orthography, and its frequency of occurrence in a given language. Sentence-level processes refer to the influence of the syntactic and informational structure of the current sentence on the processing of the sentence. Concept-level processes refer to the influence of prior semantic context on the processing of the current text unit, whether it is a word, phrase, or sentence. Finally, text-level processes produce the unified meaning representation of the text as a whole. This representation is the reader's model of the text which, compared to the products of processes at other levels, has a relatively long-term duration in memory.

In subsequent sections, I shall describe each of these levels in greater detail. In reading the sections, two qualifications should be kept in mind. The first one is that the present list is not complete. These processes were selected simply because they appear to be central to an understanding of the reading process. In addition, they were the most tractable with the research methodology and analytical techniques available (see Haberlandt, 1984). Other important processes, such as sub-word-level processes (Frederiksen, 1981; Massaro, 1979), syntactic strategies (e.g., Clark & Clark, 1977; Frazier, 1983), access of knowledge representations during reading, the role of metaphors in reading comprehension (e.g., Carbonell, 1981), and processes differentiating individual readers (e.g., Daneman & Carpenter, 1980; Perfetti & Roth, 1981) are not considered here. However, a more detailed framework of reading processes should include these processes as well. The second qualification is that any of the processes introduced here is relative to the reader's goal. The goal plays a critical role in how each of these processes, including word-level processes (cf. Thibadeau *et al.,* 1982), is engaged and what the nature of the text representation will be (e.g., Aaronson & Scarborough, 1976; Just & Carpenter, 1980; Kintsch, Kozminsky, Streby, McKoon, & Keenan, 1975; Kintsch & van Dijk, 1978). In general, the more detailed the representation of a text is, the longer it takes to read.

In order to document these processes, I used a subject-paced reading situation in which reading times were the dependent variables. This choice reflects the assumption that the different processes involved in reading occur in real time. It must be remembered, however, that the reading time of a text unit is an aggregate measure that, by itself, does not reveal the component processes. Hence, the researcher must identify experimental variables that presumably affect a process, for example word length, and investigate whether it contributes to the reading time of the text unit.

This article contains five sections. The first section describes the experimental methods and the statistical techniques used in my research. The remaining four sections are devoted to the four levels of processes (word-, sentence-, concept-, and text-level processes). For purposes of exposition, these processes are described separately. It should be remembered, however, that they act collaboratively (e.g., Thibadeau et al., 1982).

II. METHODOLOGICAL CONSIDERATIONS AND STATISTICAL ANALYSES

A. Subject-Paced Reading Research

The four processing levels were investigated in reading situations which involved a continuous language context (Haber, 1978) rather than individual words. The dependent variable was reading time rather than recognition, decision, pronunciation, monitoring latencies, or recall scores. While research using other methods has yielded important findings on certain mental processes, including many implicated in reading comprehension, it remains to be determined whether those findings could be reproduced in a reading task. The research involved a set of subject-paced reading tasks in which individual sentences or words of a text were presented on the screen of a video terminal.

In reading research as in other psycholinguistic research, many factors are necessarily confounded, so that the question has been raised whether such research is possible at all (Cutler, 1981). For example, word length and normative occurrence frequency, imagery of a concept and its complexity (Thorndyke, 1975; Toglia & Battig, 1978), number of words and syntactic structure, familiarity and narrativity of passages (e.g., Graesser & Riha, 1984), and others are confounded variables. An approach recently taken is to identify these factors and control for them by a combination of multiple regression analysis, posthoc sampling, and factorial experimentation (e.g., Knight, 1984; Just & Carpenter, 1980).

The effects of these factors on the current processing load can be detected both in absolute and in relative terms. The *absolute* amount of processing time changes if the difficulty of one or more aspects of the text change. Thus, when a word is very unusual or when an inference is difficult, the processing time increases. The *relative* contribution of the components involved in processing also changes. We shall see, for example, that the word-level attributes, length and frequency, have a relatively smaller effect on word reading times at the final word of a sentence where higher level processes are assumed to occur.

Effects associated with word-, sentence-, concept-, and text-level factors were observed in a number of experiments in my laboratory. I shall draw on data from four of those experiments in order to document the processes associated with these factors. For the moment, we shall be concerned with Experiments 1 and 2. In Experiment 1, there were two task conditions: assertions and recall. In the assertions condition, 55 subjects read passages and were instructed to respond *yes* or *no* to some assertions about each passage. In the recall condition, 48 subjects were asked to recall each passage as close to verbatim as possible (see Aaronson & Scarborough, 1976). Within each condition, there were two groups that read a set of identical passages, including 3 practice passages and 6 baseline passages. Experiment 1 also included six pairs of experimental passages that differed in their degree of familiarity. The two versions of a pair were largely identical except for the principal character(s) or the title. For example, one version of a pair of passages was about Lyndon Johnson, the other version about Yoshida Ichiro, a fictitious leader. Each group received 3 familiar and 3 unfamiliar passage versions. Experiment 2 involved 12 passages, 6 narrative and 6 expository, presented to 58 readers run in an assertions condition. Additional details on these and the other experiments will be introduced later as necessary.

Most of the data to be presented here are word-reading-time results. Word reading times were collected in the "moving-window" method (Just, Carpenter, & Woolley, 1982a; Kennedy, 1983; Wilkinson, 1983). In this method, words of a text are presented on a video terminal one at a time. When text presentation begins, the video terminal is filled with strings of dashes corresponding to the words and spaces of the text. A reader proceeds through a text by pressing a key which causes the current word to appear, replacing its dashes. With the next key press, the previous word is replaced by dashes and a new word appears. Punctuation marks are presented with the preceding word. Thus, only one word is visible at any given time (for futher details, see Just *et al.*, 1982a). Word reading time was defined as the interval between successive key presses.

B. Multiple-Regression Analysis of Word Reading Times

The theme underlying the research is that several factors jointly affect the processing load of each word. Accordingly, the contribution of each factor was estimated in multiple regressions on word reading times (Graesser, Hoffman, & Clark, 1980; Haberlandt, 1980, 1984; Just & Carpenter, 1980; Kieras, 1981; Mitchell & Green, 1978; Olson, Mack, & Duffy, 1981). The factors were analyzed in a simultaneous model because there were no predictions of their relative priority. In Experiments 1 and 2, there were four classes of predictor variables: word-level, sentence-level, text-level, and layout variables. The word-level variables included the length of the word expressed in the number of characters, the logarithm of the normative occurrence frequency of the word in English (Kucera & Francis, 1967), and the word type, that is, whether the word was a content or function word (see Clark & Clark, 1977, p. 22). Content and function words were coded by the indicator weights 1 and 0, respectively. Sentence-level factors included variables such as the beginning and the end of a sentence as well as the end of a major clause. Words located at these positions were coded with a 1; the remaining words were coded with a 0. The words of a given sentence were also coded according to the number of propositions in the sentence (see Bovair & Kieras, 1981; Turner & Greene, 1977).

Text-level variables included word repetition, the serial position of a sentence in the passage, and, in Experiments 1 and 2, the rated familiarity of the passage. Each word, whether content or function, was coded in terms of its repetition in the passage, with the first occurrence coded as 1, the second occurrence as 2, and so on. The words of a sentence were also coded in terms of the serial position the sentence occupied in the passage. Finally, in Experiment 2, all words of passage were coded in terms of the narrativity and familiarity of the passage. There were two layout or page factors, the beginning and the end of a line. Words appearing in these positions were coded with a 1, the remaining words with a 0. The coding scheme is illustrated in Table I with a sentence from a passage used in Experiment 1.

As statisticians have pointed out (e.g., Cohen & Cohen, 1975; Knight, 1984) the use of multiple regressions presupposes independence between the predictor variables. Otherwise, one must show that the variables, although statistically correlated, nevertheless affect the dependent variable independently (e.g., as in Table V). To determine the degree of independence between the predictor variables used in Experiments 1 and 2, bivariate correlations between the variables were computed. Here, I present bivariate correlation coefficients from Experiment 1 as an illustration. Table II contains the bivariate coefficients for 13 variables. With the

TABLE I
Illustration of Coding Scheme for Experiment 1[a]

1	2	3	4	5	6	7	8	9	10	11	12	13	14
420	1	0	0	1	7	−14	6.7	0	0	0	2	7250	As
371	0	0	0	2	7	−14	6.7	0	0	0	1	23237	a
432	0	0	0	1	7	−14	6.7	1	0	0	6	831	little
403	0	0	0	1	7	−14	6.7	1	0	0	3	242	boy
437	0	0	0	1	7	−14	6.7	0	0	0	2	9543	he
425	0	0	0	1	7	−14	6.7	1	0	0	6	159	walked
384	0	0	0	1	7	−14	6.7	1	0	0	5	173	miles
371	0	0	0	2	7	−14	6.7	0	0	0	2	26149	to
393	0	0	0	1	7	−14	6.7	1	0	1	3	750	get
361	0	0	0	3	7	−14	6.7	0	1	0	2	26149	to
419	0	0	0	3	7	−14	6.7	0	0	0	3	6997	his
383	0	0	0	1	7	−14	6.7	0	0	0	3	3292	one
390	0	0	0	1	7	−14	6.7	1	0	0	4	383	room
702	0	1	0	1	7	−14	6.7	1	0	0	6	492	school

[a] The fourteen columns represent the following variables: (1) mean word reading time, (2) first word, (3) final word, (4) clause boundary, (5) word repetition, (6) number of propositions, (7) serial position of sentence, (8) familiarity rating for passage, (9) word type, (10) beginning of line, (11) end of line, (12) length, (13) frequency, and (14) word.

exception of relatively high correlations between word-level variables, almost all of the correlations among the other variables were relatively low. The 2 variables most highly correlated were word type and log frequency, $r = −.82$. This correlation shows that content words tend to have lower log frequency values than function words. Because of the high correlation and the possibility of collinearity between these two variables, word type was not included as a predictor variable in the regressions described later (Graesser & Riha, 1984; Knight, 1984; Nie, Hull, Jenkins, Steinbrenner, & Bent, 1975). Length and log frequency were also highly correlated, $r = −.70$. However, it will be shown that both variables affected word reading times independently.

In the first two experiments, multiple-regression analyses were computed on the mean word reading times averaged across subjects. Some results are illustrated in Table III. The table contains results from the two conditions run in Experiment 1. In the assertions condition, the multiple R^2 coefficient was .39. This is the estimated proportion of the variance in word reading times predicted by the set of predictor variables included here. Typically, the R^2 coefficient is greater when the passages or the task are more difficult. Thus, in the recall condition, the R^2 coefficient was .59. (For data from Experiment 2, see Haberlandt and Graesser, 1985.)

TABLE II

Correlation between Variables in Experiment 1[a]

	WRT[b]	1	2	3	4	5	6	7	8	9	10	11
Word level												
1 Length	.33[c]											
2 Log frequency	-.36	-.74										
3 Type	.29	.64	-.82									
Sentence level												
4 First word	.04	-.09	.12	-.15								
5 Final word	.52	.24	-.28	.27	-.11							
6 Clause boundary	.02	.10	-.11	.14	-.05	-.05						
7 Proposition	-.03	.01	-.01	-.01	-.09	-.09	.09					
Text level												
8 Repeated word	-.16	-.25	.41	-.30	.09	-.10	-.06	-.09				
9 Serial position	-.11	.01	.02	-.04	.00	.00	.03	.01	.22			
10 Familiarity	-.05	-.07	-.01	.00	.03	.03	-.02	-.24	-.01	-.05		
Layout												
11 Begin line	.11	.13	-.11	.09	.06	.09	-.02	.00	-.05	-.02	.00	
12 End line	.05	.03	.00	.00	-.03	.00	.03	.01	.01	.02	-.01	-.09

[a] Number of observations, 3970.
[b] WRT, Word reading time.
[c] $r = .042$ and is significant at $p < .01$

TABLE III
Regression Results for Two Conditions from Experiment 1

	Assertions			Recall		
	Coefficient	Standard coefficient	t	Coefficient	Standard coefficient	t
Length	6	.09	4.68	15	.08	5.00
Frequency	−24	−.19	8.93	−35	−.10	5.64
First word	71	.13	9.91	109	.07	6.59
Last word	260	.48	34.81	1079	.70	62.36
Clause	30	.03	2.19	109	.04	3.38
Number of propositions	3	.04	2.99	8	.04	3.26
Word repetition	ns[a]	ns	ns	ns	ns	ns
Ser position	−3	−.09	7.06	−13	−.12	11.26
Familiarity	−13	−.09	6.98	−23	−.06	5.17
Beginning of line	35	.06	4.71	46	.03	2.66
End of line	42	.07	5.55	37	.02	2.07
Groups	ns	ns	ns	−71	−.08	7.36

[a] ns, Not significant.

Three statistics are presented in Table III, the regression coefficient, the standardized regression coefficient, and the t-value associated with each predictor variable. The regression coefficient or slope is an estimate of the change in the reading time with one unit of change in the predictor variable assuming the presence of the other variables in the predictive equation. The standardized regression coefficent expresses the slopes standardized for the dependent and the independent variables. These coefficients are helpful in comparing the effects of a predictor variable across analyses based on reading times with different standard deviations, e.g., those collected in the two experimental conditions of Experiment 1. The t value, in conjunction with the R^2 coefficient, can be used to express the *unique* contribution of each factor to the variance in word reading times (see Cohen & Cohen, 1975, Appendix 3). In general, a greater t value indicates a greater unique contribution of the given factor to the variance in reading times.[1]

[1] The last row in Table III includes data for a group factor representing reading time differences between two groups run in each of the conditions of Experiment 1. It indicates that there were no significant reading time differences between groups in the assertions condition. However, there was a difference between groups in the recall condition. The latter difference was attributable to reading-time differences between the two groups on the baseline passages.

With this background on research methodology and data analysis, we are now ready to describe the four levels of component processes of reading in greater detail.

III. WORD-LEVEL PROCESSES

Many consider the word as the basic unit of reading. Reading researchers investigate gaze durations (Just & Carpenter, 1980) and reading times of words (e.g., Aaronson & Scarborough, 1976). When sentence reading times are used, these are normalized in terms of the number of words (Graesser & Riha, 1984; Haberlandt, Beriah, & Sandson, 1980; Kieras, 1981). Similarly, researchers collect norms of word attributes such as length, occurrence frequency, categorizability, imagery, and pleasantness (see Rubin, 1980) in order to advance research on reading comprehension.

Among word-level processes investigators have focused primarily on encoding and lexical operations (cf. Seidenberg, Tanenhaus, Leiman, & Bienkowski, 1982). Encoding involves perceptual operations which transform the input stimulus into a format that is compatible with the format of the word concept in the lexicon. Experimental variables associated with encoding include the word's physical attributes, such as its length and stimulus quality. These two factors have a direct influence on the processing times of words. Reading and recognition times of a word are proportional to the word's length and to the clarity of its letters against the background. Lexical operations refer to the accessing of a word's meaning in the mental lexicon. The variable associated with access is the normative occurrence frequency of the word in English as measured by frequency norms (e.g., Kucera & Francis, 1967). Reading and fixation times on words, as well as latencies observed in lexical decision, pronunciation, and recognition studies, are proportional to the normative frequency of the word. This effect has been interpreted by different models, including an independent-processes model (e.g., Forster, 1976) and an interactive model (e.g., Morton, 1969).

Three aspects of word-level processes are examined here: lag effects, the relation between encoding operations and lexical access, and word-type effects. Lag effects refer to the scope of word-level processes. Processing of word n could have an impact on the reading time of word n alone as claimed by the immediacy hypothesis (e.g., Carpenter & Just, 1983). In addition, there could be a lagged effect on word n from the previous word $n - 1$. The relationship between encoding operations and lexical access was investigated by evaluating the effects of word frequency at different word lengths. This analysis was based on the assumption that word-length effects reflect word encoding and word-frequency effects reflect lexical access. These variables could affect reading times either interactively or independently (Carpenter & Just, 1983). Word-type effects refer to differential effects of function and content words. Psycholinguists have identified different characteristics of these two word types and have attributed processing differences to them as shown in the following sections.

A. Immediate versus Lagged Processing

That the processing time of the current word is a function of its length and frequency has already been widely reported (e.g., Aaronson & Scarborough, 1976; Just *et al.*, 1982a; Rayner, 1978) and was observed here as well. The question of interest is whether or not lag effects can be demonstrated. Following Carpenter & Just (1983), lag effects were studied in three separate regressions on the reading times of all words that were not located at sentence, line, and screen boundaries. In the first regression, the independent variables were length and frequency of the current word. In the second regression, length and frequency of the previous word were added. In the last regression, only the latter two variables were used. Results from these three analyses are shown in Table IV for the two conditions of Experiment 1 and for Experiment 2.

For comparison, the R^2 values are listed from Carpenter & Just's (1983) eye-fixation research. The pattern of the present results and their interpretation are quite similar to those of Carpenter & Just: Lag effects from word $n - 1$ on word n are very small compared to the effects of immediate processing. However, there are two caveats. First, in these experiments, unlike the research of Carpenter and Just (1983), the lag effect did reach statistical significance. For example, the R^2 value of .004 in the second column is associated with $F(2, 2507) = 4.57$, $p = 0.01$. Second, Just, Carpenter, & Masson (1982) observed significant lag effects for special words. They found that words following numbers in a text had longer gaze

TABLE IV
Variance in Processing Times of Word N Accounted for by Regression

	Experiment 1		Experiment 2	Carpenter and Just (1983)
	Assertion	Recall		
Word n	.183	.156	.270	.238
Word n and $n - 1$	.223	.178	.307	.240
Word $n - 1$	.011	.004	.012	.004

durations than would be expected on the basis of their length and frequency.

B. Relationship between Encoding and Lexical Access

Because the two variables associated with encoding and access, length and frequency, are inversely correlated (see Table II; Zipf, 1949), it is not clear from the results in Table III that they affect reading times independently. For example, Kliegl, Olson, and Davidson (1982) have argued that it is possible that most of the variance attributed to length may be due to word frequency, or vice versa, since these two factors are confounded. In order to meet this objection, I computed separate multiple regressions for several levels of length. The results from these analyses are shown in Table V, which illustrates frequency effects at different levels of word length for the assertions and recall conditions. These results were obtained in multiple-regression analyses computed separately for each length from 3 to 7 on reading times of words appearing for the first time in passage. Comparison of columns 1 and 2 demonstrates the inverse correlation of word length and frequency. The t values show that there were significant frequency effects at each length from 3 through 6 in both conditions of Experiment 1.

A similar result was observed in Experiment 2. These results replicate a finding reported by Carpenter and Just (1983) for gaze durations. They found parallel effects of word frequency at word lengths ranging from 2 to 11 characters per word. Based on those results, Carpenter *et al.* argued that length and frequency affected different processing mechanisms, with length influencing the *encoding* of words and frequency influencing *lexical access* (see also Glanzer & Ehrenreich, 1979).

C. Content and Function Words

Linguists distinguish between content and function words of a vocabulary (e.g., Clark & Clark, 1977; Hoerman, 1979). Content words are said to convey the meaning of a sentence by referring to objects and events and their attributes. They include nouns, verbs, adjectives, and adverbs. Function words, on the other hand, serve to connect content words in the surface structure of a sentence. They include pronouns, auxiliary verbs, determiners, and prepositions (for examples see Clark & Clark, 1977, Table 1-1). Content and function words are distinguished on a number of dimensions, including their length and occurrence frequency in English.

It is of psychological interest whether or not content and function

TABLE V

Frequency Effects for Words of Different Length (Experiment 1)

			Assertions				Recall			
Length	Number of cases	Mean log frequency	WRT[a]	Coefficient	Standard coefficient	t^b	WRT	Coefficient	Standard coefficient	t
3	272	3.468	465	−9	−.10	1.66	580	−33	−.21	3.44
4	394	2.679	490	−47	−.35	7.10	614	−77	−.33	6.73
5	271	2.252	492	−32	−.26	4.39	632	−74	−.27	4.57
6	255	1.893	516	−60	−.32	5.16	645	−93	−.28	4.55
7	156	1.804	521	−31	−.19	2.25	ns[c]	ns	ns	ns

[a] WRT, Word reading time (msec).
[b] Significance of frequency effects is reflected by t.
[c] ns, Not significant.

words are processed differently. One important difference between them is that the corpus of content words known by a person continued to expand during the person's lifetime, while the number of known function words does not. Another difference is that function words are more context dependent than content words. The greater dependence on context of function words has even been shown in a paired-associate learning experiment (Glanzer, 1962). Specifically, function words were remembered better than content words when they were presented with the context of two nonsense syllables, e.g., *TAH - of - ZUM* vs *YIG - food - SEB*. On the other hand, content words were remembered better when associated with only one nonsense syllable, as in *food − YIG* and *TAH − of*. The conclusion drawn by Glanzer (1962) was that isolated function words are psychologically incomplete units. Schindler (1978) found that in reading prose, subjects attended more to content than to function words. This was evidenced by a greater search accuracy of target letters in content than in function words. Finally, in the context of word recognition it has been claimed that content and function words involve a different mechanism of lexical access. Thus, Bradley, Garrett, and Zurif (1980) reported that in normal speakers, frequency influences recognition latencies of content but not of function words. However, in our research, frequency had a significant effect on reading times of both content and function words (see also Gordon & Caramazza, 1982). Nevertheless, there were differences in the processing of content and function words. For example, there was a word-repetition effect in content but not in function words. Since this effect depends on the presence of a passage context, it will be considered in greater detail in the section on text-level processes. Similarly, we shall revisit the effects of word length and occurrence frequency in the sections on sentence-level and text-level processes.[2]

In summary, this section investigated word-level processes in a reading situation involving entire texts rather than individual words or sentences. It was shown that encoding and lexical access make independent contributions to the aggregate reading time, although the empirical measures of these processes, word length and occurrence frequency, are correlated statistically. A reader encodes a word and accesses its meaning as he or she first encounters it with only a minimal processing lag extending to subsequent words. Controlling for word length and occurrence frequency, content and function words behave differently in a variety of research paradigms, including the moving-window method. This suggests

---

[2] In subsequent research, we found that reading times of content words, but not of function words, increase with the cumulative amount of new information in a sentence (Haberlandt & Graesser, 1986).

that the two different word types invoke different psychological processes. Their specific nature, however, remains an issue for the future.

IV. SENTENCE-LEVEL PROCESSES

The sentence is the text unit which contains the elementary ideas that a
writer seeks to communicate. These ideas are embodied in the phrases
and clauses of the sentence, which constitute its surface form. The reader
uses sentence-level processes in order to "translate" the surface form of
a sentence into its meaning representation. These processes add "new
predications" to the growing text model (cf. Perfetti & Lesgold, 1977;
Jarvella, 1979). Sentence-level processes include *syntactic-parsing strategies* (e.g., Clark & Clark, 1977), a *propositional-mapping process* (e.g.,
Kaplan, 1975), and a *sentence-modeling process* (e.g., Kieras, 1981).

A. Parsing

The parsing strategies are used to segment the sentence into its syntactic constituents. In one form or another, these strategies have been a topic
of continuing interest to psycholinguists (e.g., Clark & Clark, 1977; Fodor, Bever, & Garrett, 1974; Kimball, 1973). The principal issue has been
an empirical one, namely, whether or not listeners are sensitive to the
constituent boundaries in sentences. After nearly two decades of research,
there is plenty of evidence that listeners segment sentences presented
individually in terms of their constituents (e.g., Foss & Hakes, 1978).
However, whether *readers* segment sentences and whether they do so for
sentences in intact texts have not yet been determined experimentally.

B. Propositional Mapping

The propositional mapping process maps clauses into propositional relations (Kaplan, 1975) of the format

$$\text{Relation, Argument}_1, \text{Argument}_2 \ldots, \text{Argument}_n.$$

Here, *relation* represents a predicate, and *arguments* represent cases such
as agent, object, and recipient. The mapping process is intrapropositional.
Readers are assumed to access their knowledge of the conceptual structure of a propositional predicate and presumably predict the cases associated with that predicate (e.g., Birnbaum & Selfridge, 1981; Thibadeau *et*

al., 1982). In this fashion the mapping process yields information not necessarily stated in the text but implied by it.

C. Sentence Modeling

The interpropositional modeling process produces a sentence model which is the unified representation of the propositions of the sentence, including the relationships between the propositions. The model also includes references (or pointers) to concepts introduced in previous sentences. It is the presence of such cross-references which enable the reader to pick up the development of ideas across different sentences, whether they are adjacent or not. The function of the sentence model is to provide a set of propositions from which propositions can be selected for the growing text model. The duration of the sentence model in working memory depends on the length of the text and the nature of the task. At the minimum, it lasts for as long as it takes to add the current information to the text model (see Jarvella, 1979). It lasts for a longer period of time if the reader, due to instructions to recall the text, encodes the model into long-term memory.

At present, one can only speculate on the relationship between sentence parsing, mapping, and modeling, that is, whether they are executed successively or not. Currently, the view is being entertained that parsing and mapping, at least, occur continuously as successive words of a sentence are read. This means a word is assigned to a constituent as soon as it is read rather than at some later point when several words have been read and buffered (see Just & Carpenter, 1980; Thibadeau *et al.,* 1982). On the other hand, the modeling process is assumed to take place at the boundaries of clauses, including the sentence boundary. Specifically, Kintsch and van Dijk (1978) argued that since a text is too large as a whole, a reader must process it sequentially from left to right *in chunks* of several propositions at a time; citing the work of Aaronson and Scarborough (1977) and Jarvella (1971), they noted that the chunking probably occurs at sentence and clause boundaries. Furthermore, they proposed that abstract propositions rather than surface phrases are chunked.

Of the three sentence-level processes named here, I have thus far investigated only the modeling process. Adopting Kintsch and van Dijk's (1978) hypothesis that the chunking is propositional, I studied the sentence-modeling process by examining the relationship between reading times and the propositional structure of a sentence.

There is ample evidence that the reading times of sentences depend on the propositional structure of the sentences as measured by their number of propositions. Specifically, sentence reading times, controlled for the number of words, increase linearly with the number of propositions in the sentence (Graesser & Riha, 1984; Kieras, 1981; Kintsch & Keenan, 1973; Kintsch *et al.*, 1975). However, since sentence reading time is a rather global processing measure, it does not reveal the location(s) at which the propositional complexity exerts its influence. The processing of propositionally more complex sentences could be reflected in the reading times of individual words, at least after several propositions have been introduced (see Chang, 1980). On the other hand, as Kintsch and van Dijk (1978) hypothesized, the effect could manifest itself at syntactically defined locations such as clause and sentence boundaries.

Kintsch and van Dijk (1978) were concerned with text recall. Consequently, the chunking process they conceived of referred to the encoding of propositions for long-term recall. Nevertheless, it may be assumed that sentence modeling takes place in other reading situations, including the present assertions condition. This is (1) because readers are thought to create a text model in all reading situations except in those where strictly lexical goals dominate, such as in proofreading, and (2) because in creating the text model the reader is assumed to select propositions from the sentence model. However, since the sentence model presumably endures longer with recall rather than with other instructions, readers were expected to devote more resources to the modeling process in the recall than in the assertions condition.

1. End-of-Sentence Processing as a Function of Task and Propositional Structure

The strategy in studying the modeling process was to compare reading times of sentence-final words with those of other words and to evaluate final-word reading times as both a function of the number of propositions in the sentence and a function of the task. In the assertions condition, mean word reading times for nonboundary words and final words were 483 and 776 msec, respectively. In the recall condition, the corresponding means were 605 and 1739 msec, respectively. In order to characterize the special end-of-sentence processing more closely, I computed regressions on the reading times of sentence-final words and on the reading times of a set of control words chosen randomly from nonboundary locations in the sentence with the following constraint. The set of control words was comparable to the set of sentence-final words in terms of word length and frequency as well as in terms of the proportion of content words. This proportion was .89 and .86 among final and control words, respectively. The regression results for sentence-final and control words are shown in Table VI for the two conditions of Experiment 1.

The pattern of factors affecting the reading times of words in boundary

TABLE VI
Standardized Regression Coefficients for Sentence-Final and Control Words (Experiment 1)

	Assertions				Recall			
	Final words		Control words		Final words		Control words	
	Standard coefficient	t	Standard coefficient	t	Standard coefficient	t	Standard coefficient	t
Length	ns[a]	ns	ns	ns	ns	ns	ns	ns
Frequency	−.23	4.37	−.28	4.88	ns	ns	−.25	4.36
Number of propositions	.13	6.81	ns	ns	.18	3.95	ns	ns
Word repetition	−.12	2.43	−.21	4.24	−.10	2.14	−.15	2.99
Serial position	−.32	6.81	ns	ns	−.37	8.08	ns	ns
Familiarity	−.15	3.11	−.13	2.55	−.14	3.00	−.11	2.23

[a] ns, Not significant.

and nonboundary locations was different. There was an effect of sentence serial position on final words but not on control words. Similarly, there was a proposition effect for sentence-final words but not for control words. The effect was significant in both conditions. However, as expected, it was more pronounced in the recall condition. This interaction is illustrated in Fig. 1. It was also evident in a multiple-regression analysis.[3]

Figure 1 represents the proposition effect in the assertions and recall conditions. Reading times are shown for final words of sentences containing two through five propositions from six baseline and six experimental passages. This set of sentences was used because it provided a sufficiently large number of cases at each sentence length. The apparent interaction in Fig. 1 was confirmed by a significant proposition × task interaction term ($t = 21.83$, $p < .001$) observed in a regression on last-word reading times with serial position, passage familiarity, word length, and word frequency as additional factors.

The proposition effect in the recall conditions suggests that the sentence modeling process is propositional, at least in part. In order to evaluate this hypothesis, I correlated regression coefficients reflecting the proposition factor with subjects' mean recall. The regression coefficients were derived from 48 regressions computed on final-word reading times of

[3] Subsequent research established that the number of new arguments per sentence captures reading-time variance better than the number of propositions (see Haberlandt & Graesser, 1985).

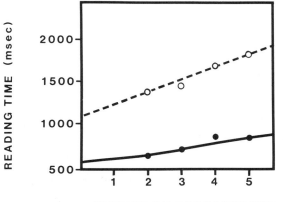

Fig. 1. Mean reading times on sentence-final words as a function of propositions and task. ○, Recall; ●, assertions.

each of the 48 individual subjects. The regression included sentences with two through five propositions of baseline and experimental passages. The predictor variables were the number of propositions, the serial position of the sentence, passage familiarity, and the length and frequency of the final word. The correlation between the regression coefficient for propositions and mean recall was significant, albeit small: $r = .30$, $p < .05$. This correlation indicates that the better recallers tend to encode sentences in terms of propositions and that they do so at the last word of a sentence. Of course, the sentence-final word is not the only location subjects use for encoding or sentence modeling. Other opportunities exist at topic shifts, at episode and paragraph boundaries (e.g., Haberlandt *et al.*, 1980), at physically marked locations such as the beginning and the end of a line, and at clause boundaries, as predicted by Kintsch and van Dijk (1978).

2. End-of-Sentence Processing and Clausal Processing

The presence of a clause in a sentence should provide the reader with an opportunity to generate the sentence model incrementally at the clause and at the sentence boundary. Consequently, reading times of final words should be shorter in sentences with a clause than in sentences without a clause. Analysis of data from Experiments 1 and 2 suggests that the clausal structure modified end-of-sentence processing as predicted. Specifically, final-word reading times were longer in sentences that did not contain a major clause than in sentences that did. This effect is shown for Experiment 2 in Fig. 2, where mean word reading times of the last word of

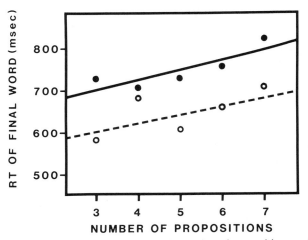

Fig. 2. Mean reading times on final words as a function of propositions and presence or absence of clause (Experiment 2). RT, Reading time; ○, clause present; ●, clause absent.

sentences are graphed as a function (1) of the presence or absence of a clause and (2) of the number of propositions from 3 through 7. The numbers of sentences with and without subordinate clauses were 87 and 171, respectively. The minimum number of cases was 8 sentences per cell (sentences containing a clause and 7 propositions).[4]

Figure 2 indicates that for each sentence length, processing of the final word is shorter in sentences with a clause than in sentences without one.

The observation that end-of-sentence processing is less in sentences with a major clause supports the expectation that in those sentences the sentence modeling process is distributed over several locations in the sentence.

As Fig. 3 indicates, one such location is the last word of a major clause (see also Fodor *et al.*, 1974; Hurtig, 1978; Jarvella, 1971; Kaplan, 1975; Miller & Kintsch, 1980; Thibadeau *et al.,* 1982). In Fig. 3, mean word reading times are graphed for words at the clause boundary and for the two surrounding words.

The left and right panels of Fig. 3 depict the clausal effect for the assertions and recall conditions of Experiment 1, respectively. While the clausal effect is due, in part, to the fact that last words of clauses tend to be longer and less frequent than the surrounding words, the effect reaches statistical significance in both the recall and assertions conditions even

---

[4] The following pair of sentences containing four propositions illustrates the presence and absence, respectively, of a subordinate clause: *When the bell rang a judge went down to hear the complaint. At that time a dog used to visit the elephant stable.*

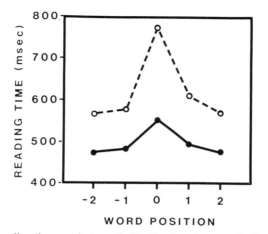

Fig. 3. Mean reading times on last words (0) of major clauses and of surrounding words. ○, Recall; ●, assertion.

after word length and frequency have been partialed out. The clausal effect is more pronounced in the former than in the latter condition, which is not surprising in view of long-term encoding processes required in recall (see Aaronson & Scarborough, 1976).

In this section, I presented results that gave evidence of additional processing at sentence and clause boundaries. The additional processing at the end of the sentence was attributed to a sentence-modeling process which produces a propositional representation of the sentence. Special end-of-sentence processing is in accord with a variety of views which hold that the sentence boundary can be used to resolve within-sentence ambiguities, integrate the current information with information from preceding sentences, and, in recall situations, to rehearse the current sentence (Aaronson & Scarborough, 1976; Carpenter & Just, 1977, 1983; Dee-Lucas, Just, Carpenter, & Daneman, 1982; Jarvella, 1971, 1979; Juola, Ward, & McNamara, 1982; Just & Carpenter, 1980; Masson, 1982).

The clausal processing observed here indicates that readers create the sentence model in stages if the sentence is too long or too complex to be represented in one operation at the sentence boundary. What makes the clausal effect interesting is the fact that it was obtained with intact texts rather than with individual sentences (e.g., Aaronson & Scarborough, 1976). The additional processing at clause and sentence boundaries shows that readers are sensitive to the syntactic structure of the sentences of a text. The results, then, call into question those views which consider syntax as unimportant for reading comprehension (e.g., Birnbaum & Selfridge, 1981, p. 325). Rather, they support Kieras' (1983) claim that the comprehension process relies upon the syntactic information in the input (see also Frazier, 1983). Of course, syntactic information by itself is not sufficient without the conceptual information conveyed by sentences (e.g., Schank & Abelson, 1977). I turn to the role of conceptual information and concept-level processes in the next section.

V. CONCEPT-LEVEL PROCESSES

Concept level processes refer to dependencies among words (e.g., Thorndyke, 1976) across and within sentence boundaries. Concept-level inferences are triggered by word and propositional concepts, *the primes*, and connect concepts within and between sentences. The effect of either type of inference is to facilitate the processing of a text unit, *the target*, appearing sometime later in the text. The utility of such priming has been described by Foss (1982) in terms of the text model the reader constructs of the text. He argued that the reader saves processing resources by exploiting semantic relationships between the priming and target units. Constructing the text model, the reader searches for structures in memory that are similar to the one which is currently being processed. Those structures need only be expanded or copied (see also Bower, Black & Turner, 1979) rather than created de novo. Foss (1982) left the question open as to whether such facilitative concept-level processes are forward or backward inferences, where a forward inference is initiated at the point of reading the prime and a backward inference is initiated when reading the target.

A. Forward and Backward Inferences

Birnbaum and Selfridge (1981) advocated forward inferences. According to their theory, upon reading a word, the reader constructs an incomplete conceptual structure representing the meaning of the word in short-term memory. The incompleteness of the structure is manifested by slots or requests for cases. For example, when one encounters the word *eat* in a sentence, one expects that an edible object such as an apple will be introduced shortly. When the word does appear in the text, it is already expected and, hence, processed relatively quickly. Forster (e.g., 1979) proposed a mechanism of backward inferences. According to his proposal new concepts introduced in the text must be integrated into the text representation created thus far. Upon reading a concept, the processor "looks backward" for a fitting structure. If prime and target are related, such a structure is easily located and, hence, the target is processed relatively fast.

B. Are There Concept-Level Effects in Reading?

Which scenario, forward or backward (or even both in combination) provides a better account for the data is not clear. Indeed, it is not clear at all to what extent there are priming effects in reading situations as opposed to a variety of other situations, including the lexical-decision, pronunciation, and phoneme-monitoring studies (see Fischler, 1977; Foss, 1982; Perfetti, Goldman, & Hogaboam, 1979; Schuberth & Eimas, 1977; Stanovich, 1981). The purpose of my research on concept-level effects was to investigate whether such effects could be demonstrated in subject-paced reading situations. This investigation is important because it has been argued that lexical-decision, pronunciation, and phoneme-monitoring tasks may not have adequately reflected processes occurring in a reading situation (see Becker, 1980; Gough, 1983; Eisenberg & Becker, 1982; Haber, 1978; Mitchell & Green, 1978; Stanovich, 1981). Stanovich (1981) argued that the context effects obtained in sentence priming studies may be confined to "unusually long intervals between context and target" and, "as the interval between context and target words is brought more into line with that obtained in normal reading, contextual effects diminish" (p. 260). Once these empirical questions have been addressed, there remains the problem of devising a research strategy which could illuminate the nature of the concept-level processes causing the facilitation.

C. Experimental Paradigms

The experimental paradigms to investigate concept-level effects are the *lexical-* and *sentential*-priming paradigms (see Forster, 1981). In the lexical-priming paradigm, both the prime (e.g., *bread*) and the target (e.g., *butter* or *nurse*) are individual words (Meyer & Schvaneveldt, 1976). In the sentential-priming paradigm, the prime is a sentence and the targets are either words or other sentences (e.g., Tulving & Gold, 1963; Tulving, Mandler, & Baumal, 1964). For example, Tulving and Gold (1963) used incomplete sentences such as *The actress received praise for being an outstanding . . .* as a prime and words such as *performer* as a target. This section describes some data from the literature and two experiments, Experiments 3 and 4, from my lab on lexical and sentential priming. Experiment 3 was a lexical-priming study examining the extent to which reading times of individual words are influenced by a priming word in the same sentence. Experiment 4 used a sentential-priming paradigm. The semantic environment was defined in terms of scripts which represent the knowledge a person has of everyday events (for further details see Haberlandt & Bingham, 1984; Experiment 3).

1. Lexical Priming in Comprehension

Only a few studies have addressed this question, and the evidence they yielded is equivocal. In this section, I review results from Watson (1976) and Carroll (1983) and describe Experiment 3. Carroll's dissertation provided evidence of lexical priming, Watson's did not. Watson (1976) used sentence classification as an orienting task and sentence processing time as the dependent variable. He presented sentences to subjects that contained pairs of associatively related words, e.g., *teacher* and *pupil* in (1a), and control sentences like (1b).

(1a) The *teacher* kissed the *pupil*.

(1b) The *teacher* kissed the *woman*.

If lexical priming took place, (1a)-type sentences should have been read faster than (1b)-type sentences. However, this was not the case in Watson's experiment.

On the other hand, Carroll (1983) found lexical priming in an eye-fixation study where subjects read sentences such as (2a) and (2b).

(2a) The salesman said that the *cloth* was actually *cotton* which had been dyed.

(2b) The salesman said that the *stuff* was actually *cotton* which had been dyed.

In Carroll's study, target words were read faster in related (2a) than in unrelated sentences (2b). Carroll found this priming effect both for category and associative relationships. He also found that it was stronger when prime and target words belonged to the same rather than to different clauses. Unlike Carroll, I did not observe such effects in Experiment 3, which was quite similar to his.

In Experiment 3 the moving-window condition described previously was used. The stimulus materials included 56 experimental and 56 control sentences in which pairs of critical words were embedded. In experimental sentences the word pairs were high associates selected from the Bousfield norms (Bousfield, Cohen, Whitmarsh, & Kincaid, 1961). In the control sentences the first member of a pair, the prime, was substituted by another word. The following sentences illustrate the stimulus materials used.

(3a) The *fox* was *sly* enough to get away from the hunters.

(3b) The *animal* was *sly* enough to get away from the hunters.

(4a) I have to *mail* a *letter* at the post office.
(4b) I have to *take* a *letter* to the post office.

Stimulus materials were randomized so that each subject received 28 experimental and 28 control sentences with the constraint that no target word be repeated. The experimental and control sentences were embedded in a sequence of buffer sentences. Four sets of 60 sentences, including experimental, control, and buffer sentences, were presented to a subject during an experimental session. Subjects were instructed to read the sentences for the purpose of recognizing them after completing a set of 60 sentences.

Mean reading times of targets in experimental and control sentences were almost equal, namely, 282 and 284 msec, respectively. Of the 56 prime-target pairs used in Experiment 3, 8 pairs had also been used by Carroll. For the sentences containing these prime-target pairs, the mean reading times for experimental and control words were 285 and 289 msec, respectively (not significant). These results, then, do not support a lexical-priming effect. The discrepancy between Carroll's and my results may be due to the choice of different stimulus sentences, to different orienting tasks, or to the different dependent measures. In any case, further experimental work on lexical priming in reading tasks is necessary.

2. Sentential Priming in Comprehension

Whereas results on lexical influences are inconclusive, there are several studies showing facilitation due to units larger than individual words (e.g., Ehrlich & Rayner, 1981; Haberlandt & Bingham, 1984; Sharkey & Mitchell, 1981). Ehrlich and Rayner (1981) used a relatively large amount of context consisting of several sentences. In two eye-fixation studies they found that target words which were highly predictable from the context had shorter eye fixations than control words of equal length and shape. Similarly, in Experiment 4 (Haberlandt and Bingham, 1984) we observed facilitation when the context consisted of full sentences which were causally related to the target sentence. The experiment was based on the expectation that casual links are important for integrating new propositions into the emergent text representation. When successive sentences reflect the causal dependencies, the building of a text representation and integration across successive sentences should be easier. We confirmed this expectation in Experiment 4 in which pairs of script-related sentences such as (5a) and (5b) were used.

(5a) He got some logs.
(5b) He lit the wood.

The independent variable was the input direction of the stimulus sentences, which could either be forward [as in (5a) and (5b)] or reverse [as in (6a) and (6b)].

(6a) He blew on the flame.

(6b) He lit the wood.

In the forward pair, the sequence of the sentences reflects the enabling relationship between them. For example, in sequence (5a) and (5b), getting logs enables one to light them. By contrast, sequence (6a) and (6b) violates the enabling relationship because one cannot blow on a fire that has not been lit. In our study, 28 forward and 28 reverse pairs selected from Galambos's (1983) scripts were used. Forward and reverse pairs derived from the same script had the same target sentence as illustrated by (5b) and (6b).

Each subject was presented with 14 forward and 14 reverse pairs derived from different scripts. These pairs were randomly embedded in a sequence of related and unrelated buffer pairs. Each trial consisted of the successive presentation of a context sentence, a target sentence, and an advance statement. On seeing the target sentence, the subject was to decide whether the two sentences were related or not. Response times were significantly faster for forward, $X = 2310$ msec, than for reverse pairs, $X = 2537$, $t(37) = 3.12 p < .01$. We replicated this forward effect in two further studies using different stimulus pairs and a different task. The different stimulus pairs involved identical sets of sentences for both forward and reverse pairs derived from the same script as is illustrated by (7a)/(7b) and (8a)/(8b).

(7a) He paid for the postage.

(7b) He mailed the box.

(8a) He mailed the box.

(8b) He paid for the postage.

The fact that facilitation was observed in pairs such as (7a) and (7b), but not in pairs such as (8a) and (8b), indicates that the directionality effect cannot easily be attributed to lexical priming between the concepts in the statements, e.g., between *postage* and *box,* unless one assumes that the association between concepts is stronger in forward than in reverse pairs. The different task involved a recognition test rather than a relatedness judgment as an orienting task. In this study, pairs were presented within a long sequence of other sentences rather than as explicit pairs. Again, we found a directionality effect.

In sum, conceptual dependencies between words in reading are typically investigated in lexical- and sentential-priming experiments. The evidence on lexical priming is mixed, with some studies supporting it (e.g.,

Carrol, 1983) and others not (e.g., Experiment 3 discussed previously; Watson, 1976). Sentential priming has been observed more widely, including in Experiment 4 discussed here (see also Ehrlich & Rayner, 1981; Haberlandt & Bingham, 1984). Experiment 4 involved sentences derived from empirical script norms. They were paired either in their normal forward order or in a reverse order. As one would expect from the causal structure of scripts, facilitation was shown only in forward pairs. The agenda for subsequent studies on concept-level processes in reading includes several issues. Research should specify different types of conceptual dependencies, such as causal, associative, and referential relations, and experimental tests should be devised to discriminate between forward and backward accounts of concept-level facilitation.

VI. TEXT-LEVEL PROCESSES

The processes considered thus far are based on segments shorter than the entire text. In contrast, text-level processes apply to the entire text. Experimental variables associated with text-level processes are features ranging over the full text, such as its genre, its structural well formedness, its imagery value, the density of its local topics, and its familiarity.

A. The Reader's Text Model

The reader creates the text model by formulating hypotheses as to what the text is about and by extracting certain pieces of information from the propositional representation of each sentence, the sentence model. The information in the text model is based on propositions derived from the current text and on references to the reader's world knowledge (e.g., Black, Turner, & Bower, 1979; Schank, 1980). These references are necessary because the writer of a text assumes that the reader accesses and uses his or her world knowledge in interpreting the text. In this respect the present text model differs from Kintsch and van Dijk's (1978) text base which contains literal information from the current text but hardly any inferential information. The text model is assumed to be hierarchical (see Kintsch & van Dijk, 1978; also Meyer, 1975; Thorndyke, 1977), with the topic and the key ideas represented at the top and elaborations and details farther below, if at all. To the extent that the reader's text model models the information in a text, it is similar to a scientific model which seeks to account for a given body of data (see Collins et al., 1980). Similarly, the text model may undergo some change with new input very much like a scientific theory which may have to be changed as a result of new observations.

Text-level processes include *topic identification* (Kieras, 1981), *model refinement* (Collins *et al.*, 1980), *continuity monitoring* (see Kintsch, 1976), and *knowledge application* (see Bisanz & Voss, 1981). The reader continuously abstracts certain propositions from successive sentence models by applying macrooperators such as deletion, generalization, and construction (Kintsch & van Dijk, 1978).

Topic identification is a kind of abstraction process that yields propositions which form the temporary topic. It serves as the organizing focus for the growing text model. If the subsequent sentences are related to the current topic, the reader maintains it. Otherwise, the topic is changed. The fate of the growing text model depends on the topic choice. If the topic remains the same, the reader keeps the current model and merely adds new propositions to it as he or she continues reading a text. This means that, once abstracted, the relative importance of propositions is maintained. On the other hand, if subsequent segments of text contain information inconsistent with the current topic and the ranking of key propositions in the model, it has to be restructured. This involves changing the importance of some propositions and may lead the reader to reread some previous sections of the text. This process changes the existing model to varying degrees. Hence, it is called model refinement.

At the beginning of reading a text, revisions are likely to be the norm rather than the exception. Research by Collins *et al.* (1980) and Olson, Duffy, and Mack (1981) indicates that the initial fragments of texts may give rise to several topics. At first the reader may maintain several topics, simultaneously checking each for an optimal fit with the text. In addition, at the beginning of reading a text, most characters and concepts are new. Consequently, the reader must generate new nodes in working memory corresponding to these new concepts. Since the initial model exploration and node generation are resource consuming, the reader presumably spends more time processing the initial segments of a text than subsequent ones. Later, the reader is likely to have settled on a more permanent model. Then he or she can insert successive segments of the text into the growing model and thereby refine it (see also Foss, 1982; Haberlandt, 1980; Kieras, 1981; Olson *et al.*, 1981).

Well-written texts deal with a global topic which is developed as the text progresses. They deal also with certain entities, both characters and objects, which frequently appear throughout the passage. Following Kintsch (1976), I assume that the reader monitors the continuity of such entities. Their continuity is signaled by surface cues which include the repetition of content words, the use of pronouns, and of other anaphoric proforms. Of these cues, the one examined here is the repetition of content words. Such repetitions help the reader to create a coherent discourse model in either a forward or a backward fashion as described previously for the case of related concepts (see also Foss, 1982; Thibadeau *et al.*, 1982). In either case, the repeated word should be processed relatively fast.

A reader does not construct a text model in a vacuum but against the background of relevant linguistic and pragmatic information (e.g., Bisanz & Voss, 1981; Schank & Abelson, 1977). Authors implicitly assume such reader knowledge in composing a text. It follows that the construction of the text base should be easier and, hence, comprehension should be faster, the more readily the reader can relate the content of a given passage to pertinent knowledge sources. This process is called knowledge application. It is evaluated here by investigating word reading times of texts with different degrees of familiarity.

Three text-level processes investigated thus far are continuity monitoring, model refinement, and knowledge application. I evaluated continuity monitoring by examining reading times of repeated content words, model refinement by investigating reading times as a function of the serial position of sentences within a passage, and knowledge application by comparing reading times of familiar and less familiar passages.

B. Continuity Monitoring and Word Repetition

A text is coherent to the extent that its sentences relate to the text's global topic and to topics of a more local scope. The local topics may include the development of an idea or the characterization of a person and his or her fate. The continuity of the local topics in the text is expressed by the repetition of content words and by other surface cues not examined here. The local topic is represented by a set of propositions relatively high in the hierarchy of the text model. This means it should be relatively easy to access them if the text refers to them. As a consequence, processing of a content word should be facilitated on repeated occurrences (see also Thibadeau *et al.*, 1982). Table VI indicates that repetition of content words speeded processing of those words by 12 ms for each repetition. Since function words do not provide independent meaning, they are not assumed to be facilitated, and as Table VI shows, there was no speedup for repeated function words. This account of the repetition effects follows Thibadeau *et al.* (1982) in assuming that the effect depends on the relationship between the repeated word and a local topic. However, the nature of this relationship has not yet been spelled out. Further research is needed to sharpen the definition of a local topic and to explicate the relationship between a topic and a particular content word.

The repetition effect invites two further questions, one regarding the contribution of text-level processes per se and the other regarding the locus of the effect. The effect not only occurs in the moving-window condition and in other reading situations (e.g., Just & Carpenter, 1980; Kolers, 1976), but also in such nonreading situations as the lexical-decision task (e.g., Scarborough, Gerard, & Cortese, 1979), the word-completion task (Tulving, Schacter, & Stark, 1982), and the word-identification task (Feustel, Shiffrin, & Salasoo, 1983). Hence, it is important (1) to distinguish between list- and text-level processes contributing to the repetition effect and (2) to determine to what extent the latter contributes to this effect. As for the locus of the repetition effect, several theorists (e.g., Dixon & Rothkopf, 1979; Just & Carpenter, 1980) attribute it to savings in the lexical-access operation. If this were the case, the relative contribution of word frequency to the reading-time variance of repeated words should decrease with each repetition. The present research did not evaluate this hypothesis because the corpus of words repeated at least three times was too small.

C. Model Refinement and the Serial Position of Sentences in the Text

When starting to read a new text, the reader does not know "what the text is about" (Collins *et al.*, 1980, Olson *et al.*, 1980)—it is the model of the text created by the reader which captures the reader's evolving knowledge of what the text is about. Since it is easier to refine an existing model than to create one, let alone several, from scratch, processing should become progressively easier. This hypothesis was evaluated by measuring word reading times as a function of the serial position of a sentence. With the other factors shown in Table III being partialed out, there was indeed a speedup of word reading times with serial position as Tables III and VI indicate. This effect was most pronounced for sentence-final words whose reading times declined by 20 ms with each successive sentence. For the remaining words the serial position effect amounted to 1 ms. In Experiment 2 the serial-position effect was somewhat larger. This effect replicates results from several labs (Cirilo & Foss, 1980; Haberlandt, 1980, 1984; Olson *et al.* 1981; Reynolds, Standiford, & Anderson, 1978). Graesser *et al.* (1980), however, argued that the serial-position effect is an artifact of argument repetition and reported that it was no longer evident after argument repetition had been partialed out. Similarly, in the present research, the word-repetition factor could be responsible for the serial position effect. However, the bivariate correlation between serial position and word repetition was only $r = .22$, which means that only 4 percent of the variance in serial position was accounted for by word repetition. Furthermore, the serial-position effect was significant even when word repetition was partialed out by being included as a factor in these regressions.

The serial-position effect, the forward effect observed by Haberlandt and Bingham (1984; Experiment 4 discussed previously), and an analysis of speak-aloud protocols collected during reading (Collins et al., 1980; Olson et al., 1981) suggest that readers access knowledge structures such as scripts and plans while reading the early sections of a text and that processing becomes easier once the knowledge structures have been accessed. Since narratives involve scripts and plans to a greater extent than expositions, this factor should be more pronounced in the former than the latter. This possibility may be viable as data from Experiment 2 and from a study by Olson et al. (1980) indicate. In these studies the serial position effect was larger in narratives than in expositions. This result suggests that readers generate expectations about input more readily with stories than with essays. However, even in narratives, the serial-position effect is not continuous. In narratives involving shifts of topic or point of view, the serial-position effect is interrupted by temporary increases in processing difficulty (Haberlandt et al., 1980; Mandler & Goodman, 1982; Olson et al., 1981). At these points the reader is assumed to adjust his or her text model by incorporating new characters or a new goal into the representation. In certain "garden-path" texts (for example, in detective novels or humorous passages), readers often have to abandon an existing model altogether because the author intentionally introduces some surprising information relatively late in the text. Since the reader must alter his or her model substantially, such surprises, however suspenseful and enjoyable, should be associated with an increase in the temporary processing load.

D. Knowledge Application and Passage Familiarity

Every act of reading requires knowledge of the reader, including general linguistic and world knowledge as well as more specific, domain-related knowledge (Bisanz & Voss, 1981). Several studies have employed the assumption that the processing difficulty of a passage should vary with the amount of knowledge the subject can apply to the passage. To the degree that familiarity ratings measure this knowledge, it should be possible to study processing difficulty of a text as a function of the rated familiarity of the text. However, while it is easy to have a text's familiarity rated, the effects of familiarity on processing load and reading speed are far from being understood. Familiarity could increase the speed because it would be easier for the reader to generate inferences and expectations. On the other hand, familiarity could decrease comprehension speed because, with more knowledge, it may take the reader longer to generate the inferences and images (Denis, 1982). The experimental evidence on familiarity effects is inconclusive, with Kintsch *et al.* (1975), Birkmire (1982), and Schmalhofer (1982) reporting faster reading times for familiar than unfamiliar texts and Graesser and Riha (1984) and Johnson and Kieras (1982) reporting only very small differences, if any.

In Experiment 1, I investigated the effects of familiarity on word reading times, with familiarity being both experimenter- and subject-defined. The experimenter wrote two versions of a passage differing in familiarity as explained previously. In a subsequent norming phase, subjects rated the familiarity of the passages they had read previously. Familiarity effects were observed for both definitions of familiarity, although to a lesser extent for experimenter-defined familiarity. The effects of subject-rated familiarity on reading times across all but last words are exhibited in Fig. 4 for the two conditions of Experiment 1. In the assertions condition of Experiment 1 the effect of familiarity was comparable for nonfinal and sentence-final words (see also Table VI).

Figure 4 shows that reading times decrease with an increase in familiar-

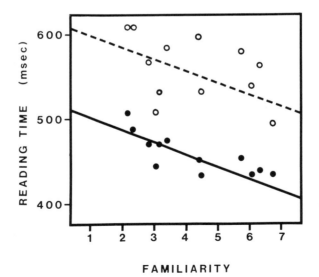

Fig. 4. Mean word reading times on passages as a function of subject-rated familiarity. ○, recall; ●, assertions.

ity. Furthermore, the fact that the regression coefficients associated with familiarity (see Tables III and VI) were significant indicates that the familiarity effect is not due to some potential confounding with other factors such as word length, word frequency, or sentence length.

The familiarity effects observed here replicate similar effects observed by Kintsch *et al.* (1975) and by Birkmire (1982). These familiarity effects can be described in terms of the model-building view advocated here. According to this view the reader creates a growing text model based on the information in the text as well as on world and domain knowledge. The domain knowledge can be used in order to establish links between sentences that are not explicitly linked in the text. These links are assumed to be represented as propositions in the emerging text model. It becomes easier to generate such propositions as the reader's knowledge about the content of the text becomes richer. In addition, model building is more efficient since certain structures, which could be used as part of the current text model, may already be available in long-term memory (e.g., Foss, 1982; Johnson *et al.*, 1982). In the case of highly familiar and ritualized action sequences, the reader can draw on relatively complete preexisting structures which are instantiated by the text (Bower *et al.*, 1979).

The effect of savings due to familiarity is that word reading times of all words, whether sentence-final words or not, are speeded up. Again, the question arises as to which specific processes are speeded up. Are such word-level processes as encoding and lexical access being facilitated? To date, one can only speculate about the relationship between passage familiarity on the one hand and encoding and access on the other. One possibility is that encoding and access are independent of the level of familiarity. In this case the slopes associated with length and frequency would be parallel in familiar and in less familiar passages, according to an additive-factors logic. Given such a result, one would have to assume that the knowledge application process operates in parallel with the word-level processes, contributing a constant level of background load at each point of a passage (see Thibadeau *et al.*, 1982). Another possibility is that the relative contributions of encoding and access change with familiarity, resulting in different slopes of length and/or frequency. Analysis of the results to date gives an inconclusive picture, as the coefficients tabulated in Table VII indicate.

On the one hand, standardized coefficients in the top three panels of Table VII suggest that the slope for length is steeper for familiar than less familiar passages, while the slope for word frequency is less steep for the more familiar passages. This pattern implies that word access is easier relative to encoding in familiar than in less familiar passages. On the other

TABLE VII
Effects of Length and Frequency in Familiar and Less Familiar Passages

	Familiar			Less familiar		
	Coefficient	Standard coefficient	t	Coefficient	Standard coefficient	t
Assertions						
Length	15	.37	7.40	8	.21	4.30
Frequency	−11	−.14	2.60	−16	−.23	4.21
Recall						
Length	20	.23	4.47	15	.20	4.03
Frequency	−31	−.19	3.43	−35	−.23	4.25
Experiment 2						
Length	17	.41	13.87	12	.26	7.72
Frequency	−7	−.09	2.78	−20	.25	6.96
Experiment 2 (max length 8)						
Length	8	.20	5.41	8	.16	3.92
Frequency	−14	.27	7.12	−20	−.28	6.74

hand, inspection of these patterns at different levels of length suggests that this reversed pattern was only evident for longer words, of which there were relatively few cases, but not for words of up to eight letters long. A regression analysis from Experiment 2 based on words of length up to eight letters showed that the effects of length and frequency were quite similar in familiar and less familiar passages. Whatever this relationship turns out to be, the overall result is that in the present tasks, familiar passages are read faster, word for word, than less familiar passages.

In sum, three text-level processes were examined here: continuity monitoring, model refinement, and knowledge application. There was a word-repetition effect which is consistent with the continuity-monitoring hypothesis. However, any contributions of word-level processes to the repetition effect still need to be controlled. Model refinement was revealed by a speedup of reading times with the serial position of sentences within passages. Similarly, the knowledge-application hypothesis was supported by facilitated reading times in more familiar passages.

VII. CONCLUSION

The goal of this article has been to list certain word-, sentence-, concept-, and text-level processes involved in reading comprehension, to document their effect on reading behavior, and to delineate their scope within different text units. At several points, I have also considered the relationship between certain component processes.

Of the word-level processes, encoding and lexical-access operations were examined. The impact of these processes is primarily confined to the current word, although there is a small significant effect on the processing of word $n + 1$. This means that word-level processes triggered by a word are not buffered until several subsequent words have been processed (see Carpenter & Just, 1983; Just & Carpenter, 1980). Since the variables associated with word-level processes, length and log occurrence frequency, are easily quantified, it is a relatively straightforward task to investigate several relationships involving these processes. One of these is the relationship between encoding and access itself. Based on the present data, the two processes are independent as revealed by significant effects of frequency for different levels of length (Carpenter & Just, 1983). Of course, this does not answer the question of whether these two processes occur sequentially or serially, or whether they are partially overlapping. New research methodologies and analytical techniques must be developed to make these questions tractable.

Among sentence-level effects, I focused on the influence of the propositional complexity on word reading times. I identified a specific sentence-level process, called the sentence-modeling process. This process establishes a sentence model in working memory which, unlike the text model, applies only to the current sentence. The sentence model includes the propositions of the current sentence and represents the relationship between them. The sentence modeling process was revealed by the proposition effect occurring at sentence-final words, but not elsewhere. The data indicated that the modeling process was more pronounced in the recall than in the assertions condition, thus reflecting the greater encoding load in a recall situation. The modeling process at the sentence boundary was reduced in sentences with a major clause, suggesting that some portion of the sentence model is created at clause boundaries.

Thus far, my research has not been concerned with syntactic parsing processes per se. These processes lead to a structural description of the sentence (Frazier, 1983; Thibadeau et al., 1982). Although not documented here, such processes must occur continuously throughout a sentence, if only in order to enable the reader to detect clause and sentence boundaries (for further arguments, see Frazier, 1983). Future research should investigate such syntactic processes in their own right and their relationship to the sentence-modeling process postulated previously.

Regarding concept-level effects, I found evidence of sentential but not of lexical priming. Because of the wealth of lexical-priming effects in a variety of experimental situations, including lexical-decision, naming, phoneme-monitoring, and eye-fixation (Carroll, 1983) studies, and because of the influence of these results on the development of interactive reading theories, it is important that more research be done on lexical priming in reading situations. For such research, intact texts rather than individual sentences should be used. Similarly, more natural sentences rather than those containing an unusually large number of highly predictive pairs of context and target pairs should be investigated (see Gough, 1983). Sentential priming was obtained in pairs of sentences which were presented in their natural forward order rather than in a reverse order. Since the lexical relatedness between concepts was controlled in forward and reverse pairs, the forward effect could not be attributed to more effective lexical priming in forward than in reverse pairs. Rather, the information in the sentences as a whole must have caused the forward effect. An unresolved question is this: At what point does the facilitation occur, early in the processing of a text unit (for example, at the point of encoding) or late in processing (for example, when the reader integrates the target sentence with the previous sentence)?

Three text-level processes were examined experimentally: continuity monitoring, model refinement, and knowledge application. Continuity monitoring was demonstrated by faster reading times of repeated content words. Model refinement was shown by the increase in reading speed of successive sentences with word repetition being partialed out. At first, when the reader has no model of the text, he or she has to create one, a process which is relatively difficult (e.g., Olson *et al.*, 1981). Later, the model merely needs to be augmented, which is less demanding. Since the speedup is greatest at the sentence-final word, we may assume that this is the place where information from the current sentence is integrated into the text model. This, in turn, suggests that the reader condenses the propositions of a sentence into a unit and adds the unit, or a subset thereof, to the growing text model. Alternatively, a proposition could be added to the model as it is extracted from a sentence. Knowledge application was demonstrated by faster reading times for familiar than unfamiliar passages, with other factors being partialed out. I attributed this effect to the greater ease with which a reader can generate inferential links between sentences not explicitly linked in the text. The familiarity effect was of similar magnitude for sentence-final and nonfinal words (see Table VII), suggesting that the process of recruiting knowledge for interpreting a passage is distributed evenly over all words of a sentence. Further research should improve on the characterization of the processes introduced here by collecting converging evidence using different techniques and by evaluating alternative accounts for the different empirical effects I have reported. While one or the other process may not weather the additional tests, their introduction will nevertheless stimulate new research including research on the relationship between the processes.

ACKNOWLEDGMENTS

This research was supported, in part, by NSF Grant BNS-8104958. I am grateful to Myron Gudz, Allen Lepore, Camille A. Pane, and P. Phiansunthon, who assisted with the research, and to Dina Anselmi, Geoff Bingham, Art Graesser, Bill Mace, Jennifer Sandson, and the volume editors for their comments on earlier drafts.

REFERENCES

Aaronson, D., & Scarborough, H. S. (1976). Performance theories for sentence coding: Some quantitative evidence. *Journal of Experimental Psychology: Human Perception and Performance, 2,* 56–70.

Adams, M. J., & Collins, A. (1979). A schema-theoretic view of reading. In R. O. Freedle (Ed.), *New directions in discourse processing.* Norwood, NJ: Ablex.

Becker, C. A. (1980). Semantic context effects in visual word recognition: An analysis of semantic strategies. *Memory & Cognition, 8,* 493–512.

Birkmire, D. P. (1982). *Text structure, background knowledge and purpose in text engineering.* Paper presented at the meeting of the Psychnomic Society, Minneapolis.

Birnbaum, L., & Selfridge, M. (1981). Conceptual analysis of natural language. In R. C. Schank & C. K. Riesbeck (Eds.), *Inside computer understanding: Five programs plus miniatures.* Hillsdale, NJ: Erlbaum.

Bisanz, G. L., & Voss, J. F. (1981). Sources of knowledge in reading comprehension: Cognitive development and expertise in a content domain. In A. M. Lesgold & C. A. Perfetti (Eds.), *Interactive processes in reading.* Hillsdale, NJ: Erlbaum.

Black, J. B., Turner, T. J., & Bower, G. H. (1979). Point of view in narrative comprehension, memory, and production. *Journal of Verbal Learning and Verbal Behavior, 18,* 187–198.

Bousfield, W. A., Cohen, B. H., Whitmarsh, G. A., & Kincaid, W. D. (1961). *Studies on the mediation of verbal behavior.* (Technical Report No. 35). University of Connecticut, Storrs, CT.

Bovair, S., & Kieras, D. E. (1981). *A guide to propositional analysis for research and technical prose.* (Technical Report No. 18). University of Arizona, Tucson, AZ.

Bower, G. (1975). Cognitive psychology: An introduction. In W. K. Estes (Ed.), *Handbook of learning and cognitive processes* (Vol 1). Hillsdale, NJ: Erlbaum.

Bower, G. H., Black, J. B., & Turner, T. J. (1979a). Scripts in memory for text. *Cognitive Psychology, 11,* 177–220.

Bradley, D. C., Garrett, M. F., & Zurif, E. B. (1980). Syntactic deficits in Broca's aphasia. In D. Kaplan (Ed.), *Biological studies of mental processes,* Cambridge, MA: MIT Press.

Cairns, H. S., Cowart, W., & Jablon, A. D. (1981). Effects of prior context upon the integration of lexical information during sentence processing. *Journal of Verbal Learning and Verbal Behavior, 20,* 445–453.

Carbonell, J. G., Jr. (1981). *Metaphor comprehension.* (Technical Report). Department of Computer Science, Carnegie-Mellon University, Pittsburgh, PA.

Carpenter, P. A., & Just, M. A. (1977). Reading comprehension as the eyes see it. In M. A. Just & P. A. Carpenter (Eds.), *Cognitive processes in comprehension.* Hillsdale, NJ: Erlbaum.

Carpenter, P. A., & Just, M. A. (1983). What your eyes do while your mind is reading. In K. Rayner (Ed.), *Eye movements in reading: Perceptual and language processes.* New York: Academic Press.

Carroll, P. J. (1983). *A study of semantic and synactic control of fixation in reading.* Unpublished dissertation, University of Massachusetts.

Chang, F. R. (1980). Active memory processes in visual sentence comprehension: Clause effects and pronominal reference. *Memory & Cognition, 8,* 58–64.

Cirilo, R. K., & Foss, D. J. (1980). Text structure and reading time for sentences. *Journal of Verbal Learning and Verbal Behavior, 19,* 96–109.

Clark, H. H., & Clark, E. V. (1977). *Psychology and language: An introduction to psycholinguistics.* New York: Harcourt.

Clark, H. H., & Haviland, S. E. (1977). Comprehension and the given-new contract. In R. O. Freedle (Ed.), *Discourse production and comprehension.* Norwood, NJ: Ablex.

Cohen, J., & Cohen, P. (1975). *Applied multiple regression: Correlation analysis for the behavioral sciences.* Hillsdale, NJ: Erlbaum.

Collins, A., Brown, J. S., & Larkin, K. M. (1980). Inference in text understanding. In R. J. Spiro, B. C. Bruce, & W. F. Brewer (Eds.), *Theoretical issues in reading comprehension.* Hillsdale, NJ: Erlbaum.

Cutler, A. (1981). Making up materials is a confounded nuisance, or: Will we be able to run any psycholinguistic experiments at all in 1990? *Cognition, 10,* 65–70.

Daneman, M., & Carpenter, P. A. (1980). Individual differences in working memory and reading. *Journal of Verbal Learning and Verbal Behavior, 19,* 450–466.

Dee-Lucas, D., Just, M. A., Carpenter, P. A., & Daneman, M. (1982). What eye fixations tell us about the time course of text integration. In R. Groner & P. Fraisse (Eds.), *Cognition and eye movements.* Amsterdam: North Holland Publ.

Denis, M. (1982). Imagining while reading text: A study of individual differences. *Memory & Cognition, 10,* 540–545.

Dixon, P., & Rothkopf, E. Z. (1979). Word repetition, lexical access, and the process of searching words and sentences. *Journal of Verbal Learning and Verbal Behavior, 18,* 629–644.

Ehrlich, S. F., & Rayner, K. (1981). Contextual effects on word processing and eye movements during reading. *Journal of Verbal Learning & Verbal Behavior, 20,* 641–655.

Eisenberg, P., & Becker, C. A. (1982). Semantic context effects in visual and word recognition sentence processing and reading: Evidence for semantic strategies. *Journal of Experimental Psychology: Human Perception and Performance, 8* 739–756.

Feustel, C. F., Shiffrin, R. M., & Salasoo, A. (1983). Episodic and lexical contributions to the repetition effect in word identification. *Journal of Experimental Psychology: General, 112,* 309–346.

Fischler, I. (1977). Semantic facilitation in a lexical decision task. *Memory & Cognition, 5,* 335–339.

Fodor, J. A., Bever, T. G., & Garrett, M. F. (1974). *The psychology of language: An introduction to psycholinguistics and generative grammar.* New York: McGraw-Hill.

Forster, K. I. (1976). Accessing the mental lexicon. In R. J. Wales & E. Walker (Eds.), *New approaches to language mechanisms.* Amsterdam: North-Holland Publ.

Forster, K. I. (1979). Levels of processing and the structure of the language processor. In

W. E. Cooper & E. C. T. Walker (Eds.), *Sentence processing: Psycholinguistics studies presented to Merrill Garrett.* Hillsdale, NJ: Erlbaum.

Forster, K. I. (1981). Priming and the effects of sentence and lexical contexts of naming time: Evidence for autonomous lexical processing. *Quarterly Journal of Experimental Psychology, 33A,* 465–495.

Foss, D. J. (1982). A discourse on semantic priming. *Cognitive Psychology, 14,* 590–607.

Foss, D. J., & Hakes, D. T. (1978). *Psycholinguistics: An introduction to the psychology of language.* New York: Prentice-Hall.

Frazier, L. (1983). Processing sentence structure. In K. Rayner (Ed.), *Eye movements in reading: Perceptual and language processes.* New York: Academic Press.

Frederiksen, J. R. (1981). Sources of process interactions in reading. In A. M. Lesgold & C. A. Perfetti (Eds.), *Interactive processes in reading.* Hillsdale, NJ: Erlbaum.

Galambos, J. A. (1983). Normative studies of six characteristics of our knowledge of common activities. *Behavior Research Methods and Instrumentation, 15,* 327–340.

Glanzer, M. (1962). Grammatical category: A rote learning and word association analysis. *Journal of Verbal Learning and Verbal Behavior, 1,* 31–41.

Glanzer, M., & Ehrenreich, S. L. (1979). Structure and search for the internal lexicon. *Journal of Verbal Learning and Verbal Behavior, 18,* 381–398.

Gordon, B., & Caramazza, A. (1982). Lexical decision for open- and closed-class words: Failure to replicate differential frequency sensitivity. *Brain and Language, 15,* 143–160.

Gough, P. B. (1983). Context, form, and interaction. In K. Rayner (Ed.), *Eye movements in reading: Perceptual and language processes.* New York: Academic Press.

Graesser, A. C., Hoffman, N. L., & Clark, L. F. (1980). Structural components of reading time. *Journal of Verbal Learning and Verbal Behavior, 19,* 135–151.

Graesser, A. C., & Riha, J. R. (1984). An application of multiple regression techniques to sentence reading times. In D. Kieras & M. Just (Eds.), *New methods in comprehension research.* Hillsdale, NJ: Erlbaum.

Haber, R. N. (1978). Visual perception. *Annual Review of Psychology, 29,* 31–59.

Haber, R. N. (1983). The impending demise of the icon: A critique of the concept of iconic storage in visual information processing. *The Behavioral and Brain Sciences, 6,* 1–54.

Haberlandt, K. (1980). Story grammar and reading time of story constituents. *Poetics, 9,* 99–118.

Haberlandt, K. F. (1984). Components of sentence and word reading times. In D. Kieras & M. Just (Eds.), *New methods in comprehension research,* Hillsdale, NJ: Erlbaum.

Haberlandt, K., Berian, C., & Sandson, J. (1980). The episode schema in story processing. *Journal of Verbal Learning and Verbal Behavior, 19,* 635–650.

Haberlandt, K., & Bingham, G. (1984). The effect of input direction on the processing of script statements. *Journal of Verbal Learning and Verbal Behavior, 23,* 162–177.

Haberlandt, K., & Graesser, A. C. (1985). Component processes in text comprehension and some of their introductions. *Journal of Experimental Psychology: General, 114,* 357–374.

Haberlandt, K., & Graesser, A. C. (1986). *Buffering new information during reading.* Unpublished manuscript.

Hoermann, H. (1979). *Psycholinguistics: An introduction to research and theory.* New York: Springer-Verlag.

Hurtig, R. (1978). The validity of clausal processing strategies at the discourse level. *Discourse Processes, 1,* 195–202.

Jarvella, R. J. (1971). Syntactic processing of connected speech. *Journal of Verbal Learning and Verbal Behavior, 10,* 409–416.

Jarvella, R. J. (1979). Immediate memory and discourse processing. In G. H. Bower (Eds.), *The psychology of learning and motivation.* New York: Academic Press.

Johnson, W., & Kieras, D. E. (1982). *The role of prior knowledge in the comprehension of simple technical prose.* (Technical Report No. 11). University of Arizona, Tucson, AZ.

Juola, J. F., Ward, N. J., & McNamara, T. (1982). Visual search and reading of rapid serial presentations of letter strings, words, and text. *Journal of Experimental Psychology: General,* **111,** 208–227.

Just, M. A., & Carpenter, P. A. (1980). A theory of reading: From eye fixations to comprehension. *Psychological Review,* **87,** 329–354.

Just, M. A., Carpenter, P. A., & Masson, M. (1982). *What eye fixations tell us about speed reading and skimming.* (Technical Report). Carnegie-Mellon University, Pittsburgh, PA.

Just, M. A., Carpenter, P. A., & Woolley, J. D. (1982a). Paradigms and processes in reading comprehension. *Journal of Experimental Psychology: General,* **3,** 228–238.

Kaplan, R. M. (1975). On process models for sentence analysis. In D. A. Norman & D. E. Rumelhart (Eds.), *Explorations in cognition.* San Francisco: Freeman.

Kennedy, A. (1983). On looking into space. In K. Rayner (Ed.), *Eye movements in reading: Perceptual and language processes.* New York: Academic Press.

Kieras, D. E. (1981). Component processes in the comprehension of simple prose. *Journal of Verbal Learning and Verbal Behavior,* **20,** 1–23.

Kimball, J. P. (1973). Seven Principles of surface structure parsing in natural language. *Cognition,* **2,** 15–47.

Kintsch, W. (1976). Memory for prose. In C. N. Cofer (Ed.), *The structure of human memory.* San Francisco: Freeman.

Kintsch, W., & Keenan, J. (1973). Reading rate and retention as a function of the number of propositions in the base structure of sentences. *Cognitive Psychology,* **5,** 257–274.

Kintsch, W., Kozminsky, E., Streby, W. J., McKoon, G., & Keenan, J. M. (1975). Comprehension and recall of text as a function of content variables. *Journal of Verbal Learning and Verbal Behavior,* **14,** 196–214.

Kintsch, W., & van Dijk, T. A. (1978). Toward a model of text comprehension and production. *Psychological Review,* **85,** 363–394.

Klatzky, R. L. (1980). *Human memory: Structures and processes.* (2nd ed.). San Francisco: Freeman.

Kliegl, R., Olson, R. K., & Davidson, B. J. (1982). Regression analysis as a tool for studying reading processes: Comments on Just and Carpenter's eye fixation theory. *Memory & Cognition,* **10,** 276–296.

Knight, G. P. (1984). Multiple regression analysis in reading research. In D. Kieras & M. Just (Eds.), *New methods in comprehension research.* Hillsdale, NJ: Erlbaum.

Kolers, P. A. (1976). Buswell's discoveries. In R. A. Monty & O. W. Senders (Eds.), *Eye movements and psychological processes.* Hillsdale, NJ: Erlbaum.

Kucera, H., & Francis, W. N. (1967). *Computational analysis of present-day American English.* Providence, RI: Brown University Press.

Levy, B. A. (1981). Interactive processing during reading. In A. M. Lesgold & C. A. Perfetti (Eds.), *Interactive processes in reading.* Hillsdale, NJ: Erlbaum.

Mandler, J. M., & Goodman, M. S. (1982). On the psychological validity of story structure. *Journal of Verbal Learning and Verbal Behavior,* **21,** 507–523.

Marslen-Wilson, W. D., & Welsh, A. (1978). Processing interactions and lexical access during word recognition in continuous speech. *Cognitive Psychology,* **10,** 29–63.

Massaro, D. W. (1979). Reading and listening. In P. A. Kolers, M. Wrolstad, & H. Bouma (Eds.), *Processing of visible language* (Vol. 1). New York: Plenum.

Masson, M. E. J. (1982). Cognitive processes in skimming stories. *Journal of Experimental Psychology: Learning, Memory, and Cognition,* **8,** 400–417.

Masson, M. E. J., & Sala, L. S. (1978). Interactive processes in sentence comprehension and recognition. *Cognitive Psychology,* **10,** 244–270.

Meyer, B. J. F. (1975). *The organization of prose and its effects on memory.* Amsterdam: North Holland Publ.

Meyer, D. E., & Schvaneveldt, R. W. (1976). Meaning, memory structure, and mental processes. In C. N. Coffer (Ed.), *The structure of human memory,* San Francisco: Freeman.

Miller, J. R., & Kintsch, W. (1980). Readability and recall of short prose passages: A theoretical analysis. *Journal of Experimental Psychology: Human Learning and Memory,* **6,** 335–354.

Mitchell, D. C., & Green, D. W. (1978). The effects of content on the immediate processing in reading. *Quarterly Journal of Experimental Psychology,* **30,** 609–636.

Morton, J. (1969). Interaction of information in word recognition. *Psychological Review,* **76,** 165–178.

Nie, N. H., Hull, C. H., Jenkins, J. G., Steinbrenner, K., & Bent, D. H. (1975). *Statistical packages for the social sciences* (2nd ed.). New York: McGraw-Hill.

Oden, G. E., & Spira, J. L. (1983). Influence of context on the activation of ambiguous word senses. *Quarterly Journal of Experimental Psychology,* **35A,** 51–64.

Olson, G. M., Duffy, S. A., & Mack, R. L. (1980). Knowledge of writing conventions in prose comprehension. In W. J. McKeachie & K. Eble (Eds.), *New directions in learning and searching.* San Francisco: Jossey-Bass.

Olson, G. M., Mack, R. L., & Duffy, S. A. (1981). Cognitive aspects of genre. *Poetics,* **10,** 283–315.

Perfetti, C. A., Goldman, S. R., & Hogaboam, T. W. (1979). Reading skill and the identification of words in discourse context. *Memory & Cognition,* **7,** 273–282.

Perfetti, C. A., & Lesgold, A. M. (1977). Discourse comprehension and sources of individual differences. In M. A. Just & P. A. Carpenter (Eds.), *Cognitive processes in comprehension.* Hillsdale, NJ: Erlbaum.

Perfetti, C. A., & Roth, S. (1981). Some of the interactive processes in reading and their role in reading skill. In A. M. Lesgold & C. A. Perfetti (Eds.), *Interactive processes in reading.* Hillsdale, NJ: Erlbaum.

Rayner, K. (1978). Eye movements in reading and information processing. *Psychological Bulletin,* **85,** 618–660.

Reynolds, R. E., Standiford, S. N., & Anderson, R. C. (1978). *Distribution of reading time when questions are asked about a restricted category of text information.* (Technical Report No. 83). Urbana, IL: University of Illinois.

Rubin, D. C. (1980). 51 properties of 125 words: A unit analysis of verbal behavior. *Journal of Verbal Learning and Verbal Behavior,* **19,** 736–755.

Rumelhart, D. E. (1977). Toward an interactive model of reading. In S. Dornic & P. Rabbitt (Eds.), *Attention and performance, VI.* Hillsdale, NJ: Erlbaum.

Sanford, A. J., & Garrod, S. C. (1981). *Understanding written language.* New York: Wiley.

Scarborough, D. L., Gerald, L., & Cortese, C. (1979). Accessing lexical memory: The transfer of word repetition effects across task and modality. *Memory & Cognition,* **7,** 3–12.

Schank, R. C. (1980). Language and memory. *Cognitive Science,* **4,** 243–284.

Schank, R. C., & Abelson, R. (1977). *Scripts, plans, goals, and understanding.* Hillsdale, NJ: Erlbaum.

Schindler, R. M. (1978). The effect of prose context on visual search for letters. *Memory & Cognition,* **6,** 124–130.

Schmalhofer, F. J. (1982). *Comprehension of a technical text as a function of expertise.* Unpublished doctoral dissertation, University of Colorado.

Schuberth, R. E., & Eimas, P. D. (1977). Effects of content on the classification of words and nonwords. *Journal of Experimental Psychology: Human Perception and Performance,* **3,** 27–36.

Seidenberg, M. S., Tanenhaus, M. K., Leiman, J. M., & Bienkowski, M. (1982). Automatic access of the meaning of ambiguous words in context: Some limitations of knowledge-based processing. *Cognitive Psychology,* **14,** 489–537.

Sharkey, N. E., & Mitchell, D. C. (1981). *Match or fire: Contextual mechanisms in the recognition of words.* Paper presented by the Experimental Psychology Society, Oxford.

Sperling, G. (1960). The information available in brief visual presentions. *Psychological Monographs,* **74,** (Whole No. 498).

Stanovich, K. E. (1981). Attentional and automatic content effects in reading. In A. M. Lesgold & C. A. Perfetti (Eds.), *Interactive processes in reading.* Hillsdale, NJ: Erlbaum.

Thibadeau, R., Just, M. A., & Carpenter, P. A. (1982). A model of the time course and content of reading. *Cognitive Science,* **6,** 157–203.

Thorndyke, P. W. (1975). Conceptual complexity and imagery in comprehension and memory. *Journal of Verbal Learning and Verbal Behavior,* **14,** 359–369.

Thorndyke, P. W. (1976). The role of inferences in discourse comprehension. *Journal of Verbal Learning and Verbal Behavior,* **15,** 437–446.

Thorndyke, P. W. (1977). Cognitive structures in comprehension and memory of narrative discourse. *Cognitive Psychology,* **9,** 77–110.

Toglia, M. P., & Battig, W. F. (1978). *Handbook of semantic word norms.* New York: Wiley.

Tulving, E., & Gold, C. (1963). Stimulus information and contextual information as determinants of tachistoscopic recognition of words. *Journal of Experimental Psychology,* **66,** 319–327.

Tulving, E., Mandler, G., & Baumal, R. (1964). Interaction of two sources of information in tachistoscopic word recognition. *Canadian Journal of Psychology,* **18,** 62–71.

Tulving, E., Schacter, D. L., & Stark, H. A. (1982). Priming effects in word-fragment completion are independent of recognition memory. *Journal of Experimental Psychology: Learning, Memory, and Cognition,* **8,** 336–342.

Turner, A., & Greene, E. (1977). *The construction and use of a propositional text base.* (Technical Report No. 63). Boulder, CO: Institute for the Study of Intellectual Behavior.

Watson, I. J. (1976). *The Processing of implausible sentences.* Unpublished doctoral dissertation. Monash University.

Wilkinson, A. C. (1983). Learning to read in real time. In A. C. Wilkinson (Ed.), *Classroom computers and cognitive science.* New York: Academic Press.

Zipf, G. K. (1949). *Human behavior and the principle of least effort.* Cambridge, MA: Addison-Wesley.

VERBAL EFFICIENCY IN READING ABILITY

CHARLES A. PERFETTI

Learning Research and Development Center
University of Pittsburgh
Pittsburgh, Pennsylvania 15260

In this article, my purpose is to make clear the central features of a theory of reading ability. The theory, the verbal efficiency theory of reading ability, has been described previously, most recently and most thoroughly in Perfetti (1985). It has also been described in piecemeal fashion in Perfetti and Hogaboam (1975), Perfetti and Lesgold (1977, 1979), and Perfetti and Roth (1981). However, its basic theoretical structure, its underlying assumptions, and its implications have not been argued in detail. In what follows, therefore, the central features of the theory will be spelled out. Following that will be a report of evidence, some unpublished, that is necessary (but not sufficient) to demonstrate the plausibility of the theory. Finally, there will be some discussion of the practical implications of the theory. The first step is to make explicit the components of reading comprehension and then to define the scope of a theory of reading comprehension.

I. COMPONENTS OF READING COMPREHENSION

There are two major components to reading comprehension: local text processing and text modeling. To demonstrate these components of comprehension, consider the following simple story excerpt, taken from Perfetti (1985):

(1) Joe and his infant daughter were waiting for the doctor to get back from lunch.
(2) The room was warm and stuffy so they opened the window.
(3) It didn't help much.
(4) Why wasn't there an air conditioner?

109

(5) Strange for this part of Manhattan.
(6) Suddenly the door swung open.

First, the comprehension of any text depends upon *local text processes* that (1) encode the contextually appropriate meanings of the words in the text, (2) encode the propositions that the text contains, and (3) integrate these propositions across the text. Second, comprehension depends on the construction of a *text model* by the reader. *Text modeling* refers to the processes by which the reader combines knowledge about concepts, including scriptal and schematic knowledge, with the text propositions to form a representation of the text meaning. In the following sections, these component processes are described briefly and exemplified for the text excerpt.

A. Semantic Encoding

The reader's semantic representation of concepts and their associated lexical realizations are the basis for semantic encoding. He or she must know something about the meanings for the words of the text. The form of this representation can be considered a semantic network, with words and concepts as nodes and relationships among concepts as links. Many, if not most, words in natural language are polysemous. They enter into multiple semantic relationships, and context dictates which meaning the reader encodes. However, the best assumption we have is that the context does its selection work after an automatic activation of several, and perhaps all, of a word's meanings (Swinney, 1979). It is possible that the most common meaning has some priority in the activation process (Hogaboam & Perfetti, 1975). In any case, the assumption is that semantic encoding proceeds in two phases. The first phase, lexical access, results in the very brief activation of all meanings associated with a word. In the second phase, the continued activation of the meaning appropriate to the context results in a semantic encoding for the proposition. In the previous text example, *room* (2) is eventually encoded as referring to *area enclosed by walls*. Initially, its sense of *open space without restriction, c.f. room for expansion,* may also be activated.

This conception of contextually appropriate meaning selection has implications for reading ability. The idea of the skilled reader as one who uses context to guide word encoding may be correct only in a restricted sense. There is some suggestive evidence that, compared with less skilled readers, skilled readers more quickly "discard" the inappropriate meaning of a word (Merrill, Sperber, & McClauley, 1981). At the same time, the skilled reader will have a word-identification process of such strength that lexical access will automatically trigger word meanings independent of context.

B. Propositional Encoding

The encoding of individual words as contextually appropriate semantic objects enables the encoding of elementary text units or propositions. Each proposition represents the elementary units of a text in terms of a predicate and one or more arguments (Kintsch 1974; Kintsch & van Dijk, 1978). A text representation, as a semantic object, is a list of propositions. Thus, this representation of what the text "says" may be distinct from the reader's representation of the situation described by the text. The latter, which van Dijk and Kintsch (1983) term the "situation model," may be constructed only with the addition of many inferences based on knowledge of the world.

As the reader encounters the words in a text, he assembles them into propositions. As subsequent text is read, new propositions are assembled and integrated with previous ones held in the reader's memory. The assembly of propositions and their integration occurs within a limited-capacity processing mechanism, i.e., working memory. The reader can hold only a few propositions. The trick is to quickly integrate the assembled propositions into a representation that can survive in memory.

C. Integrative Processes

Processes that integrate text material are a continuous part of reading. As a local process, integration refers to combining successively occurring propositions with each other. One mechanism for this local integration is the recurrence of an element in different propositions ("argument overlap," Kintsch & van Dijk, 1978). For example, two propositions of sentence (2) contain *room,* and they quickly integrate in working memory— the room that is *warm* is also the room that is *stuffy.* Another example of integration is in the anaphoric connection between *they,* in *they opened the window,* and the antecedent found in sentence (1), *Joe and his daughter.* These integrations depend, in part, on linguistic signals that trigger attachments in memory. These include not only repetition of a word and pronouns anaphoric to an antecedent, but also definite articles (e.g., *the*) that compel the establishment of a prior proposition for linkage. For example, sentence (2) refers to *the window,* which, since there are no previous propositions containing *window,* triggers the inference of a window. This interference is enabled, in large part, because of the reader's knowledge concerning rooms and a previous sentence that establishes the existence of a particular room [sentence (1)].

Fairly quickly, a proposition is displaced from working memory by subsequent processing. If this proposition is needed as an antecedent for a later proposition, a reinstatement is required (Kintsch & van Dijk, 1978; Lesgold, Roth & Curtis, 1979). When this occurs, the reader expends some processing effort to forge the linkage. Lesgold *et al.* (1979) demonstrated that such reinstatement is easily accomplished when the subsequent text has kept the antecedent proposition implicitly foregrounded. Otherwise, a memory search is required.

D. The Reader's Text Model

There is more to comprehension than constructing a list of propositions, even an integrated list. The reader adds relevant knowledge that not only fills in the text's propositional base, but also allows interpretation of it. When a reader is required to recall a text, there are typically many propositions in the recall that reflect knowledge-based additions to the text. Such recalls typically combine information from the propositional base and the situation model. Perhaps more basically, the reader's comprehension is possible only through creating inferences based on his knowledge in combination with the text propositions.

One kind of knowledge important in this modeling process is the schema. The concept of schema has had a venerable history and an elusive definition. This elusiveness has caused some psychologists to consider schemata as, at best, a pretheoretical approximation to something of interest. However, it is useful to say that a schema is a conceptual abstraction containing slots (or variables) that are instantiated in various ways. It can apply to single-word concepts and to action sequences, such as the much discussed restaurant script (Schank & Abelson, 1977). A visit to the doctor's office—to use a schema activated by the example text—includes variable slots relating to appointments (essential or advisable?), receptionists (is the receptionist also a nurse?), and waiting rooms (*Reader's Digest* or *National Geographic?*).

The importance of schemata as organizing knowledge structures in comprehension has been amply demonstrated. Dooling and Lachman (1971) showed that recall of a metaphorical passage was highly influenced by the availability of a title presented before, but not after, the text. And Bransford and Johnson (1973) showed that comprehensibility ratings and recall of vague passages were increased by titles. It is likely, as Anderson, Spiro, and Anderson (1978) put it, that a schema serves as "scaffolding" on which to construct the meaning of a text.

E. Discourse Types

Another source of knowledge useful to a reader is the form of the discourse. Reading a story, a scientific report, and a newspaper report of an accident all involve conventions that correspond to the semantic structures being described. More work has been done on the structure of stories than any other discourse form (Rumelhart, 1975; Mandler & Johnson, 1977; Stein & Glenn, 1979). The structures of stories, both in terms of their action and causal sequences (Omanson, 1982) and in terms of their syntactic constituents, are forms of knowledge the reader uses in reading. Other text types also provide such knowledge, although in a less universal form than stories, where forms become familiar to most children within a culture.

F. Summary

Comprehension in reading includes a number of local processes and text modeling. Local processes are those that operate to produce propositional meaning from sentences and to integrate these meanings over relatively short ranges of text, that is, a few clauses or sentences. They include the encoding of word meanings, a process that depends on semantic representation of words in memory and the constraint provided by the local context. Propositional assembly and integration rely on these encoded meanings. The reader constructs a text model by continuously applying schematic knowledge and inference processes to the results of local processing. These schemata include a wide range of conceptual structures deriving from everyday knowledge, specialized knowledge, linguistic knowledge, and knowledge of discourse types. The reader's text model is updated by the local processes in combination with this knowledge and expectations.

II. INDIVIDUAL DIFFERENCES IN READING ABILITY

If reading ability is defined so as to include comprehension as well as written-word identification, then individual differences can arise from any of the component processes described previously. In fact, there are reasonable grounds to resist such a broad scope. If comprehension is the target performance, then the description of reading ability may be nondistinct from the description of language comprehension ability. Crowder (1982), for one, makes a valiant attempt to keep comprehension out of the scope of reading. He points out that the psychology of reading has no particular claim on descriptions of how, for example, metaphor is understood. Such descriptions are part of a theory of language comprehension. However, there are several reasons for accepting the larger scope definition. One is fairly practical, whereas three others are theoretical–empirical.

The central theoretical–empirical reason is that the comprehension of written language and the comprehension of spoken language have both shared and distinctive features. In principle, the comprehension of written language follows from the ability to understand spoken language plus the ability to identify written words. Those of us who take a linguistic approach to reading have sometimes taken this obvious principle to be the end of the matter and then claimed that printed-word identification is the only proper study of reading. However, differences between printed and spoken language must also be taken into account. There are many such superficial differences that seem to derive from two somewhat more fundamental differences. These two fundamental differences can be considered design features, following Hockett's (1960) design features of language, that distinguish spoken from written language. The features are these: (1) the physical signal features of the two media and (2) the social–asocial features governing the relationship between the message sender and the message receiver. From the first derive differences such as the greater coding demands of reading and the greater memory demands for speech, among others. From the second derive differences such as the reduced availability of pragmatic (nonlinguistic) cues for print and the greater implicitness of speech. These design features are potentially important for comprehension as well as other components of language use. However, the consequences of these differences are just beginning to be explored (see Hildyard & Olson, 1982, for an empirical demonstration of some effects on children's text processing; see Perfetti, 1988, for a more speculative discussion of the design features).

A second theoretical reason for bringing comprehension into the definition of reading has to do with the theory of reading ability. To the extent that ability in reading and ability in spoken language comprehension share explanatory mechanisms, the descriptions of reading ability need to include comprehension components. Similarly, to the extent that word-identification processes and both spoken and written language comprehension are interrelated, ability differences can best be understood within a framework that links them.

Finally, there is a practical reason for including comprehension in a definition of reading ability. In schools, children are expected to learn through reading, and individual differences in reading comprehension emerge early and dramatically. More important is the fact that these individual differences can emerge even after students have completed reading instruction. Thus, a theory of reading ability that does not address comprehension will have limited application to individual differences beyond the first two years of schooling. This, of course, is a priori a very weak reason, but if the word-identification processes and the comprehension processes are highly interconnected, as I believe they are, the application of the theory of reading ability to older children and adults is plausible.

Thus, although a narrow concept of reading ability is appropriate for many cases and more neatly circumscribes the problem than a definition that includes comprehension, the broader definition is adopted here. One of the consequences of permitting this broader definition is that it allows reading ability, in principle, to depend on things such as knowledge and inference ability. This possibility is considered in the following section along with other possible sources of individual differences that could explain reading comprehension ability.

Schema Factors Are Insufficient

Given the broad definition of reading ability, one approach to ability is to focus on higher level text-modeling processes, especially the reader's use of schemata. This approach has become quite popular along with the generally increasing importance assigned to higher level cognitive structures. However, whereas the emphasis on schemata as important cognitive structures *in general* is well placed, *an emphasis on schemata as a source of individual differences in reading ability may be misplaced.*

To see why this is true, it is necessary to understand the role of schemata, or knowledge structures, in reading comprehension. (Fortunately, it is not necessary to clearly define schema in order to do this at a sufficiently general level.) Basically, the comprehension of even a minimal passage depends on constructing a model of the text. The knowledge structures or schemata available to the reader determine, in a fairly strong sense, the text model he or she will construct. Demonstrations of this principle are well known (e.g., Anderson *et al.,* 1978; Bransford & Johnson, 1973; Dooling & Lachman, 1971).

A schema theory of individual differences in reading ability needs more than this, of course. It needs a demonstration that individuals who have certain knowledge structures will comprehend texts not understood by readers who lack these knowledge structures. There are two kinds of relevant demonstrations. In one, individuals of different presumed knowledge read texts which lack specific unambiguous reference. The understanding and/or recall of these individuals are shown to be dependent upon their presumed knowledge. This is the demonstration of Anderson, Reynolds, Schallert, and Goetz (1976), who presented readers with a passage about "Rocky," who, according to possible alternative interpretations of a vaguely phrased text, was in the midst either of a prison escape or wrestling match. Anderson *et al.* (1976) found that students from a class in educational psychology tended to understand Rocky as a prisoner, whereas physical education students in a weight-lifting class tended to understand Rocky as a wrestler.

The second kind of demonstration is more direct. It shows that individuals who have knowledge important for comprehension of a text outperform individuals who have little of this knowledge. This demonstration has been made by Voss and collaborators in studies of baseball texts (Chiesi, Spilich, & Voss, 1979; Spilich, Vesonder, Chiesi, & Voss, 1979). In these experiments, subjects differed in their knowledge of the rules of baseball but not in their general reading comprehension level. When subjects listened to a half-inning account of a fictitious game, they recalled the account in accord with their prior knowledge. High-knowledge subjects recalled more information about events important for the structure of the game, as described in terms of its goal hierarchy (Spilich *et al.*, 1979). Other experiments seem to suggest that the baseball schemata are used during comprehension to construct a more accessible game-event structure (Chiesi *et al.*, 1979). In other words, individuals who have the knowledge use it to construct a text model that corresponds to the event structure of a game. We can summarize this research by noting that it demonstrates that memory, and probably comprehension, depends on individual knowledge. It is evidence sufficient to make the minimal case for a schema-based theory of reading comprehension ability: Comprehension depends on knowledge.

This conclusion is correct but not very powerful when applied to individual differences in reading ability. It extends to reading ability only by assuming that individuals who are high in general reading ability have more useful knowledge in more situations than do readers of low ability. Notice that schema theory cannot extend to reading ability without this generalization. Otherwise, there would be no general ability differences. Some individuals would be better at reading about baseball, others would be better at reading about fly-fishing, and still others would be better at reading about gothic romances. By this account there would be no such thing as general reading ability—merely different reading performances dependent upon the match between a text and individual knowledge. Thus, there is an issue here of whether there is a general reading ability or strictly individual, knowledge-dependent skill. If one follows the "knowledge-rich'' approach to cognitive processes frequently taken by artificial expert systems, the answer may surprise us: Beyond some minimal, widely acquired word identification skills, there is no such thing as general reading comprehension skill. I don't assume that this conclusion is beyond plausibility, but neither do I see any reason to accept it at present. Until it is proved otherwise, I assume the existence of a generalized reading ability. Given this assumption, individual differences in specific knowledge cannot be the central explanatory factor in reading ability.

The line of retreat for schema theory is that reading ability depends not just on having schemata, but also on using them. Thus, a reader can acquire a sufficient number of schemata, but somehow fail to have the right schema activated at the right time when a text is encountered. Spiro (1980) has referred to this problem as one of schema *selection*. It is, in fact, a critical comprehension process. However, it might be more accurate to refer to it as schema *activation*. If things are working the way they should, appropriate schemata are not so much selected as activated by the text. For a well-written text and a skilled reader, at least, the text itself is a trigger for the reader's knowledge.

It is possible that schema selection (or activation) is a source of general reading ability differences. Some individuals may often fail, despite sufficient knowledge, to have this knowledge activated by the text. However, a direct demonstration of this possibility, as far as I know, is lacking. Moreover, any demonstration of this phenomenon would have to meet two criteria: It would need to be demonstrated that (1) the individual has the knowledge structure needed and (2) he or she has facile word-identification skills. A reader who identifies words only with effort might very well fail to ''select'' the schemata demanded by the text. This is an implication of verbal-efficiency theory. Schema theory needs to say something more than this.

Spiro (1980) discussed other things can go wrong with schemata. A reader can have a schema-instantiation problem (failing to accommodate his knowledge to specific text information) or a schema refinement problem (failing to switch schemata when necessary). Such a reader apparently can be characterized as too ''top down,'' failing to incorporate information that deviates from his selected schema. This is an interesting possibility. However, is it anything different from describing a reader as ''not understanding sentences,'' ''failing to connect propositions,'' ''not being sensitive to changing text demands,'' or not performing some other local text processing successfully? To the extent that it is different from such descriptions, it seems to leave the domain of cognitive reading analysis for the domain of personality or cognitive style.

Despite all this, knowledge application is a potent source of differences in reading ability. There is no reason to assume that readers routinely apply knowledge appropriately, and to the extent these application failures are individually systematic rather than "noise," then, to that extent, they may have some explanatory force. There is, as yet, little to demonstrate this explanatory force. However, one line of analysis is promising. It might turn out not to be a matter of having schemata or even selecting the right one. It may be a matter of the reader having control processes to apply to text that help get schemata activated appropriately. Examples of this are the "metacognitive" knowledge that a reader has concerning (1) strategies to apply to text (e.g., allocation of processing resources), (2) levels of text importance, and (3) text inference demands. The reader's control of his processing makes such knowledge very important, and it is clear that at least some individual differences can be expected in this knowledge or in its application (see, for example, Smiley, Oakley, Worthen, Campione, & Brown, 1977).

One other application of schema theory concerns discourse types. The point is that only if a reader is familiar with a discourse type will he or she be able to comprehend a text of that type. This is very reasonable, but the work so far has been on stories. There is every reason to assume that young children are familiar with stories (Stein & Glenn, 1979) and little reason to assume that individual differences in reading ability depend in any fundamental way on differences in knowledge of story forms (Weaver & Dickinson, 1982), although it is possible that some readers do not use their story knowledge when appropriate (cf. Ryan, 1982).

The general conclusion from these observations is this: Schemata are critical to comprehension. It does not follow, however, that failures of schemata are a major explanatory mechanism for a general theory of reading ability. Metacognitive skills may be more promising as a source of reading ability differences. However, there may be still more general processing sources of ability, as the next section argues.

III. VERBAL EFFICIENCY THEORY

Verbal efficiency theory is a general theoretical framework for explaining individual differences in reading ability. Like schema theory, it assumes that comprehension is part of what a theory of reading ability will account for. Unlike schema theory, it assumes that highly generalized processes—processes not dependent upon specific knowledge structures—are central to the explanation of individual differences in ability.

The central claim of the theory of verbal efficiency is that individual differences in reading comprehension are produced by individual differences in the efficient operation of local processes. The local processes are those by which temporary representations of text segments are established. In terms of the components of reading described previously, verbal efficiency assumes that construction of a quality text model depends critically on the assembly and integration of propositions in working memory. Therefore, any processing factor that contributes to the encoding of these propositions will affect overall reading comprehension. Individual differences in reading comprehension are produced by these local processing factors. This is not to say that comprehension differences are not also produced by schema-related processes. Other things being equal, differences in appropriate schema activation will produce large differences in reading comprehension. One of the important empirical questions is the extent to which other things, that is verbal efficiency, tend to be equal among individuals.

A. General Assumptions of the Theory

There are certain assumptions of the theory that are very general and widely validated in work on cognitive processes. These include the following:

1. Some mental processes operate under constraints imposed by a processing system that is limited either by its capacity or by its resources. This is the assumption of a limited-capacity working memory system (Baddeley & Hitch, 1974). Whether this system is a structurally separate short-term memory or some functionally distinctive part of a general memory system is not important. Working memory can be thought of as the limited-capacity system that is constrained by the number of memory elements that can be simultaneously activated. For reading, these elements include permanent memory nodes, such as words, plus temporarily constructed links among nodes. That is, working memory is used for sentence comprehension, storing, for example, results of incompletely parsed sentences.

2. A related assumption concerns *attention*. The limited resource problem applies only to attention-demanding processes. The important additional attention assumption is that the extent to which a process requires attention is affected by overlearning or practice (LaBerge & Samuels, 1974; Schneider & Shiffrin, 1977). It is not assumed that overlearning leads to attention-free processing, only that it leads to reduced attention demands.

3. The third assumption, closely related to the first two, is the *resource allocation* assumption. The demands on attention of competing elements are met, but only in part, by an individual's control procedures. These procedures essentially lead to more processing resources being allocated to one process rather than another (Kahneman, 1973; Norman, 1976).

B. Central Features of Verbal Efficiency Theory

The core proposal of verbal efficiency theory is that the comprehension of a text is partly limited by the efficient operation of local processes. Individual differences in general reading ability are a result of efficient operation of these local processes. There are two specific components to this theoretical claim. The first concerns the definition of verbal efficiency, and the second concerns the range of efficiency for different processes.

1. Verbal Efficiency

Verbal efficiency is a concept of product and cost. The product is some reading process outcome, and the cost is the processing resources required to achieve the outcome. The outcome of a reading process can be the identification of a word, a semantic decision about a word or a phrase, or the comprehension of any text unit. It can, in fact, be any reading outcome. The reason it is *verbal* efficiency is that the outcome of the reading process is verbal. More important, however, is the claim that what must be efficient are processes that are in large part verbal; that is, they prominently include semantic, orthographic, and phonetic components.

Definition: Verbal efficiency is the quality of a verbal processing outcome relative to its cost to processing resources.

2. Processes that May Vary in Efficiency

In principle, any of the component processes of reading can contribute to overall efficiency. The question is whether some processes are more likely candidates than others to achieve high efficiency.

a. Schema Activation. The very use of the word *activation* implies a potentially high efficiency process. Efficient schema activation is "text driven" in part. That is, a familiar text form and a familiar topic "automatically" activate appropriate schemata. On the other hand, there are many cases of inefficient schema activation. In such cases, the processes may include several search and comparison processes. The text continues to activate candidate schemata, but subsequent text samples fail to fit. The situation in vague texts can be described as the *weak activation of multiple schemata.* However, inefficient processes occur as the reader compares these schemata with text samples. This is process-costly reading work.

It is an important practical implication of verbal efficiency that efficient schema activation is not only possible but reasonably likely for mundane texts and reasonably experienced readers. As for individual differences in schema activation, they are less likely as general characteristics. That is, individuals, irrespective of reading ability, ordinarily can be expected to have schemata automatically activated provided two conditions are met. (1) They have the necessary knowledge in the first place. (2) Their low-level text processes are sufficient to trigger their activation. It is an important consequence of verbal efficiency theory that *inefficient local processes will often cause schema activation to misfire.*

b. Proposition Encoding. The efficiency of proposition encoding is variable because it involves multiple lexical processes. Several words may be needed for a working memory representation that can be linked up with the reader's current representation. It is possible that proposition encoding could, in some sense, be automatic, but it is probably better to say it this way: The encoding of text propositions can range from fairly high to extremely low in efficiency. The integration of encoded propositions into underlying text structures, for example, establishing causal links, may be especially resource costly.

As for individual differences, the limiting factor is working memory capacity. However, the assumption is that this is a *functional* limitation that is only partly due to structural limitations. That is, two individuals may have equivalent short-term memory capacity (whatever that might mean exactly) and different functional memory limitations. The individual with the larger functional capacity will be a more efficient processor of text.

c. Lexical Access. In reading, lexical-access processes range from automatic to resource costly. However, these processes are the most likely candidates for becoming uniformly high in efficiency. This assumption can extend also to encoding the semantic information stored with a word. An activation mechanism potentially enables semantic information required by context to be triggered automatically. Also, importantly, the speech code for a word can by automatically activated, enabling a reference-secured code for memory (see Perfetti & McCutchen, 1982).

The potential for high-efficiency lexical access is important for working memory. To the extent that lexical access is resource efficient, the encoding of propositions in working memory can be achieved more efficiently. This means that individual differences in working memory can arise either because of factors characteristic of proposition encoding (e.g., ordering elements and encoding predicate relations) or from inefficient lexical processes that compete for the same resources.

3. The Text Work

The specific claim of verbal efficiency theory is that the text work, the composite resource expenditure of the reader, is made easier to the extent that those processes which *can* be at high efficiency *are* at high efficiency. Those processes that, by their nature, demand the most resources include these: (1) the encoding of propositions, especially the integrating of propositions within and across sentences; (2) some inference processes that are not automatic, for example, memory searches initiated by gaps in the text and reinstatement needed for information no longer foregrounded (Lesgold *et al.*, 1979); and (3) the interpretative and critical comprehension of text. These three comprehension activities are temporally overlapping and, perhaps, fundamentally nondistinct. They are all resource demanding.

In contrast, those processes that are especially good candidates for high efficiency are lexical access and, perhaps, *elementary* propositional encoding. This elementary encoding is distinct from the high-cost integrative and inferential proposition work. It is essentially the assembling of a single proposition from only a few words.

To illustrate the possible cost of various text-work components, Fig. 1 shows a representation of hypothetical text work for the sentence, "The room was warm and stuffy, so they opened the window," (This is the second sentence of the doctor's visit text presented in Section I). A time line indicates plausible times for four different kinds of text work: lexical access, proposition assembly, proposition integration, and text modeling. The last provides the basis for the interpretive, inferential, and critical comprehension referred to previously. The processes are represented as overlapping in time. (Lexical access can be influenced by prior activation, so this is not a strictly bottom-up model.) For convenience, it is assumed that lexical access occurs for 8 of the 11 words in the sentence, and the reader must assemble 6 propositions, including an integrative one. An integrative proposition is one that requires some links to be established with prior propositions. (Argument overlap is assumed to be nonintegrative except when anaphora are involved.) Finally, there is an estimation of the resource cost of the processes. More than average text work is indicated by an asterisk; even greater text work is indicated by two asterisks. Assuming a skilled reader, the suggestion in Fig. 1 is that the most costly single piece of text work is constructing the *because* proposition. It links two assembled propositions that are separated by several words.

Notice that it is assumed that incomplete assembly processes occur.

Time	Access	Assembly	Integration	Text Modeling
	The room	(1) *exists (room)*		$\begin{bmatrix} wait\ (they,\ doctor,\ \phi\ ) \\ \phi = room \end{bmatrix}$
	was	*was room*		
	warm	(2) *warm (room)*		
	and stuffy	(3) *stuffy (room)*		
	so	*so?*		
	they	*so they*	*they = Joe & infant daughter*	
	opened	*open they*		? *complication for visit*
	the window.	(5) *open (they, window)*	**because (5, 2 & 3)*	? *significance in event structure*
		(4) *exists (window)*		

Total Resource Cost: A   P   I   M

Fig. 1. A representation of hypothetical text work for the sentence *The room was warm and stuffy, so they opened the window* when it is the second sentence of the visit-to-the-doctor's-office story. Represented are lexical access, assembly and integration of propositions, and text modeling. Resources needed for the text work are represented at three levels. Unmarked processes are low and roughly equal. Asterisks indicate processes that may require more work. Reprinted from Perfetti (1985).

These incomplete processes (unnumbered in Fig. 1) occur for at least four words. Thus, *so* triggers an incomplete proposition and *they* is attached to it until, finally, *opened* is encoded to fill in the proposition. Presumably, delay in final proposition assembly can be a significant source of text work. (Imagine, for example, an embedded clause between a noun subject and its verb.) This is because working memory must try to retain partially assembled propositions until they can be completed.

The last row of Fig. 1 is a hypothetical distribution of text work. The assumption is that for any processing outcome, there has been a distribution of effort among lexical access, assembly of propositions, integration of propositions, and text modeling. These are the parameters A (access), P (assembly of propositions), I (integration), and M (text modeling) of Fig. 1. These parameters vary widely from one sentence to another (or some other work unit). They can also vary from one individual to another. If the total text effort is T, then $A + P + I + M = T$.

Of general interest, over large sections of text, are the relative magnitudes A/T, P/T, I/T, M/T. In cases of easy texts and skilled readers, I/T should be high relative to the others, A/T and M/T should be low. The normal high-efficiency resource allocation may produce $I/T > P/T > A/T = M/T$. To put it another way, in arriving at a text representation over, say, two or three sentences, schema activation, text-driven inferences M, and lexical activation A can be relatively easy. Integration of propositions I will be somewhat more difficult.

All of this should be taken only as a generally plausible description because no serious estimation of these parameters is available for a given text and reader. However, the following additional consideration is of interest. Suppose a text is made more difficult by substituting less frequent words for familiar words without changing anything else. For the same two or three sentences, T (the total difficulty) will increase. Furthermore, every component of T will increase, not just A. Schema activation will be more effortful, insofar as it depends on easy word recognition, and may now require active memory search. Thus, M will increase. So, too, will P and I. Propositions are more difficult to assemble and integrate partly because the words are more difficult to access.

There is an important assumption about text work not reflected in Fig. 1. The text work of proposition assembly and proposition integration overlap in time with lexical access. This overlap assumption holds also for text modeling. The processes of proposition encoding, however, are not completed until case assignment of lexical items is made. Thus, the various components of text work do not have to be thought of as a series of independent processing stages. They can be considered processes in cascade (McClelland, 1979). However, the most important point is that some of these components are more likely to achieve low resource cost than others. Lexical access is perhaps the prime candidate because it involves the activation of a single memory node. All other processes require multiple activation and the construction of temporary links.

4. Reading Ability and Text Work

The application of the text-work analysis to reading ability assumes that the text-work components vary with texts and given text j is a function of the idealized work components of the text (T_j) averaged over individuals and the idealized work resources of the individual (T_i) averaged over texts, i.e., $T_{ij} = f(T_i, T_j)$. This is a straightforward and very weak assumption. It says nothing about f, the function relating ideal individual ability and ideal text difficulty.

However, it does have some interesting implications. For example, assume a series of texts are ordered according to increasing difficulty, such that $G < H < I < J < K < L$, and a series of individuals are ordered according to decreasing ability, such that $g > h > i > j > k > l$, etc. This means that there exist many individuals for whom text J is more easily read than text K. Also, it means that there exist many texts such that reader i reads them more easily than reader j. This is the essence of a concept of reading ability. It is just the sort of thing that text-specific knowledge does not yield. It also implies that there exist two different texts of difficulty J and K, such that individual h reads the more difficult text K as well as individual i reads the less difficult text J. (For text J, $h > i$, and for text K, $h > i$). The number of such texts depends on the limits of the function relating text difficulty to individual ability, but there must exist at least one such text for any two individuals within a narrow range of ability.

This scheme provides a general way for describing ability differences and text difficulty. It depends on the assumption that text difficulty should be described by reference to known processing factors (Kintsch & Vipond, 1979). It probably also depends on measuring text difficulty in terms of comprehension product per unit effort (or time). Within limits, it is possible for two individuals to show equal comprehension when time is uncontrolled, but not when time is kept short. In fact, this trade-off may not apply commonly to the range of ability differences between children that we have considered. For many low-ability children, it is not likely that mere increases in time for reading will produce comprehension equivalent to a high-ability reader.

It is worth emphasizing that neither text difficulty nor verbal efficiency, which are complementary concepts, is to be equated only with processing of single words. In both text difficulty and verbal efficiency, the critical feature is the extent to which local text processes are made easier. Difficult words can make proposition assembly and integration more difficult. However, the general principle is that any text feature that increases the effort of proposition encoding affects text difficulty. For reading ability, the corresponding principle is that any local process that increases the effort needed for proposition encoding can produce comprehension failure. This can happen because the reader abandons the difficult job of construction of a coherent text representation or because severe compromises with the text meaning must be made in order to construct any representation at all. The importance of lexical access is that it is a potentially high efficiency process that, when it is efficient, can enable the reader to work more on propositional integration even as the text becomes more difficult. Other local processes are also critical in this respect.

C. Specific Ability Hypotheses within Verbal Efficiency Theory

There are several possibilities for specific sources of ability differences within the framework of verbal efficiency. To explain low levels of ability, the most prominent hypotheses concern inefficiency of lexical access and inefficiency of proposition encoding. Both hypotheses would be capable of explaining the local-comprehension and working-memory problems observed commonly in low-ability readers.

1. Lexical-Access Hypotheses

One way to elaborate verbal efficiency theory is to assume that lexical access is the critical process. Efficient lexical access, rapid and low in resource cost, enables working memory to carry out the propositional text work. Inefficient lexical access, slow and effortful, makes it more difficult for working memory to do this work. The general lexical-access hypothesis can have several specific forms. Two of these are that (1) inefficient access is interfering and (2) lexical access produces low-quality codes.

a. Lexical-Access Interference. The specific manner in which comprehension depends on lexical access can be described as follows. The assembly and integration of propositions are interfered with by a process that competes for processing resources. Inefficient lexical access disrupts the temporary representation of text in working memory. To illustrate, we can refer back to Fig. 1, which shows the hypothetical text work for, *The room was warm and stuffy so they opened the window.* When the reader encounters *opened,* he is holding onto propositions about the room being warm and stuffy that will have to be linked to the *so* clause. He has also begun to assemble the *so* proposition and the *they* proposition (see Fig. 1). With this text work going on in working memory, the word *opened* is accessed. A rapid, effortless access of *opened* produces the semantic (and phonetic) codes necessary for two propositions, and *window* quickly follows to complete all the partially assembled propositions. If the reader has trouble with *opened*, that is, if it takes significant processing resources away from retaining the already assembled and partly assembled propositions, then memory for the latter is at risk. The same story applies to the access of *window*, except that at *window* there is more text work to perform. It completes two propositions. This particular text is very easy for an adult. If we imagine a slightly more difficult text, it is easy to see how minor problems with a single word can explode to disrupt the text representation.

b. Code Quality. The second specific mechanism for how comprehension depends on lexical access focuses on lexical access itself. It's not just that inefficient access interferes with working memory. Rather, the code that results from inefficient lexical access is of low quality. This low quality can be described as insufficient semantic activation, insufficient phonetic activation, or code asynchrony. Although these descriptions of quality seem to be different, they are unified by the common assumption that a quality code includes phonetic and semantic information being optimally available to the working memory processes. If either semantic or phonetic activation is insufficient, more effort is required for proposition assembly.

Actually, the general problem of code quality can be seen by considering *code asynchrony.* The assumption is that the longer a lexical process takes in its total execution, the greater the possibility that the activation of its component codes will be *out of phase.* In particular, phonetic and semantic codes activated during access may be out of phase with each other. If access is rapid, this means that all codes are quickly available and that the semantic code and phonetic codes can immediately enter into proposition assembly. However, if access is slow, either semantic or phonetic activation may come too late to give the fully specified word code required by proposition encoding.

This asynchrony may be a way to understand two problems sometimes observed with low-ability readers. Immediately after reading a word in a text, the reader may be able to repeat the word but not "know its meaning"—even though he or she "knows" its meaning in some other situation. Or, immediately after reading a word in a text, the reader may have a vague memory for its gist that may result in recalling a semantically related word rather than the word itself. Or, on some occasions in oral reading, the "wrong" word is actually produced, reflecting semantic activation and phonetic–semantic asynchrony. Because of the asynchrony, the activation of the phonological representation of the "wrong" word is momentarily higher than for the representation of the actual printed word. This can occur occasionally in high-ability readers as well. Moreover, something very like this asynchrony is quite striking among "deep dyslexic" patients who, for example, misread the word *negative* as *minus* (Patterson & Marcel, 1977).

A related implication of the asynchrony hypothesis is that the context-appropriate meaning may be less active for the low-ability reader on occasion. All meanings of a word may be activated before the required one is selected. The principle of autonomous lexical access is that a context-appropriate meaning is not preselected by context, but follows the brief activation of multiple meanings. In such a case, all possible meanings should retain activation long enough to allow following context to select the correct one. Semantic asynchrony may put all meanings at a lower level of activation at exactly the moment that the context can make its best contribution.

2. Intrinsic Memory Hypothesis

The lexical-access hypotheses attempt to explain how something goes wrong in working memory because of inefficient lexical processes. An alternative explanation is that lexical processes execute their work efficiently enough, but that the efforts of working memory itself are at fault. For reasons lying beyond lexical access, working memory fails to retain words or the propositions it is encoding. There are two general possibilities. One assumes a *functional* memory problem that is especially vulnerable to propositional encoding (ordered language coding generally). The other assumes a structural memory problem, a quite general capacity limitation.

a. Proposition Encoding. The major alternative to the lexical-access hypothesis, within verbal efficiency theory, is that some process intrinsically responsible for proposition encoding produces ability differences. The assumption is that lexical-access processes have achieved a word code with relatively high efficiency. That is, several words have been efficiently accessed, but the demands of propositional encoding are not met efficiently. For example, integration of propositions may be a problem because the reader makes unnecessary memory searches trying to make links that should be made automatically in short-term memory. Another possibility is that the reader has too many *active* inferences because schemata are not activated efficiently. Perfetti and Lesgold (1977) discuss the possibility that schemata can be optimally "bound" to individual words. For example, in the *opened the window* example, the reader does attach *open* to *window,* namely the window-opening schema. In this case, it binds *they* as well. It is efficient to have the schema variables (the agent and the recipient of *opening*) specified as part of the schema, so that they can be used in the next sentence. For example, if the next sentence says something about the window breaking, or Joe sticking his head out the window, etc., these are easily comprehended because the window opening schema is available. On the other hand, if too much information is activated with the schema, this would be inefficient, adding useless information to the memory representation.

Individually, these proposition-encoding possibilities are difficult to demonstrate clearly. However, there is a common underlying process description that has plausibility. It is the *manipulation of language codes* in memory that is the major source of efficiency differences. Once they are activated, words and their components are vulnerable to memory loss. Two possible memory-loss mechanisms were described by Perfetti and Lesgold (1977): *hysteresis* and *specificity ordering.* Hysteresis is the possibility that memory mechanisms are insufficiently labile. The memory system is still working on one word—assembling a proposition for it— when the next word enters the system. It fails to react in synchrony, much like the semantic asynchrony possibility already discussed. The *specificity-ordering* possibility is that the quality of the code is low. Its specific semantic properties and its ordering position are vulnerable. These two possibilities describe things in complementary ways, one emphasizing the *system's* reactivity (hysteresis) and the other the *code's* quality.

Notice that these two possibilities are very close to describing a lexical access problem. They refer to things being out of phase in memory or to codes being of low quality. This reflects an important fact about processing descriptions of this kind. These are overlapping and interdependent processes. If a low criterion for lexical access is accepted in order to have rapid access, it is possible that some of these memory differences will be observed.

b. Short-Term Memory Capacity. The simplest memory mechanism that will produce efficiency differences is the capacity of short-term memory. We have pointed out that reading ability differences can exist in the absence of demonstrable differences in a possible primary memory. However, they will surely exist when such structural memory differences are present. This is a simpler explanation and needs no recourse to such things as asynchrony. It just stipulates a system that cannot hold enough information. In a sense, such problems are beyond the domain of verbal efficiency theory. A system-limited reading process, by definition, would be operating efficiently if its structural capacity is being used fully. Even so, there would be the question of whether we should be content with a mechanism solely dependent on abstract capacity. That, too, might deserve explanation in terms of function. Indeed, it seems reasonable to reject memory capacity as a purely structural concept, since capacity depends upon the familiarity, for a particular subject, of the items stored (Chi, 1976).

3. Linguistic Code Manipulation

Any of the previous hypotheses is a reasonable elaboration of verbal efficiency. Of course, none of them is necessarily correct. They are simply logical possibilities consistent with the general assumptions of verbal efficiency.

Are they equally plausible? When the salient facts of reading ability are considered, there are grounds for distinguishing among these hypotheses. One salient fact is that lexical-access and decoding differences are pervasive. Memory differences among readers are not generally found in isolation from lexical and decoding differences. This fact favors a lexically based explanation of efficiency.

However, a second salient fact of reading ability is that ability differences are often found for speech processing as well as print processing (for example memory for spoken language and memory for printed text). This fact seems to favor a functional memory elaboration of verbal efficiency. Alternatively, it requires a lexical explanation that is indifferent to input modality.

Thus, if there is to be a single mechanism, it will have to accommodate two facts that are, superficially at least, not compatible. However, if we assume a general linguistic coding process, things fall into place. The essential characteristics of this linguistic coding process are as follows: *In an ideal system, an inactive memory responds to a linguistic symbol, in any modality, by a rapid retrieval of codes that are part of that symbol's memory location.*

To the extent that these codes are retrieved rapidly and are high in quality, the system is efficient. To the extent that retrieval is effortful and the retrieved codes are low in quality, the processing is inefficient. Since effort and speed have already been discussed, only a sense of *code quality* is needed.

Definition: A linguistic code is high in quality to the extent that it contains both semantic information and phonetic information sufficient to uniquely recover its memory location.

The code does not have to be high in quality for a long period of time. It must be of high quality long enough for subsequent processes to perform their work. Thus, a "name" without meaning and a meaning without a "name" are both low quality.

Notice also the assumption of an inactive memory. That means the memory system has not been primed. This retrieval from inactive memory is a critical feature of high levels of reading ability. Thus, *inactive* memory, *effortless retrieval* (effortless retrieval is "activation" rather than retrieval), and *quality code* are the three essential features of the concept of efficient linguistic coding. The manipulation of such codes in memory—first their retrieval, then their manipulation in memory—are the essential local processes of reading.

Can this linguistic coding concept handle the two basic facts of (1) pervasive ability differences in lexical access and (2) modality-independent ability differences in memory (at least in many cases)? The second fact is easily handled, because a system with low quality codes or one that spends effort at code manipulation will show general memory problems, independent of input modality. The first fact eventually needs more data for interpretation. One possibility is that lexical-access differences studied in print will also be found in speech recognition. However, assuming any such differences are either negligible or smaller than differences in reading, this fact is explained as follows: Lexical access from print (or decoding from print) depends on linguistic code manipulation more than does access from speech. For the low-ability reader, lexical access from print, in effect, demands an early process of code translation. This process, *at minimum,* involves access to and manipulation of linguistic symbols at the letter and word level. The simplest model is that activation pathways between the letter level and the word level are not as easily activated. However, a fuller account will have to take into account activation of subword units, that is, orthographic and/or phonetic pathways to the word. In other words, visual word recognition requires from the low-ability reader more of what he or she is not good at—retrieval and manipulation of linguistic codes.

Finally, it is possible to link the concept of an efficient linguistic coding process to the various elaborations of verbal efficiency previously discussed. That is, an inefficient linguistic coding process can cause each of the following. (1) Lexical interference: it results from an inefficient code retrieval that places verbal memory at risk. (2) A low-quality code: the inefficient linguistic coding operation either fails to activate all of the needed semantic and phonetic codes in synchrony, or a quality code is at risk because of competing memory demands. (3) Proposition encoding failure: functional working memory is limited by inefficient code manipulation. Thus, the three elaborations of verbal efficiency each predict processing "hitches" that might be observed under any particular situation. What seems to be the best description in any particular case will depend on how the reader is trading off the costs of his or her inefficiency.

D. Summary

Verbal efficiency theory gives a comprehensive account of reading ability (defined by comprehension) by focusing on the resource cost of different components. It assumes that general constraints on memory and attention place a premium on efficient processing. It assumes that the reader can reduce, through learning and practice, the resource demands of some processes. It also assumes that allocation of resources contributes to efficiency.

The core proposal is that comprehension is limited by the efficient operation of local processes. Efficiency is defined as the quality of processing outcome in relation to the cost to processing resources. The various components of reading vary in their potential for efficiency. Schema activation and lexical access are potentially very low in resource cost, while proposition encoding is high.

These aspects of efficiency are demonstrated in the text work necessary for understanding a brief text segment. The various components—lexical access, propositional assembly, propositional interaction, and text modeling—are overlapping processes. Most of the text work goes to propositional encoding in the ideal case. Ability differences and text differences are described in similar terms, in reference to the text-work components.

The more specific components of verbal efficiency depend on how observed differences in local processes are explained. One possibility is that lexical-access inefficiency is responsible for observed differences in memory as well as lexical processes. The other is that intrinsic working memory differences are responsible. The salient facts may be explained by a generalized *linguistic coding* process that affects the speed and quality of both the lexical access and the manipulation of codes in memory. An inefficient linguistic coding mechanism can produce access interferences with the current contents of memory, lower quality word codes, and functional linguistic memory problems.

IV. EVIDENCE FOR THE THEORY

There is ample evidence linking reading comprehension ability to local processing abilities. Thus, the general predictions of verbal efficiency, that there is a linkage between local and global processing abilities, has been confirmed. The causal evidence is weak, however, because it is largely correlational. I will very briefly review some of the previously published evidence before describing some unpublished data.

A. Lexical Access

A consistent research result is that when reading ability is defined according to a reader's score on a reading comprehension test, and when word identification accuracy is controlled, high-ability readers are faster at isolated word identification (naming) than low-ability readers. This result was first reported by Perfetti and Hogaboam (1975) and has been replicated many times (Hogaboam & Perfetti, 1978; Perfetti, Finger, & Hogaboam, 1978).

There have emerged several informative facts that help interpret this speed of word identification difference:

1. It does not depend upon specific word knowledge or vocabulary. Perfetti and Hogaboam (1975) found that the word identification latencies of high-ability readers did not depend on whether they knew the meaning of the word, controlling for frequency. By contrast, low-ability readers' latencies were faster for words with known meanings.

2. The difference between the word-identification latencies of high- and low-ability readers increases for infrequent words and is greater for pseudowords than real words (Perfetti & Hogaboam, 1975; Hogaboam & Perfetti, 1978). It also increases for longer words when frequency is controlled for (Hogaboam & Perfetti, 1978).

3. The word identification difference does not extend to identification latencies for color and pictures (Perfetti *et al.*, 1978), although such differences may exist for some reading-disabled populations.

4. When words are identified in discourse context, ability differences in latencies decrease (Perfetti, Goldman, & Hogaboam, 1979). However, when the discourse context is anomalous or incompatible with the word to be identified, the ability difference increases (Perfetti & Roth, 1981).

Thus, the picture one gets from this line of research is that high-ability readers in the elementary grades differ from low-ability readers (ability defined by comprehension) in terms of context-free word identification. Low-ability readers are more affected by context and by intrinsic lexical-access factors (length and frequency). It is not a general speed-of-access factor but may depend, in part, on linguistic properties of a stimulus.

One way to look at this body of research is to consider, over different studies, the magnitude of the ability factor as a function of the intrinsic difficulty of lexical access. This is what is shown in Fig. 2, which is based on several different published studies in this series of experiments with the same population. Variables such as word vs pseudoword, number of syllables, frequency, and context–no context have been ignored.

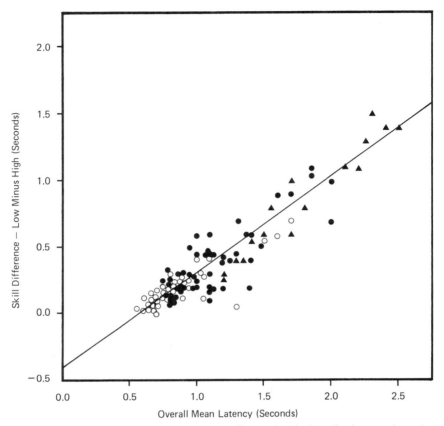

Fig. 2. Differences between high- and low-ability readers in decoding latency depend on the mean decoding latencies for all subjects. Data are from different experiments using vocalization latency to words or pseudowords as the dependent measure. ●, Isolated word; ○, word in context; ▲, pseudoword. $r = .92$, slope $= .71$, y intercept $= -0.41$, $n = 107$. Reprinted from Perfetti (1985).

As Fig. 2 shows, there is a strong relationship ($r = .92$) between the ability difference in latency and the overall mean latency for reading groups combined. As a letter string, for whatever reason, increases in intrinsic identification difficulty, ability differences in identification increase. This relationship (which could, of course, have a statistical explanation) reflects the point made previously that text difficulty (here, word difficulty) and individual ability are complementary concepts.

There is evidence from tasks other than naming, and they converge on the same conclusion: The hallmark of the skilled reader is rapid access to a word in inactive memory. The low-ability reader is characterized by a slower access that is more dependent upon context and more affected by lexical-accessibility factors. Individual differences in comprehension among adult readers have also been found to be correlated with speed of lexical access (Hammond, 1984).

B. Working Memory

There is also evidence that links working memory to reading ability measured by comprehension. For example, Perfetti and Goldman (1976) probed children's memory for recently heard words from a story. Compared with high-ability children, low-ability children showed a lower retention, even when words to be recalled had occurred in the sentence that the subject had just heard. Goldman, Hogaboam, Bell, and Perfetti (1980) applied this probe memory task to reading with the same result. For both listening and reading, the retention advantage of the high-ability reader increased as the number of intervening words increased. The conclusion from these studies, and others, is that high-ability readers have a better *verbatim* representation of the local text than do low-ability readers. This provides a needed link to global comprehension, as measured, for example, by story recall or question answering. Comprehension differences are present during processing, not merely in the retrieval of information (see also Berger & Perfetti, 1977). As in the case of lexical access, these working memory links to reading skill are found also for adults (Daneman & Carpenter, 1980).

C. Sentence Verification

A direct link between simple comprehension and general reading comprehension ability has been established in unpublished experiments using sentence verification. In these experiments, subjects verified simple semantic category sentences of the form, *An apple is/is not a fruit.* (False version: *An apple is a sport.*)

This task yields an unusually simple comprehension situation. A model of the class developed by Trabasso, Rollins, and Shaughnessy (1971) and Clark and Chase (1972) is sufficient to describe the three stages of comprehension: (1) encode the written proposition: *is (apple, fruit)*; (2) retrieve information from memory: *is (apple, fruit)*; (3) compare representations: match → *yes*, mismatch → *no*.

Even in this most simple of comprehension tasks, verifying a true affirmative sentence containing only two content words, there was a substantial difference of some 970 msec between the decision times of high- and low-ability readers. This time can be taken to include lexical-access, proposition assembly, fact retrieval, and comparison processes. But true affirmative sentences do not include any of the more costly work of mismatch and negation processing that the other sentences require. In fact, differences in decision times between high- and low-ability readers increased when sentences contained negation or when they were false (e.g., "An apple is not a fruit"). A two-parameter model, with one parameter for encoding negation and a second parameter for a mismatch in a comparison process, provided a good fit for the verification times of high-ability readers. Low-ability readers were more variable, some subjects fitting this two parameter model and some not.

Although low-ability readers were more affected by any kind of sentence complexity, the comparison between true and false affirmatives is most straightforward. (It requires no assumptions about how negatives are processed.) The difference between groups was dramatic. High-ability readers required an additional 220 msec for falsification. Low-ability readers required an additional 590 msec. My interpretation of this is that it reflects the *inactive memory* principle of verbal efficiency. In a true affirmative sentence, there is a spread of activation from *apple* to *fruit*— *fruit* is accessed more easily. In a false affirmative such as *An apple is a sport,* there is no prior activation of the category term. This is the condition in which the low-ability reader has most difficulty, just as lexical access is most difficult without context.

D. Verbal Arithmetic

While the verification research demonstrates a link between simple sentence comprehension and overall reading ability, a second kind of experiment demonstrates what happens when sentence integration is involved. In this task, fourth-grade subjects solved problems of verbal arithmetic. For example

(1) Mary had seven marbles.
(2) Then Fred gave her two marbles.
(3) How many marbles does Mary have now?

Two important features of such problems are that their semantic representation is reliably expressed in terms of basic set combination structures (Heller & Greeno, 1978) and that the arithmetic is trivial. Thus, it is a situation with a clear ideal text model, and the subjects' performance in problem solution can be taken to reflect construction of this model, i.e., comprehension.[1]

[1] The text model in this case is a representation of states (e.g., the number of marbles Mary starts with is seven) and state changes (e.g., increment by two). Thus, the text model is a mental model of a world described by the text. Van Dijk and Kintsch (1983) refer to such a model as a "situational model." In general, my use of "text model" is a model of what the text is about and, thus, can be identified with their situational model.

In one verbal arithmetic experiment, subjects were presented with all lines of the problem (either three or four lines) at once, and their time to problem solution was measured. The basic result of this experiment, ignoring some variables concerning the language of the problems, was that high-ability readers were faster at problem solution than were low-ability readers. With the problems described in terms of propositions, high-ability readers averaged about 865 msec per proposition, and low-ability readers averaged about 1255 msec per proposition. When subjects solved corresponding nonverbal number problems, for example, $7 + 2 = X$, speed differences between groups were not significant. Independent measures were taken of the subjects' word-identification speed, numerical computation speed, and a standard math achievement measure of mathematical concept speed. The best predictor of individual word problem solution times was word identification speed ($r = .72$), even with numerical computation speed and mathematical concept knowledge controlled. Thus, we have a needed demonstration that lexical-processing efficiency is linked to comprehension in a case in which it is difficult to argue that knowledge-related factors might have been responsible for observed comprehension differences.

In a second verbal arithmetic experiment, the problem was presented one line at a time. The reader paced himself through the lines, and the measure was the time to read each line. Every problem requires the *integration* of a state change in the second line with an initial problem state of the first line (see the example problem given previously). Thus, although the possibilities for which line-allowed computation varied across problems, there was always a line which forced proposition integration. This is essentially an example of the reader's updating his text model. The lines of a problem were analyzed to assign this *integration* component and a *computation* component. Linear-regression equations were then constructed to predict reading time per line in terms of *basic reading* time plus integration plus computation. (The first line involves neither *integration* nor *computation* and reflects only basic reading time.) The important result is that there was a reading time advantage for high-ability readers in two components: an intercept component (reflecting basic reading time) of about 0.5 sec and an integration component of about 0.3 sec. There was no difference in the computation component.

Thus, the verbal arithmetic experiments show a link between simple proposition encoding time and reading ability, just as the verification studies do. They go beyond this, however, in also demonstrating that the integration of propositions is an additional component of differences in comprehension skill. We thus see a chain of evidence, albeit correlational, that links global comprehension ability, measured by paragraph reading and question answering, to the "on-line" comprehension of sentences. This linkage includes lexical access, proposition encoding, and proposition integration as components of comprehension skill that produce reading ability differences in on-line comprehension and global comprehension.

V. INSTRUCTIONAL IMPLICATIONS OF VERBAL EFFICIENCY

The evidence for verbal efficiency is both very strong and very weak. It is very strong in this sense: It is very difficult to find two individuals who differ in global comprehension ability who do not also differ in local processing ability, including speed of lexical access. Not only are there data of the kind reviewed here; there are somewhat more "clinical" data. Many people, including teachers, report informally that there are many children who are poor at reading comprehension but who are adequate in word reading. We have tried to find some of these children by asking teachers in grades two through eight to identify children who had trouble comprehending what they read but who had no trouble reading words. The second-grade teacher, logically enough, identified no such problems, but teachers in fourth through seventh grades did. We tested eight children thus identified on isolated word identification, vocabulary, and listening comprehension. We also tested a large norming sample matched to the age of each child. The result was that all of the children, except one, were significantly below average in speed of word identification or in listening comprehension. (For the exception, we tested reading comprehension and found the child to be at grade level.)

On the other hand, the evidence is weak because it is largely correlational.[2] Instructional experiments provide a stronger test of the claim that local processing factors produce differences in comprehension ability. There have been attempts to train children to read words faster in order to observe their effects on comprehension. However, experiments of this sort have failed to produce comprehension gains from speeded word identification training (Fleischer, Jenkins, & Pany, 1979; Piggins & Barron, 1982).

There are several important additional considerations that are relevant for instructional implications. First, there are some important theoretical considerations, the main one being that a theory of skilled performance (e.g., verbal efficiency theory) is not the same as a theory of skill acquisi-

---

[2] There is somewhat stronger evidence from a longitudinal study of early reading reported by Lesgold and Resnick (1982). Using path analysis, they found that gains in comprehension were better predicted by earlier gains in speed of word processing than vice versa.

tion. A skill-acquisition theory will have as its scope (1) the conditions of learning and (2) specification of what is learned. The conditions-of-learning component would have to address at least these issues: reading words in context vs reading words in isolation, reading accuracy vs reading speed, and amount of practice. In short, both the quality and quantity of instructional events are important aspects of reading instruction that demand thoughtful analysis. It may turn out, for example, that practice at reading and rereading texts is superior to isolated word practice. Samuels (1979) has, in fact, demonstrated the value of a rereading method for improving reading fluency.

As for the amount-of-practice component, it should come as no surprise that an hour or two of training is simply not enough. The fluency of a skilled reader has been achieved over hundreds of encounters with specific word forms and thousands of encounters with specific letter patterns. There are not likely to be dramatic gains from quick "training experiments," but there may be gains from useful instructional events extended over much larger periods.

The second component of an acquisition theory is a specification of what is learned. I suggest that what is learned is not fast responding to words nor even attention-free responding to words. What is learned is thousands of specific word forms (the lexicon) and thousands of orthographic patterns that support access to the lexicon. Speed of processing and low-attention processing are by-products of this overlearning. This naturally has some implication for the conditions of learning. Speeded practice may not be critical, although it could turn out to be beneficial. Perhaps the control of attention by print is part of what gets learned, and speeded practice may help bring this about. In any case, the point is that this question of what is learned in skilled reading beyond elementary word recognition needs thoughtful analysis independent of a theory of skilled reading. An example of such an analysis is provided by Ehri and Wilce (1983), who point out that incomplete knowledge of word structure by many low-ability readers will limit the effects of speeded practice.

Finally, it should be clear that there are no implications of verbal efficiency concerning the direct teaching of comprehension. It is quite possible, and even likely, that children who are not good at reading can be taught compensatory skills, skills that might come more easily for children who read well. For example, instruction in inference making (Bransford, Stein, Vye, Franks, Auble, Mezynski, & Perfetto, 1982) and instruction in comprehension monitoring (Palinscar & Brown, 1984) both seem to work, at least in producing short-term gains. Even story grammar instruction, which otherwise seems quite superfluous, may produce gains in some circumstances (Short & Ryan, 1982; Fitzgerald & Spiegel, 1983).

These things seem to work by providing some compensating skills or by making more accessible skills that children already have.

The instructional issues are complex in their own right. They are not addressed directly by verbal efficiency theory, but, rather, they comprise a separate set of problems. As these problems are met directly on their own terms and as creative long-term instruction is designed, we can expect to see some instructional gains.

VI. SUMMARY

This article describes verbal efficiency theory. The theory addresses reading comprehension as a generalized process, one not easily explained by schema theory. Within an interactive framework, it assumes that some reading processes are better candidates than others for becoming low in resource costs. These are, especially, lexical processes and, perhaps, the assembly of elementary local propositions. Its specific predictions are that there should be links to general reading comprehension ability from lexical access through propositional encoding and propositional integration. Evidence supporting these predictions is by now substantial. Instructional implications of the theory do not necessarily include speeded practice. An independent theory of skill acquisition is needed to make the link to instruction.

ACKNOWLEDGMENTS

This contribution draws freely on material published in Perfetti (1985). I am grateful to Oxford University Press for permitting this. The research has been carried out with support from the Learning Research and Development Center, University of Pittsburgh, which is supported in part by the Office of Educational Research and Improvement.

REFERENCES

Anderson, R. C., Reynolds, R. E., Schallert, D. L., & Goetz, E. T. (1976). *Frameworks for comprehending discourse* (Technical Report No. 12). Urbana, IL: University of Illinois Laboratory for Cognitive Studies in Education.

Anderson, R. C., Spiro, R. J., & Anderson, M. C. (1978). Schemata as scaffolding for the representation of information in connected discourse. *American Educational Research Journal, 15,* 433–440.

Baddeley, A. D., & Hitch, G. T. (1974). Working memory. In G. A. Bower (Ed.), *The psychology of learning and motivation* (Vol. 8). New York: Academic Press.

Berger, N. S., & Perfetti, C. A. (1977). Reading skill and memory for spoken and written discourse. *Journal of Reading Behavior, 9,* 7–16.

Bransford, J. D., & Johnson, M. K. (1973). Considerations of some problems of comprehension. In W. G. Chase (Ed.), *Visual information processing*. New York: Academic Press.

Bransford, J. D., Stein, B. S., Vye, N. J., Franks, J. J., Auble, P. M., Mezynski, K. J., & Perfetto, B. A. (1982). Differences in approaches to learning: An overview. *Journal of Experimental Psychology: General, 111*, 390–398.

Clark, H. H., & Chase, W. G. (1972). On the process of comparing sentences against pictures. *Cognitive Psychology, 3*, 472–517.

Chi, M. T. H. (1976). Short-term memory limitations in children: Capacity or processing deficits? *Memory & Cognition, 4*, 559–572.

Chiesi, H. L., Spilich, G. J., & Voss, J. F. (1979). Acquisition of domain-related information in relation to high and low domain knowledge. *Journal of Verbal Learning and Verbal Behavior, 18*, 257–274.

Crowder, R. G. (1982). *The psychology of reading*. New York: Oxford University Press.

Daneman, M., & Carpenter, P. A. (1980). Individual differences in working memory and reading. *Journal of Verbal Learning and Verbal Behavior, 19*, 450–466.

Dooling, D. J., & Lachman, R. (1971). Effects of comprehension on retention of prose. *Journal of Experimental Psychology, 88*, 216–222.

Ehri, L. C., & Wilce, L. S. (1983). Development of word identification speed in skilled and less skilled beginning readers. *Journal of Educational Psychology, 75*, 3–18.

Fitzgerald, J., & Spiegel, D. L. (1983). Enhancing children's reading comprehension through instruction in narrative structure. *Journal of Reading Behavior, 14*, 1–18.

Fleischer, L. S., Jenkins, J. R., & Pany, D. (1979). Effects on poor readers' comprehension of training in rapid decoding. *Reading Research Quarterly, 14*, 30–48.

Goldman, S. R., Hogaboam, T. W., Bell, L. C., & Perfetti, C. A. (1980). Short-term retention of discourse during reading. *Journal of Educational Psychology, 68*, 680–688.

Hammond, K. (1984). *Auditory and visual memory access and decoding in college readers*. Paper presented at the annual meeting of the American Educational Research Association, New Orleans, LA.

Heller, J. I., & Greeno, J. G. (1978). *Semantic processes in arithmetic word problem solving*. Paper presented at the Midwestern Psychological Association Meeting, Chicago, IL.

Hildyard, A., & Olson, D. R. (1982). On the comprehension and memory of oral vs. written discourse. In D. Tannen (Ed.), *Spoken and written language: Exploring orality and literacy*. Norwood, NJ: Ablex.

Hockett, C. D. (1960). The origin of speech. *Scientific American, 203*, 88–96.

Hogaboam, T. W., & Perfetti, C. A. (1975). Lexical ambiguity and sentence comprehension. *Journal of Verbal Learning and Verbal Behavior, 14*, 265–274.

Hogaboam, T. W., & Perfetti, C. A. (1978). Reading skill and the role of verbal experience in decoding. *Journal of Educational Psychology, 70*, 717–729.

Kahneman, D. (1973). *Attention and effort*. New York: Prentice-Hall.

Kintsch, W. (1974). *The representation of meaning in memory*. Hillsdale, NJ: Erlbaum.

Kintsch, W., & van Dijk, T. A. (1978). Toward a model of text comprehension and production. *Psychological Review, 85*, 363–394.

Kintsch, W., & Vipond, D. (1979). Reading comprehension and readability in educational practice and psychological theory. In L. G. Nilsson (Ed.), *Perspectives on memory research*. Hillsdale, NJ: Erlbaum.

LaBerge, D., & Samuels, S. J. (1974). Toward a theory of automatic information processing in reading. *Cognitive Psychology, 6*, 294–323.

Lesgold, A. M., & Resnick, L. B. (1982). How reading disabilities develop: Perspectives from a longitudinal study. In J. P. Das, R. Mulcahy, & A. E. Wall (Eds.), *Theory and research in learning disability*. New York: Plenum,

Lesgold, A. M., Roth, S. F., & Curtis, M. E. (1979). Foregrounding effects in discourse comprehension. *Journal of Verbal Learning and Verbal Behavior, 18*, 291–308.

Mandler, J. M., & Johnson, N. S. (1977). Remembrance of things parsed: Story structure and recall. *Cognitive Psychology, 9*, 111–151.

McClelland, J. L. (1979). On the time relations of mental processes: An examination of systems of processes in cascade. *Psychological Review, 86*, 287–330.

Merrill, E. C., Sperber, R. D., & McCauley, C. (1981). Differences in semantic encoding as a function of reading comprehension skill. *Memory & Cognition, 6*, 618–624.

Norman, D. A. (1976). *Memory and attention*. New York: Wiley.

Omanson, R. C. (1982). An analysis of narratives: Identifying central, supportive, and distracting content. *Discourse Processes, 5*, 195–224.

Palinscar, A. S., & Brown, A. L. (1984). Reciprocal teaching of comprehension-fostering and comprehension-monitoring activities. *Cognition and Instruction, 1*, 117–175.

Patterson, K., & Marcel, A. (1977). Aphasia, dyslexia, and the phonological code of written words. *Quarterly Journal of Experimental Psychology, 29*, 307–381.

Perfetti, C. A. (1985). *Reading ability*. New York: Oxford University Press.

Perfetti, C. A. (1987). Language, speech and print: Some asymmetries in the acquisition of literacy. In R. Horowitz & S. J. Samuels (Eds.), *Comprehending Oral and Written Language*. New York: Academic Press.

Perfetti, C. A., Finger, E., & Hogaboam, T. W. (1978). Sources of vocalization latency differences between skilled and less skilled young readers. *Journal of Educational Psychology, 70*, 730–739.

Perfetti, C. A., & Goldman, S. R. (1976). Discourse memory and reading comprehension skill. *Journal of Verbal Learning and Verbal Behavior, 14*, 33–42.

Perfetti, C. A., Goldman, S. R., & Hogaboam, T. W. (1979). Reading skill and the identification of words in discourse context. *Memory & Cognition, 7*, 273–282.

Perfetti, C. A., & Hogaboam, T. W. (1975). The relationship between single word decoding and reading comprehension skill. *Journal of Educational Psychology, 67*, 461–469.

Perfetti, C. A., & Lesgold, A. M. (1977). Discourse comprehension and sources of individual differences. In M. A. Just & P. A. Carpenter (Eds.), *Cognitive processes in comprehension* (pp. 141–183). Hillsdale, NJ: Erlbaum.

Perfetti, C. A., & Lesgold, A. M. (1979). Coding and comprehension in skilled reading and implications for reading instruction. In L. B. Resnick & P. A. Weaver (Eds.), *Theory and practice of early reading* (Vol. 1). Hillsdale, NJ: Erlbaum.

Perfetti, C. A., & McCutchen, D. (1982). Speech processes in reading. In N. Lass (Ed.), *Speech and language: Advances in basic research and practice* (Vol. 7, pp. 237–269). New York: Academic Press.

Perfetti, C. A., & Roth, S. F. (1981). Some of the interactive processes in reading and their role in reading skill. In A. M. Lesgold & C. A. Perfetti (Eds.), *Interactive processes in reading* (pp. 269–297). Hillsdale, NJ: Erlbaum.

Piggins, W. R., & Barron, R. W. (1982). *Why learning to read aloud more rapidly does not improve comprehension: Testing the decoding sufficiency hypothesis*. Paper presented at the annual meeting of the American Educational Research Association, New York.

Rumelhart, D. E. (1975). Notes on a schema for stories. In D. Bobrow & A. Collins (Eds.), *Representation and understanding: Studies in cognitive science*. New York: Academic Press.

Ryan, E. B. (1982). Identifying and remediating failures in reading comprehension: Toward an instructional approach for poor comprehenders. In G. E. MacKinnon & T. G. Waller (Eds.), *Advances in reading research* (Vol. 3). New York: Academic Press.

Samuels, S. J. (1979). The method of repeated readings. *The Reading Teacher, 32,* 403–408.

Schank, R. C., & Abelson, R. P. (1977). *Scripts, plans, goals and understanding: An inquiry into human knowledge structures.* Hillsdale, NJ: Erlbaum.

Schneider, W., & Shiffrin, R. M. (1977). Controlled and automatic human information processing. I: Detection, search, and attention. *Psychological Review, 84,* 1–66.

Short, E. J., & Ryan, E. B. (1982). *Remediating poor readers' comprehension failures with a story grammar strategy.* Paper presented at the annual meeting of the American Educational Research Association, New York.

Smiley, S. S., Oakley, D. D., Worthen, D., Campione, J. C., & Brown, A. L. (1977). Recall of thematically relevant material by adolescent good and poor readers as a function of written and oral presentation. *Journal of Educational Psychology, 69,* 881–887.

Spilich, G. J., Vesonder, G. T., Chiesi, H. L., & Voss, J. F. (1979). Text-processing of domain-related information for individuals with high and low domain knowledge. *Journal of Verbal Learning and Verbal Behavior, 18,* 275–290.

Spiro, R. J. (1980). Constructive processes in prose comprehension and recall. In R. J. Spiro, B. C. Bruce, & W. F. Brewer (Eds.), *Theoretical issues in reading comprehension* (pp. 245–278). Hillsdale, NJ: Erlbaum.

Stein, N. L., & Glenn, C. G. (1979). An analysis of story comprehension in elementary school children. In R. Freedle (Ed.), *Advances in discourse processing 2: New directions in discourse processing.* Norwood, NJ: Ablex.

Swinney, D. A. (1979). Lexical access during sentence comprehension: Reconsideration of context effects. *Journal of Verbal Learning and Verbal Behavior, 18,* 645–659.

Trabasso, T., Rollins, H., & Shaughnessy, E. (1971). Storage and verification stages in processing concepts. *Cognitive Psychology, 2,* 239–289.

Van Dijk, T. A., & Kintsch, W. (1983). *Strategies of discourse comprehension.* New York: Academic Press.

Weaver, P. A., & Dickinson, D. K. (1982). Scratching below the surface structure: Exploring the usefulness of story grammars. *Discourse Processes, 5,* 225–243.

WORD KNOWLEDGE AND READING SKILL

MEREDYTH DANEMAN

Erindale College
University of Toronto
Mississauga, Ontario L5L 1C6, Canada

I. INTRODUCTION

Recently overhearing me engaged in a conversation about cognitive theory, my seven-year-old son asked me what the word *theory* means. While I was battling to formulate in my head a definition appropriate for a seven year old, my eight-year-old son piped in, "I know what *theory* means. In my *Hardy Boys* mystery books, Frank and Joe Hardy's father Fenton is a detective and he always says he has a theory about who stole the jewels, or who kidnapped the horse. *Theory* means you have an idea or a possible explanation for what happened." Not a bad definition, I thought to myself. Being a *Hardy Boys* buff has some value after all.

Does this cute anecdote reflect any of the processes actually involved in acquiring word meanings? Werner and Kaplan would probably argue yes. In their classic monograph, (Werner & Kaplan, 1952) they proposed that

> The child acquires the meaning of words principally in two ways. One is by explicit reference either verbal or objective; he learns to understand verbal symbols through the adult's direct naming of objects or through verbal definition. The second way is through implicit or contextual reference; the meaning is grasped in the course of conversation, i.e., it is inferred from the cues in the verbal context. (p. 3)

Presumably, my seven-year-old son learned the meaning of theory in the first way—through explicit verbal reference supplied by his older brother. By contrast, my eight-year-old son displayed evidence of having learned the meaning of *theory* in the second way—through implicit contextual reference in the course of reading many a *Hardy Boys* novel. In this article, I will examine individual and age-related differences in acquiring word meanings through contextual inference and suggest how these skills might be related to reading comprehension skill.

145

II. HYPOTHESES ABOUT THE RELATIONSHIP BETWEEN
VOCABULARY KNOWLEDGE AND COMPREHENSION SKILL

Differential psychologists have long recognized the intimate connection between vocabulary knowledge and reading comprehension. Indeed, vocabulary is one of the best single predictors not only of verbal ability but even of overall intellectual ability (Anderson & Freebody, 1981; Brown, Nelson, & Denny, 1976; Davis, 1944, 1968; Jensen, 1980; Singer, 1965; Thurstone, 1946). Of course, a correlation between two variables does not permit the establishment of a direct causal link, nor does it permit the ruling out of an indirect relationship between the two through their dependence on a third, higher order variable. For this reason, a number of hypotheses, both direct and indirect, have been offered for the strong correlation between vocabulary knowledge and reading comprehension (cf. Anderson & Freebody, 1981). I will briefly outline some of these and then focus on the hypothesis that vocabulary knowledge and comprehension are related because both reflect the individual's ability to learn from context. As will become evident, the various hypotheses are not mutually exclusive, and no doubt all contribute to the relationship between vocabulary and comprehension. My concentration on the *learning-from-context* hypothesis reflects my view that it is the most theoretically interesting and, as of now, the most empirically persuasive.

A. Building-Block Hypothesis

A direct causal connection between vocabulary knowledge and comprehension is a necessary assumption of all models of reading comprehension. To the extent that words are the building blocks of connected text, constructing text meaning depends, in part, on the success of searching for individual word meanings. Readers with small vocabularies are more likely to encounter unknown words in a text, that is, words for which they have no stored meaning representation in memory. Unknown words would create gaps in the meaning of a text. Too many gaps (too few building blocks) would hinder or prevent the construction of overall text meaning and a coherent text structure. Although there is no doubt merit in this relatively intuitive assumption about the relationship between vocabulary knowledge and comprehension achievement, this cannot be the whole story. First of all, the hypothesis is silent on how some individuals come to have larger vocabularies in the first place. Second, simply increasing a reader's vocabulary does not automatically improve comprehension. Indeed, Tuinman and Brady (1974) showed that direct pretraining on vocabulary items from passages to be read did not increase the comprehension scores of children in grades four to six. Thus, while vocabulary knowledge is necessary for text comprehension, it is not sufficient. For these reasons, the building-block assumption must be complemented with other hypotheses about the relationship between vocabulary knowledge and comprehension.

B. Lexical-Efficiency Hypothesis

A direct causal connection between vocabulary and comprehension is strongly assumed by reading models emphasizing the importance of fluent (Perfetti & Lesgold, 1979) and automatic (LaBerge & Samuels, 1974) word encoding and lexical access. These models go beyond the building-block assumption by suggesting that comprehension success depends not only on the sheer size of the reader's vocabulary, but also on the facility with which the reader can access the known word meanings represented in memory. To the extent that lexical and comprehension processes share a limited resource pool, skilled reading will occur only if some component processes can be executed with relatively modest or possibly no resource demands. Consequently, reading comprehension will suffer if lexical processes use an excessive share of the limited resources. Readers may know each word's meaning but be inefficient or slow to encode the word and access its meaning from memory. Because the individual word meanings are less accessible, processing resources would have to be diverted toward individual word meaning searches rather than toward constructing the overall meaning of the text.

The lexical-efficiency hypothesis has been tested by comparing the performance of good and poor readers on tasks requiring speeded word encoding and lexical access. The general finding is that poor comprehenders are slower at recognizing words (Perfetti & Hogaboam, 1975) and slower at making single-word semantic decisions even when differences in word identification time are accounted for (Perfetti & Lesgold, 1979). Poor readers are also slower at semantic matching tasks, such as responding "same" if two words are synonyms or homonyms (Jackson & McClelland, 1979). However, it is equally important to note that speed of retrieving word names and accessing word meanings typically accounts for only about 10% of the variance between good and poor readers (Daneman, 1982; Jackson & McClelland, 1979). This proportion is substantially lower than the 36–50% typically accounted for by tests of vocabulary knowledge. Thus, while speed of verbal access may be a factor in reading, the correlation suggests that it is not the most important factor.

Besides the purely correlational design, the lexical-efficiency hypothesis can also be tested by experimentally manipulating vocabulary knowledge and processes. If, as the hypothesis suggests, there is a causal connection between vocabulary processes and reading comprehension skill, then vocabulary instruction should produce changes in comprehension achievement. Here, the empirical evidence is equivocal. Although most of the training studies have succeeded in boosting vocabulary knowledge (Beck, Perfetti, & McKeown, 1982; Draper & Moeller, 1971; Jenkins, Pany, & Schreck, 1978; Kameenui, Carnine & Freschi, 1982; Tuinman & Brady, 1974), relatively few have succeeded in demonstrating concomitant improvements in comprehension (Beck *et al.*, 1982; Draper & Moeller, 1971; Kameenui *et al.*, 1982). However, failure to improve comprehension could be a function of an inadequate training procedure. Indeed, in one of the most rigorous training programs to date, Beck *et al.* (1982) illustrated the need for an extended and intensive instructional procedure. They suggested that for vocabulary instruction to affect reading comprehension, it is not sufficient to establish accurate responses to words on a multiple-choice vocabulary test. Rather, instruction should go beyond simply increasing the number of new word meanings learned; it should be aimed at increasing processing fluency, that is, the speed of accessing the newly acquired word meanings.

After a 19-week instruction program designed, among other things, to increase lexical knowledge and lexical fluency, Beck *et al.* (1982) showed improvements in both. Moreover, and more important, there were also improvements in the comprehension of texts containing the instructed words, although such improvements were confined to recall of noncentral text content.

In sum, there seems to be some evidence from correlational and training studies suggesting that both the number of word meanings the reader knows and the accessibility of these word meanings directly influence the reader's skill at constructing overall text meaning. However, as we shall see, this is still not the whole story.

C. Knowledge Hypothesis

A more indirect connection between vocabulary and comprehension achievement is assumed by models emphasizing the importance of knowledge rather than processing differences among good and poor comprehenders. The idea is that old knowledge affects the acquisition of new knowledge (Schank & Abelson, 1977; Spilich, Vesonder, Chiesi, & Voss, 1979). Moreover, individuals differ with respect to the richness of knowledge in specific content areas, that is, in the quality and flexibility of the connections among concepts in semantic memory. Vocabulary and comprehension achievement are indirectly related because both are influenced by the reader's knowledge about specific content domains. Readers with an impoverished knowledge base would access conceptually impoverished word meanings and end up with a conceptually sparser representation of the overall text meaning.

The knowledge hypothesis has been tested by examining comprehension and recall of text as a function of the reader's prior knowledge about the text topic (e.g., baseball). Not surprisingly, results have shown that comprehension and recall are inferior for readers who know fewer concepts and know less about the relations among these concepts (Spilich *et al.*, 1979).

We can summarize the contributions of the knowledge hypothesis. Not only is it important for readers to know the individual word meanings (building-block hypothesis) and know them well (lexical-efficiency hypothesis), but they should be able to access contextually rich meanings for words; that is, they should be able to relate words to other concepts demanded by the context. This latter skill will depend on the richness of the individual's knowledge of the text topic.

I do not dispute that knowledge plays a role in vocabulary and comprehension achievement. However, an approach that focuses on knowledge at the expense of process in the development of expertise cannot account for how individual differences in knowledge states arise in the first place (see also Sternberg & Powell, 1983). As we shall see, the learning-from-context approach proposes a mechanism to account for the acquisition and accumulation of vocabulary and textual knowledge.

D. Verbal-Intelligence Hypothesis

Vocabulary knowledge and reading comprehension achievement could be indirectly related because both depend on a third factor, the individual's verbal intelligence (cf. Anderson & Freebody, 1981). Obviously, such a hypothesis is only interesting to the extent that we have some theory of verbal intelligence and how it might be involved in accumulating knowledge about word meanings and in extracting meanings from text. The learning-from-context hypothesis can be viewed as an instantiation of the verbal-intelligence hypothesis; according to this hypothesis, the ability to acquire information from context is the process mediating the relationship between vocabulary knowledge, text comprehension, and verbal intelligence.

E. Learning-from-Context Hypothesis

According to the learning-from-context hypothesis, vocabulary and comprehension are correlated because vocabulary tests and comprehension tests both reflect the individual's ability to learn or acquire new information from context.

In the case of reading comprehension, the potential importance of extracting or inferring information from context is quite transparent. After all, when we read connected discourse, it is not the same as accessing the meanings of a list of unrelated words. Successive words, phrases, and sentences are semantically and syntactically related, and a major component of skilled reading is the ability to compute the relationships between the successive words, phrases, and sentences. Only by integrating successive ideas can the reader develop a coherent and meaningful representation for the text.

In the case of vocabulary knowledge, the potential role of extracting or inferring information from context is a little less transparent since typical vocabulary tests do not interrogate word meanings in context. Rather, subjects generally have to select from four or five alternatives the best synonym for the vocabulary item in question. The clue to the connection between vocabulary knowledge and extracting information from context comes from Werner and Kaplan's (1952) observations about how vocabulary might be acquired in the first place. If people acquire many word meanings by inferring them from verbal contexts, as my eight year old acquired the meaning of *theory* by inferring how Detective Fenton Hardy was using the word in the context of his investigative pursuits, then vocabulary tests may be reflecting learning-from-context skills. A test of the extent of someone's current vocabulary knowledge would be measuring the end products of that individual's history of acquiring and accumulating word meanings through implicit or contextual reference (Jensen, 1980; Sternberg & Powell, 1983). In Jensen's own words, vocabulary may be such a good measure of verbal comprehension, or even of overall intelligence, because "the acquisition of word meanings is highly dependent on the *eduction* of meaning from the contexts in which the words were encountered" (p. 146). By *eduction,* I think Jensen had in mind rather sophisticated inferential or reasoning skills, the kinds of skills measured in tests of fluid intelligence (Horn & Catell, 1966). And, indeed, evidence suggests that subjects with low reasoning ability (Marshalek, 1981) and low scores on tests of general intelligence (Sternberg & Powell, 1983) have greater difficulty inferring meanings from contexts. Later, I will argue for the involvement of working memory processes rather than deductive-reasoning skills in acquiring information about individual words and connected discourse from context. To develop my thesis, let us first examine more closely the research that has investigated the vocabulary-acquisition skills of children and adults.

III. VOCABULARY ACQUISITION

Werner and Kaplan (1952) devised an ingenious method to study how children learn word meanings from context. Children aged 9 to 13 were presented with an artificial word embedded in six successive sentences. The children's task was to infer the meaning of the word based on the contextual cues. The sentences in each series were ordered so that the clues increased in definiteness. One example from the set of 12 artificial words coined by Werner and Kaplan was *contavish,* and it was presented in the context of the following six sentences:
(1) You can't fill anything with a contavish.
(2) The more you take out of a contavish the larger it gets.
(3) Before the house is finished the walls must have contavishes.
(4) You can't feel or touch a contavish.
(5) A bottle has only one contavish.
(6) John fell into a contavish in the road.
Children were presented one sentence at a time, although once presented, a sentence always remained in view. They were informed that the word had only one meaning throughout the six sentences and that their task was to figure out the meaning. After presentation of each sentence, the children had to tell the experimenter what they thought the word may mean; in fact, they were encouraged to say aloud everything they were thinking about the word.

Werner and Kaplan provided a very detailed quantitative and qualitative analysis of the developmental patterns. For the purposes of this article, the important results can be summarized as follows. As children got older, the number of correct solutions increased. Particularly interesting, however, were the differences in the developmental curves of the two classes of erroneous solutions, the *incomplete finals* and *incorrect completes.* Incomplete-final solutions were those which did not fit all six sentences. Incorrect-complete solutions were wrong solutions, but ones that supposedly did fit all six sentences. An example of an incomplete-final solution for *contavish* given by a nine year old was "bubble gum." The child's solution was based on the fact that he believed bubble gum fit into sentence (2): *The more you take out of bubble gum (contavish) the larger it gets.* The child's reasoning was manifested in his verbal protocol: "Because the more you take 'bubble gum' out of your mouth the larger it gets, you know when you pull on it.'' (Werner & Kaplan, 1952, p.52). The child reached this conclusion by interpreting sentence (2) somewhat egocentrically and, of course, by ignoring the fact that bubble gum did not fit into the other five sentence contexts. By contrast, incorrect completes are the products of a greater, albeit unsatisfactory, effort to integrate the cues across six sentences. An example for *contavish* supplied by a 10 year old was the final solution "hole and beam." The child employed "hole" for sentence (1): *You can't fill anything with a hole*. The solution she offered for sentence (3) was "beams": *Before the house is finished the walls must have beams*. The child reasoned that the overall solution was "hole and beams" because, to quote her, "in sentence (1) you can't fill a hole with a beam because a beam isn't round like a hole so it can't fill it up." (Werner & Kaplan, 1952, p.27).

Developmentally, the incomplete–final solutions decrease sharply between the youngest age group (9 year olds) and the next (10 year olds), with insignificant changes thereafter. By contrast, the incorrect–complete solutions increase from ages 9 to 10 and there is a gradual decrease thereafter. Thus, in the youngest age group, the proportion of incomplete finals to incorrect completes is 9 : 4; by the next age group it is 5 : 8. According to Werner and Kaplan (1952),

> This shift reflects the maturing attitude of the child toward what constitutes a solution. The younger child does not recognize the necessity for integrating, by a single solution, the cues of all six contexts. With growing age the child seeks increasingly to fulfill this demand for integration, though his attempts may still result in wrong solutions. (p. 11)

The important point to note here is that the task of inferring the meaning for the artificial word demands a rather sophisticated integration of contextual cues across the successive sentences. The youngest group shows no evidence of integration; the older group shows attempts at integration, even if the attempts are unsatisfactory. Werner and Kaplan attribute the immature responses of the youngest children to an incorrect attitude. The child fails to "recognize the necessity for integrating" (p. 11) or takes a "part-pro-toto attitude toward the task: he accepts a partial fulfillment of the task for its consummation" (p. 75).

I will return later to the issue of integration and propose a different developmental explanation than that of Werner and Kaplan. I will argue that integration processes place heavy demands on working memory resources and that individual and age-related differences in integration reflect differences in working memory capacity. Thus, the seeming lack of integration among the youngest may be attributed to a smaller working memory capacity that prevents them from integrating across sentences

(Daneman & Carpenter, 1983), rather than to some lack of "metacognitive awareness" on their part of the need for integration in order to reach the correct solution.

Since Werner and Kaplan's early work, numerous other researchers have attempted to examine how contextual learning of vocabulary takes place (Cook, Heim, & Watts, 1963; Sternberg & Powell, 1983; van Daalen-Kapteijns & Elshout-Mohr, 1981).

Van Daalen-Kapteijns and Elshout-Mohr used the Werner and Kaplan paradigm with adult subjects who were at the high and low extremes on two tests of vocabulary knowledge. One interesting new feature in their study was the kind of word to be learned. Remember, Werner and Kaplan gave children an artificial word, that is, a made-up label that could be substituted for an already existing word. So, for example, *contavish* is a novel word but the meaning assigned to it is "hole," a meaning for which there already exists a single-word label in English, the common word *hole*. In some sense, then, the Werner and Kaplan learning-from-context task involved learning new labels and learning to map these new labels onto existing English words which, for the most part, were already very familiar to the children. By contrast, van Daalen-Kapteijns and Elshout-Mohr (1981) used neologisms, new words with invented meanings. For example, one neologism was *kolper* with the assigned meaning "a window that transmits little light because of something in front of it." This task may simulate real-life vocabulary acquisition which no doubt frequently requires not only the learning of a new label and the pairing of this label with a concept, but also the learning of the concept itself.

College students saw five serially presented sentences containing the neologism *kolper* (van Daalen-Kapteijns & Elshout-Mohr, 1981, p. 387):

(1) When you're used to a broad view it is quite depressing when you come to live in a room with one or two kolpers fronting a courtyard.
(2) He virtually always studied in the library, as at home he had to work by artificial light all day because of these kolpers.
(3) During a heat wave a lot of people all of a sudden want to have kolpers, so the sales of sun blinds then reach a peak.
(4) I was afraid the room might have kolpers but when I went and saw it, it turned out that plenty of light came into it.
(5) In these houses, you're stuck with kolpers all summer, but fortunately once the leaves have fallen out that isn't so anymore.

As can be seen, the series consisted of three examples and two counterexamples for *kolper*. For all neologisms, the first sentence always indicated a superordinate for the term (here, "window"); the second and third sentences conveyed two specifications about the meaning; the fourth and fifth sentences presented counterexamples for these specifications. Subjects were given two minutes to work on each sentence before it was removed and the next presented. They were encouraged to think aloud while inferring the neologism's meaning.

According to van Daalen-Kapteijns and Elshout-Mohr, an ideal strategy for learning from context is one in which subjects form a model (a provisional representation) for the concept and then gradually modify the model in light of the examples and counterexamples. So, for *kolper,* an ideal acquisition process would form a model from the first sentence that *kolper* provisionally means "window," and the model would have slots reserved for more specific information to differentiate a *kolper* from other kinds of windows. The model could then be used to guide the search for relevant information to fill the slots. The processing of each new piece of information could lead to an adjustment or filling of one of the model's slots and, if need be, the wholesale replacement of the initial model. The processing of each new contextual statement involves two steps: reformulation and transformation. During reformulation, the sentence content is reformulated so that it bears directly on the neologism. Sentence (2), for example, would be reformulated into "Kolpers in a house mean having artificial light all day." During transformation, the reformulated information is transformed so as to fit one of the slots in the provisional model. Reformulated, sentence (2) would be transformed into "Kolpers transmit little light," causing a readjustment of the model to represent *kolper* as a window transmitting little light. The processes of reformulation and transformation can then be applied to all remaining sentences until the final meaning is acquired.

Van Daalen-Kapteijns and Elshout-Mohr suggest that the ideal acquisition process depends on the subject's ability to represent the initial model's meaning as a bundle of independent components rather than as an indivisible unit. In this way, individual components of the model can be utilized separately as the learner refines the meaning in the light of successive contextual cues. According to van Daalen-Kapteijns and Elshout-Mohr, this kind of analytic model utilization characterized the performance of their high-verbal subjects (subjects who performed well on two standardized vocabulary tests) and could be differentiated from holistic model utilization which typified the performance of their low-verbal subjects. Low-verbal subjects tend to represent the model as an indivisible unit so that processing operates on the entire model. Consequently, they have to maintain, replace, or reject the entire model; they cannot maintain, replace, or reject components of the model. Rather than using a model-based integrative search, low-verbal subjects have to resort to sentence-based processes. They perform the first step of the process; that is, they reformulate the sentence meaning so as to bear directly on the neologism. They omit the second transformational step; that is, they cannot transform the information to fit one of the provisional slots of the model. By the fifth sentence they frequently have five sentence-based word meanings that "coexist and compete with the initial model" (van Daalen-Kapteijns & Elshout-Mohr, 1981, p. 397). So, for example, one subject came up with the following separate definitions for the five successive sentences: "windows," "small windows," "blinded windows," "small windows," and "shaded windows." Before a final definition can be formulated, some weighting process must occur. Since the sentences are no longer available for inspection, the weighting process is based on information that can be retrieved from memory. Approaches like this lead to various kinds of definitions. Sometimes one of the substitutes is arbitrarily selected, for example, "small windows." Sometimes, a few are concatenated, for example, "small window or a prisonlike window—this is reminiscent of Werner and Kaplan's 10 year old whose poor attempt at integrating contextual cues resulted in the definition "hole and a beam" for *contavish*. Sometimes the low-verbal subjects select a word meaning that comprises only the information common to all the different substitutions, concluding, for example, that "a kolper is a window." Sometimes they may even reject the initial model "window," as in the case of one subject who rejected "window" because the gist of sentence (5) ("about a shadow") contradicted his notion of window since windows must transmit light. This example clearly shows that when subjects are utilizing a holistic model, conflicting evidence cannot be used constructively to refine the components of the model's meaning; rather, conflicting evidence frequently leads to a crisis situation in which a decision is made to save or abandon the model in toto.

Let me sum up the van Daalen-Kapteijns and Elshout-Mohr work. I think it provides us with important insights into qualitative differences in word meaning acquisition for individuals who show quantitative differences on vocabulary tests. It shows us that these individuals differ in the way they organize and represent knowledge, even about as simple a concept as "window." Moreover, this knowledge representation has consequences for the processes that extract information from text. If the model is represented as a bundle of separable components, processing is analytic and integrative. If the model is represented as an indivisible unit, processing is holistic and sentence based.

On a slightly more negative note, I think the van Daalen-Kapteijns and Elshout-Mohr model of vocabulary acquisition has limited generality. In daily life, contextual information about a word meaning is not neatly packaged with superordinate information presented first and conveniently followed by specifications and counterexamples. Consequently, in more naturalistic situations, the ideal acquisition process might look very different from the model-guided analytic search the authors propose. Next, we will turn to Sternberg and Powell's (1983) theory of learning from context, which is a much more general theory than that of van Daalen-Kapteijns and Elshout-Mohr and is, indeed, the most comprehensive theory of contextual learning to date. A very nice feature of Sternberg and Powell's theory is that it attempts to account for characteristics of the context and of the individual reader that might influence contextual learning. Whereas van Daalen-Kapteijns and Elshout-Mohr used a constant contextual configuration (and not a very naturalistic one at that), Sternberg and Powell's interest in context differences led them to construct many different contexts, ones that resembled the kinds of connected prose passages readers would encounter outside of the laboratory.

Sternberg and Powell (1983) recognize two important determinants of contextual vocabulary acquisition: the context and the reader. The *contextual cues* convey various types of information about a given word's meaning and dictate the quality of meaning that can *theoretically* be inferred from that context. However, the *actual* quality of the inferred meaning will also depend on a given individual's ability to exploit the relevant contextual cues. The theory attempts to specify the set of contextual cues external to the individual that can potentially facilitate meaning acquisition. The theory also attempts to specify the set of *mediating variables* that "lie at least partially within the individual" (Sternberg & Powell, 1983, p. 882) and that affect how well any given set of contextual cues will be utilized in the meaning abstraction process. Because this article addresses the question of the relationship between an individual's vocabulary knowledge and reading skill, I will describe the mediating variables in more detail. Given that these are the variables reputed "to lie partially within the individual," in them we are more likely to gain insights into the question at hand.

Contextual Cues. Sternberg and Powell (1983) differentiate external context or cues in the context surrounding the word from internal context or cues provided by morphemes within the word itself. Here, I will briefly review only their theory of external cues. They specify eight classes of cues about the unknown word concept that can be provided by the external context. These are (1) *temporal cues* regarding the unknown word concept's duration or frequency, (2) *spatial cues* regarding the general or specific location of the unknown word *or* where it can sometimes be found, (3) *value cues* regarding its worth or desirability or the affect it arouses, (4) *stative descriptive cues* regarding its physical properties, e.g., color, size, feel, and shape, (5) *functional descriptive cues* regarding the purposes of the unknown word or the actions it can perform, (6) *cause/enablement cues* regarding the possible cause of or enabling conditions for the unknown word, (7) *class membership cues* regarding the class(es) to which it belongs, and (8) *equivalence cues* regarding its meaning or contrasts (e.g., antonyms) to its meaning. Within this descriptive framework, Werner and Kaplan's context sentence (4) for contavish, *You can't feel or touch a contavish,* provides predominantly stative descriptive cues about a contavish's properties and also hints at class membership properties. Sentence (6), *John fell into a contavish in the road,* supplies additional stative descriptive information about what a contavish looks like as well as spatial information about possible locations for contavishes. Sternberg and Powell's eight classes of cues are not intended to be mutually exclusive or exhaustive. Rather, they can be used to provide useful information about the strategies people use to infer meaning from context.

Mediating Variables. Sternberg and Powell specify seven types of mediating variables that affect the perceived usefulness of the contextual cues and, hence, whether the cues will actually be utilized in the processes of meaning extraction. A list of the seven types plus a short description of each follows.

1. *Number of occurrences of the unknown word.* Multiple occurrences of an unknown word increase the number of available cues surrounding the word. Multiple occurrences would facilitate contextual learning if the reader is able to integrate the cues surrounding the multiple appearances of the word. Multiple occurrences could impede contextual learning if the reader has difficulty integrating information from separate appearances of the word.

I think Sternberg and Powell have hit on an important source of individual differences here, the ability to *integrate* the contextual cues to determine their relationship to the unknown word. In this variable, Sternberg and Powell are referring to temporal integration of information, that is, the integration of information over temporally discrete encounters with the word. Later, I will suggest how other forms of integration may be important, too.

2. *Variability of contexts in which multiple occurrences of the unknown word appear.* Different types of contexts are likely to supply different types of cues about a given word's meaning. To the extent that readers can integrate information across successive appearances of a word, this would increase the reader's ability to get a full picture of the scope of a given word's meaning as well as to detect those aspects of the word's usage that remain invariant across specific contexts. To the extent that

readers have difficulty integrating across variable contexts, variable repetitions would likely introduce ambiguities and complexities that obscure the invariant-meaning attributes and impede meaning extraction.

Again, in this variable, we encounter the idea that the integration skills of a given reader may affect his or her ability to capitalize on the wealth of cues given by variable contexts. What might account for individual differences in integration? Sternberg, Powell, and Kaye (1983) hint at the potential contributions of an individual's processing capacity limitations in the meaning-extraction process by suggesting that in some situations and for some individuals, "stimulus overload" may occur and this would result in reduced rather than increased learning. This argument is not developed in their theory, but it is the one I will be promoting later.

3. *Increased importance of the unknown word to understanding the context in which it is embedded.* The more a given word is judged to be necessary for understanding the surrounding context, the more the reader will be likely to use the surrounding context to decipher it. The ability to recognize the importance of a word to understanding context may be an important component of comprehension monitoring (Flavell, 1981; Markman, 1979), or what researchers have called "metacognitive" awareness.

4. *Helpfulness of the surrounding context in understanding the meaning of the unknown word.* A given cue may be differentially helpful, given the nature of the unknown word and given the location of the cue in the text relative to the unknown word. So, for example, to infer that *diurnal* means "daily," a temporal description of when a diurnal event occurs would be more helpful than a spatial cue describing where the event occurs. By contrast, to infer that *ing* means low-lying pasture, spatial cues would be more potent than temporal cues. As for the location of cues, there is a greater probability that a cue close in proximity to the word will be recognized as relevant to that word's meaning than a cue separated from the word by a larger chunk of text. Perceived helpfulness of any contextual cue may also vary depending on whether it occurs before or after the unknown word (Rubin, 1976). Again, in this variable, Sternberg and Powell seem to be imputing some difference among individuals in their ability to judge which cues are relevant.

5. *Density of unknown words.* When the density of unknown words in a text is high, readers may be overwhelmed and unwilling or unable to use available cues to their best advantage. Also, with a high density of unknown words, the probability of figuring out the meaning of any one of them would be reduced given that the context itself is made up of many unknown and, thus, unhelpful words. Finally, it would be difficult to figure out which of the available cues applied to which of the unknown words.

6. *Concreteness of the unknown word and the surrounding context.* Concrete concepts will be easier to understand because they have a simpler meaning structure as evidenced by the fact that it is easier for people to reach a consensus about the definitions for concrete words, such as *house* or *cat,* than for abstract words, such as *liberty* or *love.* Moreover, unknown word meanings (even if relatively concrete themselves) will be easier to infer if the surrounding context is concrete rather than esoteric.

7. *Usefulness of previously known information in cue utilization.* Here, Sternberg and Powell make provision for the role of past knowledge. They suggest that the cue's usefulness will depend on the extent to which past knowledge can be brought to bear on the cue and its relation to the unknown word. Of course, the usefulness of the prior information will in turn depend on a given individual's ability to retrieve the information, recognize its relevance, and apply it appropriately.

Empirical Tests of the Theory. To empirically test the theory, Sternberg and Powell had high school students read short prose passages containing very low-frequency words whose meanings could be inferred from the context. The 32 passages were divided among 4 different writing styles: literary, newspaper, scientific, and history. An example of a literary passage follows:

> Two ill-dressed people—the one a tired woman of middle years and the other a tense young man—sat around a fire where the common meal was almost ready. The mother, Tanith, peered at her son through the *oam* of the bubbling stew. It had been a long time since his last *ceilidh* and Tobar had changed greatly; where once he had seemed all legs and clumsy joints, he now was well-formed and in control of his hard, young body. As they ate, Tobar told of his past year, recreating for Tanith how he had wandered long and far in his quest to gain the skills he would need to be permitted to rejoin the company. Then all too soon, their brief *ceilidh* over, Tobar walked over to touch his mother's arm and quickly left.

After reading each passage, the students' task was to define as best they could each of the low-frequency words in the passage. In this case, the cues in the text could be used to infer that *oam* means "steam" and *ceilidh* means "visit."

Sternberg and Powell varied the kinds of contextual and mediating variables present in the 32 passages. For example, *density of unknown words* was varied by having 1 to 4 of the unknown words in a single passage; *number of occurrences* was varied by having the same unknown word appear in 1 to 4 of the 32 passages.

Internal validation of the theory involved the use of stepwise regression procedures to determine whether the contextual cues and mediating variables could predict the mean quality of definition for each word averaged over subjects. The correlations between predicted and observed quality ratings for definitions varied from .74 to .94 for the four writing styles; all of these values were highly statistically significant.

External validation of the theory involved correlating definition quality with student's scores on standardized tests of intelligence, vocabulary, and reading comprehension; the correlations were .62, .56, and .65, respectively. On the basis of these high intercorrelations, Sternberg and Powell (1983) concluded that their "learning-from-context task measures something closely akin to that which is measured by standardized tests of verbal intelligence in general, and of verbal comprehension in particular, and that the ability which is measured in each case is the ability to acquire new verbal knowledge" (p. 885).

Sternberg and Powell have provided an exciting theory of learning from context, but I would like to push it a little further. If we accept Sternberg and Powell's conclusions that the ability to acquire new verbal knowledge from context is the key source of individual differences and accounts for the high intercorrelations among tests of vocabulary knowledge, comprehension, and IQ, we need to ask why these differences in ability to learn from context exist in the first place. Sternberg and Powell have some interesting suggestions, but so far, these ideas have not been tested directly.

I began the description of Sternberg and Powell's theory by suggesting that their mediating variables were likely candidates for individual difference parameters because these are the variables assumed to affect the learner's ability to recognize and use potential cues in the context. And indeed, the theoretical descriptions of many of them include a number of potentially interesting loci for individual differences—differences in prior knowledge, metacognitive skills, and integrative skills. However, in empirical tests of the theory, the mediating variables functioned as or translated into context variables, that is, variables extraneous to the individual. For the most part, the mediating variables were experimentally manipulated by arrangements introduced into the texts themselves. So, for example, the density of unknown words, the number of occurrences of an unknown word, and the variability of cues associated with multiple occurrences were all introduced by systematic manipulations within and across the 32 passages. Moreover, internal validation of the variables involved an item analysis in which the dependent measure was the quality of definition inferred for each unknown word averaged over the performance of individual students. Such an analysis precludes the examination of how specific features of the context interact with specific features of the learner to influence the learning process.

Even though operationalized as contextual features, the mediating variables could still have influenced an individual subject's performance in the learning-from-context task. For example, individuals with poor ability to integrate cues might not have been able to take advantage of the multiple contextual cues in the way individuals with good ability to integrate could. Thus, the mediating variables would have contributed to the significant correlations between individual readers' learning-from-context scores and their performance on standardized tests of vocabulary knowledge and comprehension. However, this is somewhat indirect evidence for the role of the mediating variables in producing the individual differences in learning from context and certainly does not isolate the specific loci of individual differences. Thus, the main contribution of the Sternberg and Powell research with respect to individual differences was to demonstrate that individual differences in the ability to learn word meanings from context are related to individual differences in performance on standardized tests of vocabulary knowledge and comprehension. My research attempts to answer the obvious next question: What accounts for the large individual differences in the ability to learn from context?

IV. INTEGRATION SKILL AND WORKING MEMORY

A. The Theory

In Sternberg and Powell's (1983) theory, learning from context is the central explanatory construct; in my theory, working memory assumes that role. According to Sternberg and Powell, the ability to acquire new information from context is the common skill underlying tests as diverse in form and content as those measuring vocabulary, reading comprehension, and IQ. However, Sternberg and Powell do not specify precisely what factors might contribute to individual differences in contextual learning in the first place. I would like to argue that individual differences in contextual learning can be attributed, in part, to the individual learner's ability to process and store information simultaneously in working memory. There are two steps to my argument. The first is that learning from context depends, to a large extent, on sophisticated integration skills. The second is that these integration processes can be more easily accomplished by individuals with large working memories. Let me expand on these in turn.

When acquiring meaning from context, whether it is the meaning of an individual vocabulary item or the meaning of extended discourse, the learner must integrate the successive idea units represented by words, phrases, and sentences in the context. Successful contextual learning implies that the learner has not only isolated the relevant ideas, but also computed their relationships to one another.

Consider, for a start, the learning of individual *word* meanings from context. To infer from the relatively short prose passage that *oam* means "steam," Sternberg and Powell's (1983) readers had to isolate the following facts as relevant to the word's meaning: *oam* is emanating from the stew, the stew is bubbling, *oam* can be peered through, and bubbling is associated with a fire. However, simple isolation of the facts is not sufficient for inferring the word's meaning. To do this, readers must combine or integrate the cues to figure out how they relate to one another and to the unknown word; readers must figure out how bubbling relates to the fire and stew, how the fact that oam can be peered through relates to these facts, and so on (Sternberg & Powell, 1983). Successful acquisition of word meaning from context likely depends on a given learner's ability to sift through and integrate the relevant contextual information.

Like vocabulary acquisition, reading comprehension also depends on the skill of integrating successive idea units. Sternberg and Powell have elaborated their theory of contextual learning and cue integration with respect to comprehending individual words. However, there is ample evidence that similar processes are involved in comprehending sentences and extended texts. Readers process text in cycles, working with at most several sentences or propositions at a time (Kintsch & van Dijk, 1978; Kintsch & Vipond, 1979). Propositions in one cycle, however, are frequently related to propositions in previous cycles, and if the reader is to establish a coherent representation for the text, he or she must integrate the related propositions (Daneman, 1982). Most standardized tests of reading comprehension tap these integration processes. Take, for example, the following excerpt from Form 2B of the widely used Davis Test (Davis & Davis, 1962): "When Robert Oppenheimer, who supervised the making of the first atomic bomb, was asked by a committee of Congress whether there was any defense against it, his reply was 'Certainly.' (p. 9)" At the end of the passage, readers are given a pronoun question about this sentence. They are asked whether *it* refers to (a) making, (b) bomb, (c) committee, (d) Congress, or (e) defense. This question is a fairly good example of one that taps a reader's ability to determine the interrelationships among all the arguments and propositions of a sentence. Of course, other items on a reading comprehension test tap the reader's ability to integrate information *across* sentences and even larger chunks of text.

In sum, I would argue that the ability to comprehend the meanings of both new words and new texts depends, in part, on the ability to integrate successively encountered idea units. This means that the reader must be able to represent the current chunk of text in working memory and relate it to preceding ideas represented from the text.

The second step of my argument is that the quality of integration will vary as a function of a given individual's working memory capacity. Individuals with small working memories would be less likely to detect relationships between new and prior information since they would be less likely to have the preceding relevant information still accessible in working memory. Empirical evidence for my argument comes from correlational studies showing that readers with smaller measured working memory spans perform more poorly on tests of reading comprehension. Working memory span has correlated strongly with standardized tests of reading comprehension and even more strongly with specific tests of integration, such as the ability to compute a pronoun's referent, monitor for inconsistencies within and between sentences, and abstract the main theme (Baddeley, Logie, Nimmo-Smith, & Brereton, 1985; Daneman & Carpenter, 1980, 1983; Masson & Miller, 1983).

In this research, working memory was measured by variants of the *reading span test,* a measure originally devised by Pat Carpenter and I to assess a reader's conjoint effective use of the processing and storage resources of working memory. The theory behind the test is that working memory has processing and storage functions that compete for a limited capacity (Baddeley & Hitch, 1974; Case, Kurland, & Goldberg, 1982; Perfetti & Lesgold, 1977). More demanding processes consume more of the available capacity, leaving less residual capacity for storing and maintaining information in working memory. According to the theory, individual differences in working memory capacity reflect differences in the conjoint efficient use of processing and storage resources. Less-skilled individuals process less efficiently, and this has the effect of reducing their functional storage capacity. This theory of working memory can be contrasted with the more traditional theory that views working memory, more commonly labeled short-term memory, as having storage functions only, with individuals differing in the number of items or chunks they can store (Broadbent, 1975; Miller, 1956). Thus, while traditional tests of short-term memory like digit span and word span were designed to tax storage functions, the reading span test was designed to tax processing and storage. The reading span test is itself very simple. The subject is given increasingly longer sets of sentences to read aloud and, at the end of each set, attempts to recall the final word of each sentence in the set. Reading span is defined as the maximum number of sentences the subject could read aloud while maintaining perfect recall of final words. The processing and storage components of the reading span test involve the usual demands of sentence comprehension, such as word encoding, lexical access, and interclause integration, as well as an additional component of maintaining and retrieving the sentence-final words. By now the test has been administered to over 500 university students in our lab, and reading span has varied from two to five sentence-final words. The theory behind the test is that individuals with inefficient processes devote so much capacity to comprehending the sentences that they have less capacity left over to store and produce the final words. Evidence for the dynamic theory of working memory comes from the fact that the reading span test successfully predicts performance on the reading comprehension and integration tasks mentioned earlier, whereas traditional tests of static storage capacity, such as word span and letter span, do not (Daneman & Carpenter, 1980, 1983; Masson & Miller, 1983).

B. Empirical Tests of the Role of Working Memory

Given that successful integration in reading is related to an individual's working memory capacity, and given that the acquisition of new word meanings from context requires sophisticated integration skills, it follows that success at acquiring word meanings may also be related to the individual's working memory capacity. To test this, I and my co-workers have conducted a series of learning-from-context studies which incorporated some of the features of the previous vocabulary acquisition research that I have described, but which included a measure of the reader's working memory capacity. I will discuss the pertinent results here, leaving details of the methodology and data analyses for elsewhere (Cull, 1983; Daneman & Green, 1986).

The basic task was for readers to learn the meanings of 24 words, each embedded in a naturalistic prose passage of the sort used by Sternberg and Powell (1983). Each word, like those of Sternberg and Powell, had an extremely low frequency of occurrence and was unlikely to have been encountered by any of the college student subjects prior to testing. Moreover, each word, like those of van Daalen-Kapteijns and Elshout-Mohr, had an unusual meaning to the extent that no single-word synonym for it exists in English. This meant that my subjects had to learn a new concept for the new label rather than simply figure out the closest synonym to the new label. I will illustrate the materials and procedure with one of the target words—*ruelle*.

The passage for *ruelle* was the following:

Tom was exhausted. Coming home after a long, hard swimming practice he headed straight for his room with the intention of taking a short nap. In spite of the sun shining in from the window overhead he fell asleep quite easily. He was soon to be awoken, however, by his parents who had just returned from shopping. Tom looked up and sleepily viewed his parents as they moved his new desk into his room. Mrs. Johnson, after stepping back to look at the desk, suggested moving it closer to the window so that Tom would get the maximum amount of light. Tom remarked that then they would have to eliminate the ruelle and he didn't want to do that. Mrs. Johnson said that she didn't see why this should make such a big difference. "Besides," she added, "then you won't be able to get up on the wrong side in the morning." Tom said he liked being able to sleep with his legs hanging over the edge on either side. He finally gave in saying that he could probably get used to the change. Tom got up and they made the necessary moves. After all the commotion Tom was wide awake. Rather than returning to finish his nap he decided to put his things into the new desk.

As you can see from this example, there are sufficient cues in the extended context to infer that *ruelle* means "the space between the bed and the wall." While none of these cues provides the reader with direct synonyms for *ruelle,* by integrating the successively encountered contextual cues, the reader can infer the complex meaning of the unfamiliar word.

Before subjects saw the passage, the experimenter first read to them the target sentence containing *ruelle* and then asked them to try to define the word. This procedure was used to gauge the extent of the subjects knowledge about a target word prior to being exposed to the contextual cues. Having determined that the subject did not already know the word's meaning, subjects were then given the passage to read and told to use the context to infer the word's meaning. Immediately after reading the passage, subjects were to write down as precise a definition as possible. The quality of each definition was rated independently by two trained raters. In each study, interrater reliability was .90 or better; consequently, an average of the two ratings was used as a definition–goodness score for each word for each subject. A subject's total definition–goodness score summed over the 24 passages was taken as a measure of his or her ability to learn new word meanings from context.

In the first study, the 30 adult subjects were each given a sheet of cardboard to cover the lines as they read them; this prevented them from reexamining previously read information so that integration and contextual learning depended entirely upon what information the reader could easily retrieve. As predicted, learning-from-context scores were highly correlated with their ability to coordinate processing and storage in working memory, as measured by the reading span test, $r(28) = .69, p < .01$. The mean learning-from-context scores for readers with small working memories was 40%; for readers with intermediate spans, it was 46%; for readers with large spans, it was 62% (see Daneman & Green, 1986, for details). These results suggest that working memory may play an important role in the processes that infer the meaning of an unknown word by integrating successive contextual cues.

Of course, caution is required when imputing the causal relationship. An obvious limitation of this research (and most individual differences research for that matter) is that it is inherently correlational by virtue of the fact that working memory (like many other individual difference parameters) cannot be manipulated readily in the laboratory. Strictly speaking, then, I am limited to demonstrating a relationship between working memory capacity and vocabulary acquisition rather than directly supporting my theory that working memory influences vocabulary acquisition. One way to seek converging evidence for my theory, within the constraints of the inevitably correlational paradigm, is to manipulate the working memory demands of the learning-from-context task. In a second study that I will describe next, we reduced the working memory demands of the learning experience and, in so doing, eliminated the correlation between working memory span and contextual learning.

In the second study (unpublished), 30 college students, who had not participated in the previous study, were given the same set of unfamiliar words embedded in the prose contexts. The only difference this time was that the subjects were not required to cover the text as they read. Rather, they were given a maximum of two minutes to study each passage and were encouraged to backtrack and reread any part of the passage they wished. The prediction was that the learner's working memory capacity would no longer be related to his or her ability to acquire new word meanings from context since cue integration would not depend on what information the learner could easily retrieve from memory.

The mean learning-from-context scores were higher in this experiment than in the one that prohibited backtracking; it was 56% as compared to 49% for the no-backtracking experiment. More important, and as predicted, working memory span was no longer related to the ability to learn from context, $r = .25$, $p > .10$. The major effect of allowing readers to backtrack was to improve the learning-from-context performance of individuals who had small and intermediate working memory spans. The mean learning-from-context scores for readers with small working memories was 52%; for readers with intermediate spans, it was 56%; for readers with large spans, it was 59%. These differences were, of course, much smaller than the differences in the no-backtracking experiment and were not statistically significant. Sternberg and Powell have proposed a variety of contextual features that facilitate the acquisition of word meanings from context. This research supplements their findings by focusing on the contributions of the individual learner to the acquisition process. The research proposes that the individual's working memory capacity may be one factor that influences contextual learning to the extent that contextual integration relies on the learner's memory for the successive ideas supplied by that context. Later, I shall speculate on the extent to which our real-world opportunities to accumulate vocabulary knowledge indirectly through contextual inference actually occur in situations with heavy memory demands. However, first I will describe a study that investigated developmental differences in contextual learning skills.

Working memory capacity is also a good predictor of developmental differences in the ability to acquire new word meanings from context. Barry Cull and I used a similar learning-from-context task with 49 school children in the fourth to sixth grades. We chose a new set of target words, simpler than the ones used with our college students, but unlikely to be known by most elementary school children. As in the adult studies, the children's knowledge of each target word was assessed prior to exposure to the context by first reading them the stimulus sentence containing the target word and then having them attempt to define it. In the few cases where a child already knew the meaning of a word, the trials were discarded. Children read each passage aloud, a procedure that had the same effect as the covering procedure used with the adult subjects, since fluent oral reading precludes major backtracking. Immediately after reading each passage, the children provided an oral definition for the target word. The quality of each definition provided by each child was rated from 0 to 2. As predicted, working memory capacity (as measured by a simplified version of the reading span test for children) was highly correlated with learning-from-context performance, $r(47) = .66$, $p < .01$. On average, children with small spans learned 41% of the word meanings, and children with larger spans learned 58%. Of particular developmental interest was the fact that working memory span was a better predictor of contextual learning than the two standard developmental variables, age and school grade; age was not significantly correlated with learning from context, $r(47) = .26$, and grade only correlated .38 with learning from context. Moreover, working memory span was still significantly correlated with learning from context when age and grade were partialled out, .64 and .63, respectively. These results suggest that working memory capacity is a better index of vocabulary acquisition than chronological age or years of schooling.

To provide converging evidence for the view that working memory capacity influences contextual learning, we again manipulated the working memory demand of the learning-from-context task. This was achieved by varying the position of the contextual cues relative to the target word. According to my theory, the working memory demand on integration would be greater if the relevant contextual cues preceded rather than followed the target word. To understand this, consider first the case in which context follows the target word. In this case, readers would encounter the unknown word in its immediate syntactic and semantic context first, and then they could actively search the subsequent context for information that might reveal the meaning of the word. By contrast, when the context precedes the target word, readers would have no way of predetermining as they read what features might be relevant. Once they encountered the unknown word, they would have to rely on what they could retrieve of the earlier information. Children with small spans should be at a particular disadvantage in this case because less of the relevant information would still be available to them when they encounter the unknown word. In other words, when contextual cues follow the unfamiliar word, children could compensate for an inadequate working memory capacity by strategically searching for relevant cues; when contextual cues precede the unfamiliar word, they cannot.

To test our prediction that children with small working memory spans would be particularly handicapped when context preceded the target word, two context paragraphs were constructed for each target word. The two differed in whether the contextual cues appeared before or after the target word. This was accomplished by setting the target word in a neutral sentence that could be placed as the first or the last sentence of the context paragraph without altering the overall sense and cohesion of the paragraph. As an illustration, take the target word *conflagration* embedded in the sentence, *The conflagration was very large by now*. The context-after condition, where the target sentence is the first sentence of the paragraph is

> The *conflagration* was very large by now. Within no time the flames had left a trail of destruction behind. Ahead it threatened more bush and a small town. It had been raging for a few days, and the black smoke had risen and formed a large cloud which could be seen for miles. It was hard to believe that a carelessly thrown match could cause so much damage.

The context-before condition simply involved moving the target sentence to the end of the paragraph. Because subjects were questioned about the meaning of the target word immediately after reading the passage, it was important to keep the time between presentation of the target sentence and question as constant as possible. This was accomplished by having the context paragraph accompanied by a filler paragraph of equal length. When the context occurred after the target word, the filler paragraph was the first paragraph of the passage; when the context occurred before the target word, the filler paragraph was the second. The contents of the filler paragraph were consistent with the theme of the context paragraph but provided no additional cues as to the target word's meaning. Each child saw half of the target words in the context-after condition and the other half in the context-before condition. The results showed the predicted interaction between context position and working memory span. Small-span children learned more poorly than large-span children, with the difference being more pronounced when integration demanded more working memory capacity. Small-span children learned 23% fewer word meanings than large-span children when context preceded the target word; they learned 12% fewer word meanings when context followed the target word.

Werner and Kaplan (1952) suggested that developmental differences in the ability to acquire new word meanings from context may be attributed in part to the younger child's failure to integrate successive contextual cues. They attributed this failure to integrate to a failure to recognize the need to integrate. By contrast, our research suggests that failure to integrate may be part and parcel of the younger or less-experienced child's inadequate working memory capacity. Children with small working memories would be less able to maintain successively encountered contextual cues simultaneously in working memory and, therefore, less able to detect and compute the relationships among the successive cues.

C. Contributions to the Learning-from-Context Hypothesis

I began this article by endorsing the learning-from-context account of the relationship between vocabulary knowledge and reading comprehension. I then attempted to supplement this account with my own views on how individual differences in learning from context exist in the first place. I will first sum up the contributions with respect to individual differences in contextual learning and then return to the broader issue of the relationship between vocabulary knowledge and reading comprehension.

I argued that contextual learning involves the integration of successively encountered ideas in the context and that integration, in turn, is influenced by the individual learner's working memory capacity. The research I reported showed that adults and children with smaller working memories were least able to infer the meanings of new words from context (Cull, 1983; Daneman & Green, 1986). However, the research also showed that working memory only plays a role in contextual learning when the reader does not have the opportunity, or does not exercise the opportunity, to reread previously encountered text. In other words, working memory seems to be related to learning vocabulary from context only when contextual integration depends on the reader's memory for successive ideas supplied by the context. Besides making sense theoretically, this finding is, in fact, consistent with past research that has shown a relationship between working memory capacity and integration in reading comprehension tasks. On reviewing that literature, one finds that all of the strong correlations reported between working memory and reading comprehension thus far have been in situations where the reader's ability to backtrack was precluded or penalized. Backtracking was precluded when readers were required to cover each line of text as they completed it (Daneman & Carpenter, 1980) or when they were allowed to view only one word at a time on a computer monitor (Daneman & Carpenter, 1983). Backtracking was penalized when comprehension was tested under the speeded conditions of a standardized reading test, because taking time to backtrack would be reflected in lower test scores (Baddeley *et al.,* 1985; Daneman & Carpenter, 1980, 1983; Masson & Miller, 1983). To date, there has been no direct test of the relationship between working memory and reading comprehension in tasks where the working memory demand is decreased by permitting or actively encouraging extensive backtracking. However, in light of the vocabulary-acquisition data reported here, one might expect a much weaker relationship between working memory span and reading comprehension in conditions allowing extensive study time for text material. In sum, then, an individual's working memory may dictate how well that individual comprehends new *words* or new *texts* whenever the reading situation prohibits or inhibits the reexamination of previously encountered context.

To determine what role working memory plays in real-life contextual learning, we need to establish how frequently real-life opportunities for contextual learning actually occur under conditions with high memory demands. Although I know of no direct evidence on the issue, I believe that a great deal of contextual learning occurs when working memory demands, whether externally imposed or self-imposed, are high. For example, all word meanings acquired during the course of conversation are likely acquired under conditions that strain working memory. Spoken discourse does not have the permanence of written discourse, affording listeners very little opportunity to backtrack and review the earlier context. During our lives, we no doubt encounter many new words in conversation with parents, teachers, colleagues, and so on. For very young children who have not yet mastered reading, the only means to acquire new vocabulary from verbal contexts is via conversational contexts. The new vocabulary encountered during listening is more likely to be acquired by individuals with larger working memories.

It is also likely that working memory plays a role in the acquisition of word meanings from written contexts. In this case, the working memory demand may be self-imposed rather than externally imposed as in the case of spoken contexts. The evidence suggests that during normal fluent reading, regressive eye movements account for only 10% of all eye movements (Buswell, 1922; Just & Carpenter, 1980; Rayner, 1978), and a large proportion of these regressions are very local, spanning at most several words or lines of text. Unless deliberately required to learn or memorize the contents of a text, readers do not engage in extensive rereading. Consequently, the new vocabulary encountered during normal reading conditions is more likely to be acquired by readers with larger working memory capacities. The net effect is that individuals with larger working memories are at an advantage when they encounter unknown words in all verbal contexts; those with larger working memories will likely amass a larger body of vocabulary knowledge by utilizing these verbal contexts.

This study has examined the way individuals use context to construct word meanings from scratch. However, we do not only use context to comprehend unknown word meanings: we also use it to enrich our comprehension of partially known meanings. Our previous understanding of *abstemious* may have just sufficed to pass a multiple-choice vocabulary recognition test. The partial understanding could be greatly enhanced each time we encounter *abstemious* showcased adroitly in contexts such as the following:

> After Ronald Reagan became the nation's 40th President yesterday, Mrs. Reagan prepared to appear at the inaugural balls in a hand-beaded gown designed by James Galanos. Its cost is estimated by industry experts to approach five figures, and the overall price of Mrs. Reagan's inaugural wardrobe is said to be around $25,000. Limousines, white tie and $10,000 ball gowns are in; shoe leather, abstemiousness and thrift that sacrifices haute couture are out, it seems, as Nancy Reagan sweeps from fete to fete in a glistening full-length Maximilian mink (Greenman, 1983, p. 49).

Individuals with large working memory spans should be able to capitalize on multiple and variable contexts to acquire, expand, and hone their knowledge of word meanings.

If working memory is related to contextual learning and reading comprehension because it influences the outcome of the integration processes (Daneman & Carpenter, 1980; Daneman & Green, 1986), and if vocabulary knowledge is related to contextual learning and reading comprehension because it reflects a past record of integration success (Sternberg & Powell, 1983), then we should expect working memory and vocabulary knowledge to be related to one another. For adult subjects, we found a correlation of .57 between working memory span and performance on a standardized multiple-choice vocabulary test (Daneman & Green, 1986); for children we found a correlation of .45 between working memory span and the Gates–MacGinitie Vocabulary Test (Cull, 1983). In Baddeley *et al.'s* (1985) study, the results were more equivocal; in their first experiment, there was a moderate correlation of .33; in the second experiment there was no correlation at all. Of course, there is no reason to believe that vocabulary tests are pure measures of readers' abilities to accumulate word knowledge through contextual inference since many of the words on the list may have been acquired through more explicit forms of reference. It is safe to assume differences in the *proportion of items* tapping earlier contextual learning opportunities across vocabulary tests and also across subjects' taking the same vocabulary test. For these reasons, the correlation between working memory capacity and vocabulary test scores would be moderate at best, and certainly not reliable.

Given that we cannot recover the learning instances of each vocabulary item for each individual, one way to corroborate my theory would be to simulate the learning processes in the laboratory. For example, subjects could be exposed to unknown words (like *ruelle*) under a variety of conditions that mimic real-life situations and then have their knowledge of the words tested later. In one condition, they could hear an explicit oral definition of the word, much as if a parent or friend had provided the definition to them. In a second condition, they could read an explicit written definition of the word, much as if they had looked up the word in a dictionary. In yet another condition, they could encounter the word in a prose passage so that their only means for learning the meaning would be through implicit contextual reference. If working memory is only related to the kind of vocabulary acquisition that involves context-based inferences, then we will have provided stronger support for the theory.

This research has provided a theoretical link between two excellent predictors of reading comprehension—working memory capacity and vocabulary knowledge. Given that the tests to measure working memory and vocabulary differ so markedly in content and form, their relationship is not immediately apparent, and, indeed, one might have expected that they made separate contributions to reading comprehension. My goal here has been to show that their contributions are not completely independent.

V. VOCABULARY KNOWLEDGE AND COMPREHENSION SKILL REVISITED

And now come the notorious and inevitable qualifiers of a concluding section. Although I have championed the claims of a working memory–learning-from-context hypothesis, it, like its contenders, does not provide the whole story about the remarkably strong relationship between vocabulary knowledge and comprehension skill. In our contextual learning studies, vocabulary knowledge still played a role over and above the role of working memory. In the study in which readers could not backtrack and working memory was highly correlated with learning success, the correlation between vocabulary knowledge and learning success was marginally significant when the effects of working memory were partialled out statistically. In the study in which readers were allowed to backtrack and working memory was not significantly correlated with learning success, vocabulary knowledge was. Despite the theoretical and empirical attractiveness of the working memory and learning-from-context account, it is unrealistic to assume that a complex and multifaceted skill such as reading comprehension will be reduced to one or more underlying constructs. Besides, as I forewarned, learning from context can complement rather than replace other accounts of the relationship between vocabulary knowledge and comprehension. Although we do not yet have the whole story, I think we have made significant strides toward understanding why the sheer number of meanings a reader knows enables so astoundingly accurate a prediction of an individual's ability to comprehend text.

REFERENCES

Anderson, R. C., & Freebody, P. (1981). Vocabulary knowledge. In J. T. Guthrie (Ed.), *Comprehension and teaching*. Newark, DE: International Reading Association.

Baddeley, A. D., & Hitch, G. (1974). Working memory. In G. H. Bower (Ed.), *The psychology of learning and motivation* (Vol. 8). New York: Academic Press.

Baddeley, A. D., Logie, R., Nimmo-Smith, I., & Brereton, N. (1985). Components of fluent reading. *Journal of Verbal Learning and Verbal Behavior, 24, 119–131.

Beck, I. C., Perfetti, C. A., & McKeown, M. G. (1982). Effects of long-term vocabulary instruction on lexical access and reading comprehension. *Journal of Educational Psychology, 74, 506–521.

Broadbent, D. A. (1975). The magical number seven after fifteen years. In A. Kennedy & A. Wilkes (Eds.), *Studies in long-term memory*. New York: Wiley.

Brown, J. I., Nelson, M. J., & Denny, E. C. (1976). Examiner's manual: The Nelson–Denny reading test. Boston: Houghton-Mifflin.

Buswell, G. T. (1922). *Fundamental reading habits, a study of their development*. Chicago: Chicago University Press.

Case, R., Kurland, D. M., & Goldberg, J. (1982). Operational efficiency and the growth of short-term memory span. *Journal of Experimental Child Psychology, 33, 386–404.

Cook, J. M., Heim, A. W., & Watts, K. P. (1963). The Word-in-Context: A new type of verbal reasoning test. *British Journal of Psychology, 54, 227–237.

Cull, B. (1983). *The relationship of working memory to vocabulary acquisition and reading comprehension: Individual and developmental differences in school aged adults*. Unpublished master's thesis, University of Waterloo, Waterloo, Ontario, Canada.

Daneman, M. (1982). The measurement of reading comprehension: How not to trade construct validity for predictive power. *Intelligence, 6,* 331–345.

Daneman, M., & Carpenter, P. A. (1980). Individual differences in working memory and reading. *Journal of Verbal Learning and Verbal Behavior, 19,* 450–466.

Daneman M., & Carpenter, P. A. (1983). Individual differences in integrating information between and within sentences. *Journal of Experimental Psychology: Learning, Memory, and Cognition, 9,* 561–584.

Daneman, M., & Green I. (1986). Individual differences in comprehending and producing words in context. *Journal of Memory and Language, 25,* 1–18.

Davis, F. B. (1944). Fundamental factors of comprehension in reading. *Psychometrika, 9,* 185–197.

Davis, F. B. (1968). Research in comprehension in reading. *Reading Research Quarterly, 3,* 499–545.

Davis, F. B., & Davis, C. C. (1962). *Davis reading test manual.* New York: Psychological Corporation.

Draper, A. G., & Moeller, G. H. (1971). We think with words (therefore, to improve thinking, teach vocabulary). *Phi Delta Kappan, 52,* 482–484 (ERIC Document Reproduction Service No. ED 036 207).

Flavell, J. H. (1981). Cognitive monitoring. In W. P. Dickson (Ed.), *Children's oral communication skills.* New York: Academic Press.

Greenman, R. (1983). *Words in action.* New York: Times Books.

Horn, T. L., & Cattell, R. B. (1966). Refinement and test of the theory of fluid and crystallized ability intelligences. *Journal of Educational Psychology, 57,* 253–270.

Jackson, M. D., & McClelland, J. L. (1979). Processing determinants of reading speed. *Journal of Experimental Psychology: General, 108,* 1–31.

Jenkins, J. R., Pany, O., & Schreck, J. (1978). *Vocabulary and reading comprehension: Instructional effects* (Technical Report No. 100). Urbana, IL: University of Illinois, Center for the Study of Reading.

Jensen, A. R. (1980). *Bias in mental testing.* New York: Free Press.

Just, M. A., & Carpenter, P. A. (1980). A theory of reading: From eye fixations to comprehension. *Psychological Review, 87,* 329–354.

Kameenui, E. J., Carnine, D. W., & Freschi, R. (1982). Effects of text construction and instructional procedures for teaching word meanings on comprehension and recall. *Reading Research Quarterly, 17,* 367–388.

Kintsch, W., & van Dijk, T. A. (1978). Toward a model of text comprehension and production. *Psychological Review, 85,* 363–394.

Kintsch, W., & Vipond, D. (1979). Reading comprehension and readability in educational practice and psychological theory. In L. G. Nilsson (Ed.), *Perspectives on memory research.* Hillsdale, NJ: Erlbaum.

La Berge, D., & Samuels, S. J. (1974). Toward a theory of automatic information processing in reading. *Cognitive Psychology, 6,* 293–323.

Markman, E. M. (1979). Realizing that you don't understand: Elementary school children's awareness of inconsistencies. *Child Development, 50,* 643–655.

Marshalek, B. (1981). *Trait and process aspects of vocabulary knowledge and verbal ability* (NR 154-376 ONR Technical Report No. 15). Stanford, CA: School of Education, Stanford University.

Masson, M. E. J., & Miller J. A. (1983). Working memory and individual differences in comprehension and memory of text. *Journal of Educational Psychology, 75,* 314–318.

Miller, G. A. (1956). The magical number seven, plus or minus two: Some limits on our capacity for processing information. *Psychological Review, 63,* 81–97.

Perfetti, C. A. & Hogaboam, T. (1975). Relationship between single word decoding and reading comprehension skill. *Journal of Educational Psychology,* **67,** 461–469.

Perfetti, C. A., & Lesgold, A. M. (1977). Discourse comprehension and sources of individual differences. In M. A. Just & P. A. Carpenter (Eds.), *Cognitive processes in comprehension.* Hillsdale, NJ: Erlbaum.

Perfetti, C. A., & Lesgold, A. M. (1979). Coding and comprehension in skilled reading and implications for reading instruction. In L. B. Resnick & P. Weaver (Eds.), *Theory and practice of early reading* (Vol. 1). Hillsdale, NJ: Erlbaum.

Rayner, K. (1978). Eye movements in reading and information processing. *Psychological Bulletin,* **85,** 618–660.

Rubin, D. C. (1976). The effectiveness of context before, after, and around a missing word. *Perception and Psychophysics,* **19,** 214–216.

Schank, R. C., & Abelson, R. P. (1977). *Scripts, plans, goals, and understanding.* Hillsdale, NJ: Erlbaum.

Singer, H. (1965). A developmental model of speed of reading in grades 3 through 6. *Reading Research Quarterly,* **1,** 29–49.

Spilich, G. S., Vesonder, G. T., Chiesi, H. L., & Voss, J. F. (1979). Text processing of domain-related information for individuals with high and low domain knowledge. *Journal of Verbal Learning and Verbal Behavior,* **18,** 275–290.

Sternberg, R. J., & Powell, J. S. (1983). Comprehending verbal comprehension. *American Psychologist,* **38,** 878–893.

Sternberg, R. J., Powell, J. S., & Kaye, D. B. (1983). Teaching vocabulary-building skills: A contextual approach. In A. C. Wilkinson (Ed.), *Classroom computers and cognitive science.* New York: Academic Press.

Thorndike, R. L. (1973). *Reading comprehension education in fifteen countries.* New York: Wiley.

Thurstone, L. L. (1946). A note on a reanalysis of Davis' reading tests. *Psychometrika,* **11,** 185–188.

Tuinman, J. J., & Brady, M. E. (1974). How does vocabulary account for variance on reading comprehension tests? A preliminary instructional analysis. In P. Nacke (Ed.), *Twenty-third National Reading Conference Yearbook.* Clemson SC: The National Reading Conference.

van Daalen-Kapteijns, M. M., & Elshout-Mohr, M. (1981). The acquisition of word meanings: A developmental study. *Journal of Verbal Learning and Verbal Behavior,* **20,** 386–399.

Werner, H., & Kaplan, E. (1952). The acquisition of word meanings: A developmental study. *Monographs of the Society for Research in Child Development,* No. 51.

INFERENCES IN READING COMPREHENSION

MURRAY SINGER

Department of Psychology
University of Manitoba
Winnipeg, Manitoba R3T 2N2, Canada

I. INTRODUCTION

For the past twenty years, cognitive psychologists have intensively studied the problem of language comprehension. The tremendous complexity of understanding even a simple sentence has been noted by many investigators. Decoding a sentence requires a person to retrieve the meaning of each word and choose among alternative possibilities, to identify the part of speech of each word in the sentence, to identify the syntactic structure of the sentence, and to combine the concepts discussed in the sentence into units of meaning (Clark & Clark, 1977, Chapter 2).

Any comprehensive account of human language understanding must address two related realms of theory, namely, the representation of text meaning and the cognitive processes that operate on that representation. Several detailed proposals which consider both of these domains have by now been presented (e.g., Anderson, 1976; Kintsch & van Dijk, 1978; Norman & Rumelhart, 1975). These formulations are alike in their goal of striving to address a broad range of language phenomena, including language comprehension, language production, memory for complex messages, and the retrieval of the meaning of a message.

From the outset, researchers have recognized that the problem of inference constitutes a central component of language comprehension (e.g., Bransford & Franks, 1971; Potts, 1972). Theorists have argued that the representation of the meaning of a message may include ideas inferred by the listener or reader in addition to the ideas conveyed more explicitly by the message. These inferences are derived from the application of world knowledge to the content of the message by the language recipient. By

177

1976, Schank asserted that inference constitutes the "core of the understanding process" (Schank, 1976, p. 168).

Inference is so pervasive in language comprehension that it is easy to overlook its role. Consider the fact that many English nouns are ambiguous. In the sentence, *The farmer placed the straw beside the machine,* the context guides the reader to infer that *straw* refers to "hay" and not a drinking utensil (Clark & Clark, 1977, p. 80). The determination of the part of speech of each word is inferential. While *old* is usually an adjective, it is inferred to be a noun in, *The old teach the young* (Clark & Clark, 1977, p. 62). Every pronoun that appears in a text must be inferentially linked to its correct antecedent (Clark, 1977). Examples of this sort are inexhaustible.

Accordingly, this article was designed to review and integrate the inference literature from 1970 to the present. The goal of this endeavor is to identify the dimensions, variables, and principles of inference which have emerged from the research.

The label *inference* is so broad that it is necessary at the outset to identify the focus of this article. Inference will be defined here with reference to proposals concerning the propositional representation of text (e.g., Anderson, 1976; Kintsch, 1974). According to this position, the meaning of a text can be analyzed as a network of units of meaning, called propositions. For example, underlying the sentence, *The dog chased the scared cat* are two propositions, (*chase, dog, cat*) and (*scared, cat*). Each proposition consists of a predicate, typically a verb, adjective, or adverb, and one or more arguments, typically nouns. Thus (*chase, dog, cat*) has the predicate *chase* and the arguments *dog* and *cat*. Detailed principles of the propositional analysis of text have been presented by Turner and Greene (1978).

For the purposes of this article, an inference will refer to the addition of either an argument or an entire proposition, to the list of propositions that are explicitly conveyed by a text. Consider the sentence, *The nurse lit the cigarette.* Underlying this sentence is the proposition (*light, nurse, cigarette*). The inference that the nurse used a match to light the cigarette would result in the addition of an argument to the proposition, as in (*light, nurse, cigarette, match*). If one inferred that the cigarette consequently burned, the proposition (*burn, cigarette*) would be added to the list of propositions underlying the message.

What aspects of inference does this definition exclude? Corbett and Dosher (1978) have drawn a pertinent distinction between *activating* and *encoding.* The notion of activation is based upon the principles of the spread of activation in neural pathways (Anderson, 1976; Quillian, 1968). Quillian argued that the activation of a concept in semantic memory results in the spread of activation to related concepts, like from *bread* to *butter*. By now, there is extensive evidence of the spread of activation, or *priming*, in one's memory of (1) word meaning (Meyer & Schvaneveldt, 1971), (2) facts (Anderson, 1976), and (3) the meaning of a text (McKoon & Ratcliff, 1980). However, Corbett and Dosher (1978) argue that the priming of one concept by another does not guarantee that an inference is encoded. That is, when one reads *The nurse lit the cigarette,* the concept *match* may be briefly activated, but this does not necessarily result in an inference about the nurse using a match. The present article will focus on the circumstances in which there is evidence of inference encoding, rather than simply of activation.

Another aspect of inference that will be *deemphasized* is reconstructive memory for text. It is well documented that with increased test delay, people are more likely to incorrectly recognize test sentences that are consistent with the meaning of a text (Dooling & Christiaansen, 1977; Sulin & Dooling, 1974). These incorrect recognitions are said to be based on the reader's reconstruction of the text meaning. For example, Sulin and Dooling (1974) presented passages about famous characters to their subjects. Immediately after reading a passage about Helen Keller, 20% of the subjects incorrectly recognized the *new* test sentence, *She was deaf, dumb, and blind,* as having occurred in the passage. However, when the test was administered a week after reading, 50% made this incorrect recognition. Kintsch and van Dijk (1978) reported a similar trend in the free recall of text.

Sulin and Dooling's (1974) study showed that people rely heavily on their general knowledge in delayed memory tests for prose. While such reconstruction is clearly inferential in nature, it may be distinguished from the activity of drawing inferences in the course of encoding a message. The focus here will be upon the inference processes that accompany comprehension.

While the emphasis is on inference in *reading,* considerable reference will also be made on listening comprehension. There have been clear demonstrations of extensive similarity between reading and listening comprehension (e.g., Kintsch, Kozminsky, Streby, McKoon, & Keenan, 1975). Therefore, it will be assumed that studies of inference in listening comprehension carry useful suggestions for the study of reading.

To summarize, this article will inspect inferences that accompany the encoding of a message and that are derived from the representation of the explicit ideas of a message. It will deemphasize (1) the transient activation of implied ideas and (2) reconstructive memory phenomena. The remainder is organized as follows. Section II asks whether certain inferences accompany comprehension or are delayed until a later time. Section III inspects several taxonomies of inference that have been presented and identifies several dimensions that help to organize these taxonomies. Section IV examines text and reader variables that guide inference processing. Section V applies modern theories of text representation and comprehension to the problem of inference. Finally, Section VI is a summary.

II. LOCUS OF INFERENCE: A BRIEF REVIEW

In the early 1970s, Bransford and colleagues conducted a number of studies that set the stage for an intensive examination of the problem of inference. In one of these studies, Bransford and Franks' (1971) subjects heard an initial list of simple sentences such as *The ants ate the sweet jelly,* and, *The ants in the kitchen ate the jelly.* In all, the subjects heard six sentences derived from each of four complex ideas, such as, *The ants in the kitchen ate the sweet jelly which was on the table.* In an unexpected recognition test, the subjects heard sentences consistent with the complex ideas, but only a subset of which had been included verbatim in the original list. The most striking result was that a subject's tendency to report recognizing a test sentence was influenced most by the complexity of that sentence. For example, a relatively complex item such as, *The ants in the kitchen ate the sweet jelly,* was recognized more confidently than, *The jelly was sweet.* In contrast, whether or not the sentence had occurred in the original list did not have much impact on recognition.

Bransford and Franks (1971) concluded that the internal representation of the original sentences could best be characterized not as a list of sentences but as a number of holistic networks of ideas. According to this view, the reason that recognition confidence was greatest for the complex test sentences was that these were the ones that most closely resembled the stored networks. These results had some clear implications about inference in comprehension: Because Bransford and Franks (1971) showed that people integrate the ideas conveyed by a sequence of sentences, it seemed quite plausible that the resulting mental representation of these sentences might include some additional ideas, ones implied by the content of the message.

Johnson, Bransford, and Solomon (1973) conducted a study to investigate this issue. Their subjects heard messages including sentences such as, *John was pounding the nail when his father came out to watch him.* In a subsequent recognition test, the subjects heard either an identical ("old") sentence or one such as, *John was using the hammer when his father came out to watch him* (an "inference" sentence). The inference sentence referred to the concept hammer, which was implied but not stated in the original message. The subjects actually reported recognizing inference test sentences marginally more confidently than old sentences.

Johnson *et al.* (1973) were careful to identify two explanations of this result. First, the subject might have inferred the use of the hammer when they encountered the original message. In this case, the inference test sentence would resemble the internal representation of the message, and subjects would recognize it. Alternatively, the inference about the hammer might have occurred at the time of the recognition test. Johnson *et al.* (1973) stated that their results did not permit the resolution of this issue. However, these two alternative views concerning the "locus of inference," the inference-on-input and inference-at-retrieval interpretations, became the focus of many investigations.

In this vein, Paris and Lindauer (1976) conducted a developmental study of inference processes in comprehension. In one experiment, children in grades one, three, and five heard a list of sentences, each of which included either an explicit or an implicit instrument. For example, one sentence was either, *The truck driver stirred the coffee in his cup with a spoon,* or the same sentence with the phrase about the spoon omitted. Later, the children performed a cued recall task. They were given words, like *spoon,* that were either stated or implied by the sentences and were asked to state the sentence that the cue reminded them of. While first grade students performed better with explicit than with implicit cues, cue type had little effect for fifth grade students.

Paris and Lindauer (1976) reasoned that the older children inferred the implicit instruments during the listening task. Then, when presented with an implicit cue like *spoon,* these children had direct access to the internal representation of the corresponding sentence. The authors concluded that inference processing increases with developmental maturity.

By concluding that their older subjects inferred the instruments during comprehension, Paris and Lindauer (1976) favored the inference-on-input hypothesis discussed earlier. There are, however, two additional ways in which an implicit recall cue might effectively prompt recall. First, suppose that a child has *not* inferred an implicit instrument, but rather has encoded only the explicit ideas of an acquisition sentence. Then, when presented with an implicit cue like *spoon,* the child would be reminded of an action usually performed with a spoon, like stirring. This, in turn, would permit the recall of the sentence. Second, given an implicit cue, the child could simply recall as many of the acquisition sentences as possible (there were only eight of them) and respond with the one that best fit the prompt.

Without questioning Paris and Lindauer's conclusions concerning developmental trends, it may be argued that the mechanism they posited for the effectiveness of an implicit cue is in doubt. It could be that the older children, like the younger ones, did not reliably infer the implicit instruments during comprehension. Instead, the older children may have been more adept at retrieving the correct sentence because they recognized the relationship between the instrument and the corresponding action.

Corbett and Dosher (1978) performed a study which was very pertinent to these points. In one experiment, adult subjects read sentences that included probable or improbable instruments, or no instrument at all (the "implicit" condition). For example, the subjects read, *The accountant dried his hands* (implicit instrument), *The accountant dried his hands with the towel* (probable instrument), or, *The accountant dried his hands with the shirt* (improbable instrument).

After reading, the subjects received recall cues that included the probable instrument or no instrument. The most interesting result for the present considerations concerns the impact of the probable cue, *towel*. The probable cues prompted the recall of both the probable instrument sentences and the implicit instrument sentences about 72% of the time. This outcome replicated Paris and Lindauer's (1976) findings for fifth grade children. However, Corbett and Dosher (1978) also found that the probable instrument reminded subjects of the improbable instrument, *The accountant dried his hands with the shirt,* 73% of the time! (In contrast, baseline mean recall in the absence of an instrument cue was 63%).

This result carried strong implications for the interpretation of Paris and Lindauer's (1976) findings. When one reads, *The accountant dried his hands with the shirt,* there is no reason to draw the conflicting inference that a towel was used. Therefore, if *towel* is an effective recall cue for this sentence, it must be because *towel* reminds the reader of the activity of drying. Similarly, *towel* may prompt the recall of the implicit instrument sentence, *The accountant dried his hands,* by virtue of the "backward association" from *towel* to *drying* rather than by direct access to an earlier inference about the towel.

It should be noted that Corbett and Dosher's (1978) finding did not, of itself, discount the inference-on-input hypothesis. What it did show is that the effectiveness of an implicit recall cue does not clearly distinguish between the inference-on-input and inference-at-retrieval hypotheses. However, Corbett and Dosher (1978) presented other evidence that bore more directly on this issue. They argued that if people make inferences about the use of probable instruments, then they should include the instruments in their written recall of the sentences. Across three experiments and a variety of conditions, the investigators found that people seldom write down an implicit instrument like *towel* after having read, *The accountant dried his hands.* This result was obtained even when the subjects had the opportunity to forget the exact wording of the original sentences, such as when they initially read 40 complex sentences, and recall was delayed until 30 min later.

This last result clearly poses difficulties for the inference-on-input hypothesis. If people infer the use of a towel during reading, then "towel" should be included in the internal representation of the sentence. This should result in people "recalling" the use of the towel, even though it was not directly mentioned.

Singer (1979a,b) used a different technique to evaluate the inference-on-input and inference-at-retrieval hypotheses. Singer (1979a) had subjects read 20 to 24 three-sentence passages that stated or implied the use of high-probability instruments [e.g., *The worker hit the nail (with the hammer)*]. Afterwards, the subjects were timed while they made judgments about test sentences that always mentioned the instrument. The logic of the study was that if a person has inferred an instrument during reading (inference on input), it should take no longer to make an accurate judgment about the instrument than if the instrument has been mentioned explicitly. However, if the inference is not reliably drawn during reading (inference at retrieval), then it should take longer to judge implicit instruments than it does explicit instruments.

Across four experiments, Singer (1979a) varied the test task (recognition vs verification), the reading-test retention interval (0–20 min), and the degree of similarity between the message and the test sentence. Regardless of these manipulations, the readers needed between 194 and 263 msec longer to make correct judgments about implicit than explicit instruments. This outcome was viewed as being consistent with the inference-at-retrieval hypothesis that states people do not reliably infer probable instruments during reading.

In another study, Singer (1979b, Experiment 4) extended the study of inference processing in several ways. The subjects read "antecedent" sentences and then verified a test sentence after each one. The antecedents stated or implied a particular concept. In contrast with previous studies, these concepts could fill the agent or patient semantic "cases" (Braine & Wells, 1978; Fillmore, 1968) as well as the instrument case. Furthermore, the test sentence could be true or false. For example, the sequence, *the tooth was filled painlessly, a principal filled the tooth* was a false implicit item. Singer (1979b) found that, across the six conditions obtained by crossing truth × case, subjects always needed more time to verify implicit than explicit test sentences. This outcome was consistent with the results of Singer (1979a).

Frederiksen (1975) used a different technique to evaluate the inference-on-input and inference-at-retrieval hypotheses. His subjects listened to a complex passage four times and performed a free recall task after each presentation. The subjects' recall protocols included many ideas implied by the passage. Frederiksen argued that if the inferences were drawn *on input*, then they would become integrated with and, therefore, be indistinguishable from the explicit ideas of the passage. As a result, the inferences drawn during early presentations of the passage would not tend to drop out of the recall protocols that the subjects produced after later presentations. As a result, the number of inferred ideas would accumulate as a function of learning–recall trials. Accordingly, the number of inferences produced in recall would be either positively or negligibly correlated to the number of explicit passage ideas recalled (reproductions).

Conversely, Frederiksen proposed that if the inferences in question were drawn *at retrieval time,* then the number of inferences should decrease over learning-recall trials. For example, in the extreme, if the subject eventually learned an entire passage by rote, then no inferences should be intruded.

Because Frederiksen's results showed predominantly positive correlations between inferences and reproductions, he concluded that the data supported the inference-on-input hypothesis. However, there are several difficulties with this interpretation that call Frederiksen's conclusion into question. First, the proposal that the subjects should have drawn fewer inferences as they recalled more explicit ideas is questionable. This proposal might be reasonable if a reader has almost completely memorized a passage and can sense that the explicit ideas he or she generates almost exhaust the passage. However, Frederiksen's subjects reproduced only 45% of the concepts of the 503-word passage by trial 4. There was, therefore, little reason to draw fewer inferences in recall after the fourth presentation. One could, in fact, argue that the more explicit ideas one recalled, the more inferences these ideas might suggest. In this case, a positive correlation of inferences and reproductions would be consistent with the inference-at-retrieval hypothesis.

Second, Frederiksen did not take into account the possibility that inferences generated by a subject at retrieval time may themselves become integrated into the meaning of the passage. Thus, the fact that the frequency of inferences did not diminish over four recall trials might reflect retrieval inference processes rather than encoding inference processes. While Frederiksen's results provide insight into the evolving nature of the internal representation of a complex message, they do not resolve the problem of the locus of inference.

In summary, these studies revealed that listeners and readers may be quite restricted in the number and types of inferences that they can draw during comprehension (i.e., "on input"). Thus, the locus-of-inference problem was revealed to be a complex issue, one which will receive further consideration in this article. The studies examined in this section also contributed to the refinement of the principles of inference processing and the methods available to study these principles. These issues will be pursued in the remainder of this article.

III. TAXONOMIES AND DIMENSIONS OF INFERENCE

A. Taxonomies

The studies considered in Section II addressed the issue of the locus of inference, but did so only with reference to certain types of inference. In particular, many of those investigations framed their questions in the context of inferences about the instruments used to perform certain actions (Corbett & Dosher, 1978; Johnson *et al.,* 1973; Paris & Lindauer, 1976; Singer, 1979a). However, in the latter part of the 1970s, lists or taxonomies of inference were presented by several investigators (Clark, 1977; Harris & Monaco, 1978; Rieger, 1975; Trabasso, 1981). These endeavors were motivated by the assumption that different categories of inference might play different roles in language comprehension. Table I shows the list of inference types identified by each author (Trabasso's list is a summary of that of Warren, Nicholas, & Trabasso, 1979). The total number of categories listed is 44. From these, no fewer than 20 inference categories can easily be identified.

An examination of the inference categories listed in Table I reveals them to be extremely heterogeneous in nature. Consider briefly a few of these categories. (1) Clark's "necessary and inducible roles" and Harris and Monaco's "implied instruments and locations" concern the concepts that are implied by the use of particular verbs. For example, *sweeping a floor* implies the use of the instrument *broom.* (2) Categories such as causes, reasons, motives, and consequences refer to the relations that exist among the events described in a text. Frequently, a sentence, such as *The open wine bottle tipped over,* implied its cause or consequence, such as the spilling of the wine. (3) Several of Clark's (1977) categories address the inferences necessary to link a word with an earlier referent. For example, to understand *Anne opened the book, she read the first chapter,* one must infer that the pronoun, *she,* refers to *Anne.* (4) Finally, readers must infer the speech act of a sentence (Harris and Monaco's "indirect speech acts," Rieger's "utterance intent" inferences). The utterance *it's cold in here* has the direct speech act of an assertion but it may function indirectly as a request to close the window.

Clark (1977) suggested a major reason for the lack of organization and completeness in such taxonomies, namely, the absence of a theory to generate or explain the taxonomy. Actually, there are several theoretical

TABLE I
Cumulative Taxonomy of Inference Categories

Clark (1977)	Harris and Monaco (1978)	Rieger (1975)	Trabasso (1981)
Direct reference by identity	Sequential events	Specification	Informational
Direct reference by pronominalization	Implied cause	Causation	Spatial or temporal
	Implied instrument	Resultative	Script based
Direct reference by epithet	Implied location	Motivational	World knowledge
Direct reference by set membership	Antonymous adjectives	Enablement	Evaluative
	Indirect speech acts	Function	
Necessary parts	Rhetorical questions	Enablement/prediction	
Probable parts	Nonfactitive verbs	Missing enablement	
Inducible parts	Conditional linguistic	Intervention	
Necessary roles	reasoning	Action/prediction	
Inducible roles		Knowledge propagation	
Reasons		Normative	
Causes		State duration	
Consequences		Feature	
Concurrences		Situation	
Subsequences		Utterance intent	

formulations that are pertinent to subsets of the categories in Table I. The case grammar proposals of Fillmore (1968) emphasize the importance of inferences about agents, objects, instruments, and locations. Linguistic theories concerning speech acts (Clark & Clark, 1977, Chapter 3) suggest that it is important for the listener to infer the direct and indirect speech acts of utterances. Models of the representation of the meaning of complex texts, like story grammars, lead to the identification of relations, like cause and enablement, which may have to be inferred (Mandler & Johnson, 1977; Schank & Abelson, 1977; Trabasso, Secco, & van den Broek, 1984).

In general, however, there is no single theory to which all of the inference categories in Table I can be traced. Furthermore, there is the danger that the proliferation of inference categories may simply overwhelm the researcher, rather than help to organize this domain of study. Furthermore, it is possible to identify a number of dimensions and distinctions that impose some order on the categories of Table I. These dimensions will be considered next.

B. Inference Dimensions and Distinctions

Some language comprehension researchers have explicitly identified dimensions and distinctions that help to organize inference categories such as those shown in Table I. Additional dimensions of this sort may be extracted from the inference literature. The rest of this section examines four such dimensions, including logical vs pragmatic inference, forward vs backward inference, type of implied relation, and implicational probability. An attempt will be made to determine how these dimensions help to organize categories of inference. Finally, the psychological validity of the dimensions will be examined.

1. Logical versus Pragmatic Inferences

The taxonomy of inference that Harris and Monaco (1978) presented was based on a distinction that they drew between logical and pragmatic inference. Logical inferences are based upon the rules of some formal domain and are 100% certain (Harris & Monaco, 1978). For example, the sentence, *Susan had nine oranges and she gave two to Bill* logically implies that Susan was left with seven oranges. We can be certain of this because of our knowledge of arithmetic. In contrast, pragmatic implications are based upon a person's knowledge of the world and are not certain. For example, *Joe dropped the egg* implies that the egg broke, but there is some probability, however small, that the egg did not break.

The logical-pragmatic distinction appears to be a useful one. First, many of the types of inference listed in Table I clearly belong to one of these categories or the other. For example, one's ability to draw inferences about agents, objects, instruments, locations, enablements, causes, consequences, and parts are all based on world knowledge, and so constitute pragmatic inferences. On the other hand, *Jenny saw an ant* logically implies *Jenny saw an insect,* based on category relations. Similarly, spatial relations permit *B is to the right of A* to be logically inferred from *A is to the left of B*. Thus, the logical–pragmatic distinction helps to organize inference types.

A second advantage of the logical–pragmatic distinction is that it alerted Harris and Monaco to certain subtle distinctions that might otherwise have been overlooked. For example, the negation of a "discrete" adjective (*not open*) logically implies its antonym (*closed*). In contrast, the negation of a "continuous" adjective (*not hot*) may imply the antonym (*cold*), but that implication is pragmatic rather than logical. This is true because the object in question might be lukewarm rather than cold.

2. Forward versus Backward Inference

A second distinction that has been identified by inference researchers is forward vs backward inference (Clark, 1977; Just & Carpenter, 1978; Thorndyke, 1976). Consider the sequence, *the pitcher threw toward first base, the ball sailed into right field.* Even though the second sentence does not repeat any of the words of the first sentence, the sequence does not strike the reader as disjoint. This is because one can easily see the relation between *ball* in the second half of the sequence, and what precedes it. The reader accomplishes this by working *backward* in the text and deciding that the ball is what the pitcher threw. Backward inferences preserve the coherence of a text.

In contrast, the isolated sentence, *The pitcher threw toward first base* also permits the inference that a ball was thrown. In this case, however, the reader must extrapolate, or work *forward*, from the text to infer the presence of a baseball.

Like the logical–pragmatic distinction, the forward–backward distinction helps to organize the cumulative inference taxonomy shown in Table I. For example, an especially important type of backward inference is direct reference. As discussed earlier, finding the referent of the current word in a text involves inference processes (Clark, 1977; see also Kintsch *et al.*, 1975). More particularly, however, identifying a referent requires that the reader search *backward* through the text representation. Some of the factors that guide the identification of a referent have been addressed by Anderson and Hastie (1974), Clark and Lucy (1975), Corbett and Chang (1983), and Garrod and and Sanford (1977).

In his inference taxonomy, Clark (1977) specifically addressed the inference processes of linking or "bridging" of the current sentence to what has preceded. He called the set of resulting inferred propositions *implicatures,* another name for backward inferences. An examination of Table I reveals, however, that the semantic relations underlying Clark's implicatures might be pertinent to forward as well as backward inferences. For example, from the sequence, *Joe dropped the egg on the floor, the egg broke,* one can indeed arrive at the consequence implicature that dropping the egg resulted in its breaking. However, if one read, *Joe dropped the egg on the floor,* it would still be possible to conclude that the egg broke, which, in this case, would be a forward consequence inference.

3. Type of Implied Relation

Table I identifies types of inference that deal with a wide variety of semantic relations. For example, several of the authors of the taxonomies mentioned inferences concerning semantic cases, that is, the sorts of relations that link a concept to its governing verb (Fillmore, 1968). Clark's "roles," Harris and Monaco's "implied instruments and locations," and Rieger's "specifications" all refer to inferences about case relations. Other categories in Table I refer to the relations that link the propositions in the representation of complex texts. These include reasons, causes, consequences, concurrences, subsequences, sequential events, motivations, and enablement.

It is not suggested that these types of relations constitute an ordered dimension with regard to the problem of inference. However, there are important reasons to distinguish among them. For example, it might be argued that certain of these relations, such as cause, are particularly important for the understanding of a text (Schank & Abelson, 1977). If this is accurate, then it is possible that readers will more reliably draw inferences about these important relations than ones that might be judged more peripheral to text meaning.

4. Implicational Probability

Another dimension of inference that can be detected in Table I, especially in Clark's (1977) list, is implicational probability. For example, Clark distinguishes among implicatures about necessary, probable, and inducible parts. He calls a ceiling, windows, and a chandelier necessary, probable, and inducible parts of a room, respectively. Suppose that these three words are alternately substituted in the frame, *Carol entered the room, the X was dirty.* In each case, the resulting implicature would be *the room has an X*, but the ease of constructing this implicature would be a function of the probability of a room having an X.

Implicational probability applies to forward as well as backward inference. If one read only, *Carol entered the room,* it would be more reasonable to draw a forward inference about the room having a ceiling than a chandelier. Similarly, probability is pertinent to many of the types of implied relations discussed earlier. For example, implications about instruments, locations, causes, and consequences may be of high or low probability. This, in turn, may have an impact on whether or not the corresponding inference is drawn by the reader.

However, implicational probability is not relevant to the logical vs pragmatic inference distinction because logical implications are, by definition, certain. Thus, only pragmatic implications vary on the dimension of probability. This reveals that the dimensions under consideration are not entirely orthogonal to one another.

C. Evaluating the Inference Dimensions

1. Dimensional Organization of the Cumulative Inference Taxonomy

To briefly review, four dimensions of implication either have been identified by previous investigators or may be extracted from inference taxonomies: logical–pragmatic, forward–backward, implied relation, and probability. One test of the usefulness of these dimensions is to determine whether they help to organize inference categories such as those listed in Table I.

It is convenient to consider pragmatic and logical inferences separately. Table II shows a three-dimensional space of pragmatic inference defined by the dimensions forward–backward, implied relation, and probability. Three rather diverse types of implied relation have been selected for the purpose of illustration, namely, parts, case (role), and cause. The body of the table shows inference categories that correspond to the intersection of the "values" of the three dimensions. These inference categories are ones that are listed in Table I or that have been studied empirically.

Several of Clark's (1977) implicature types serve as clear examples of backward implication, examined in the first row of Table II. The top left-hand cell of the table refers to inferences about high-probability parts. This is illustrated by Clark's (1977) "necessary parts." For example, sequence (1) below permits the backward inference that the keys in question belonged to the piano. Analogously, Clark's (1977) necessary role implicature fits the backward–high-probability–case cell of the table. For example, sequence (2) permits the backward inference that the farmer used the high-probability instrument, axe.

(1a) The musician sat down at the piano.

(1b) The keys felt cold.

(2a) The farmer chopped the wood.

(2b) The axe was dull.

While Clark (1977) did not identify a category of implicature concerning necessary causes, there are some events with such causes. Thus, the

TABLE II

Application of Inference Dimensions to Categories of Pragmatic Inference[a]

| | Probability | | | | | |
| | High | | | Low | | |
Inference	Parts	Case	Cause	Parts	Case	Cause
Backward	Necessary parts implicature[b]	Necessary role implicature[b]	Necessary cause implicature	Inducible parts[b]	Inducible roles[b]	Inducible cause
Forward	Implied parts[c]	Implied instrument[d]	Implied cause[d]	—	—	—

[a] See text for explanation.

[b] Clark (1977).

[c] Chafe (1972).

[d] Harris and Monaco (1978).

sequence, *the temperature rose above freezing, the snowman began to melt,* exemplifies what might be called a necessary cause implicature.

Even when the relation among concepts has a low a priori probability, certain juxtapositions of these concepts in a text may lead to corresponding backward inferences. Thus, the exemplars of the low-probability, backward inference quadrant of Table II are inducible parts, inducible instruments, and inducible causes, respectively. For example, *the hikers put out the bonfire, the sand was blown on their clothes,* suggests that the fire was extinguished with sand, even though sand is a low-probability *instrument* for extinguishing a bonfire (Singer, 1977).

The second row of Table II concerns forward inferences. Following Harris and Monaco (1978), the high-probability forward inference cells of Table II are labeled implied parts, implied instrument, and implied cause, respectively. Chafe (1972) suggested that one may infer the existence of the highly probable parts of an object under discussion. For example, if one is told about a bicycle, it is possible to infer that it has a frame. Similarly, the sentence, *Captain Ahab shot the whale,* permits a forward inference about the instrument *harpoon* (Harris & Monaco, 1978). Finally, the sentence, *The snowman melted,* implies that the cause was that the temperature rose above freezing.

The lower right-hand quadrant of Table II is empty. The rationale for this is that it is considered unlikely that a reader will draw a forward inference about a low-probability concept or relation. If one reads that a snowman melted, it is unlikely that one would infer that a fire was lit near the snowman.

The application of the three dimensions of Table II to logical inferences is more complicated. One reason for this is that many logical inferences that may accompany text comprehension constitute examples of complex problem solving (Clark, 1977; Singer, 1976), and there is no limit to their variety. Nevertheless, some of the logical inference types listed in Table I can be interpreted in relation to the dimensions under consideration. Consider the forward–backward dimension. To understand the sequence, *Bob noticed the grasshopper in the sink, the insect startled him,* one must infer that the category name, *insect* refers to its member, *grasshopper.* This constitutes a *backward* logical inference, based on the principles of set membership (Clark, 1977). In contrast, *The lamp is to the right of the ashtray* permits the reader to infer that the ashtray is to the left of the lamp. This is a *forward* logical inference, which fits Trabasso's (1981) category of spatial inferences. The probability dimension, on the other hand, does not apply to logical implications, all of which are 100% certain.

Some inference types shown in Table I, such as indirect speech acts, do not seem to be captured by the dimensions under consideration. In general, however, these dimensions do help to organize the many types of inference that have been considered in the literature. As such, they play a useful taxonomic role.

2. *Psychological Validity of Dimensions of Implication*

Another important test of the proposed dimensions of implication concerns their psychological validity. Although there are many ways in which an inference may be reflected in behavior, the following discussion will ask whether the four dimensions under consideration help to distinguish between inferences that accompany comprehension and those that are delayed or not drawn at all.

Of the four dimensions, the forward–backward distinction appears to have the greatest impact on inference processing. Clark (1977) has argued that the coherence of a text depends upon the computation of bridging or backward inferences that link the ideas in the present sentence with what has preceded. Evidence that backward inferences occur "on line" has taken several forms: (1) people need extra time to read a sentence requiring a backward inference, (2) the time needed to verify certain backward inferences is approximately equal to verification time for corresponding direct statements, (3) people incorrectly report recognizing sentences expressing backward inferences, and (4) the ideas that are integrated in the course of backward inference processing act as powerful recall cues for one another. Each of these types of evidence will be considered in turn.

a. Reading Time. Haviland and Clark (1974) reasoned that the time needed to draw a backward inference should be reflected in sentence reading time. Their subjects viewed sentences such as either (3a) or (3b) followed by (3d). The term *beer* in (3d) provides direct access to its antecedent in (3a). In contrast, to understand (3d) in the context of (3b), one must draw a backward inference, such as "the picnic supplies included beer." Accordingly, Haviland and Clark (1974) predicted that reading time for sentence (3d) would be greater in the context of (3b) than (3a). The data clearly supported this prediction.

(3a) We got some beer out of the trunk.
(3b) We checked the picnic supplies.
(3c) Ed was desperate for a beer.
(3d) The beer was warm.

To show that the reading time advantage of sequence (3a)–(3d) was not due merely to the repetition of the word *beer,* Haviland and Clark (1974, Experiment 2) examined sequences such as (3c)–(3d). According to the authors, understanding sentence (3d) in this sequence required a backward inference such as "Ed did get a beer." This is because sentence (3c) does not specify the existence of a particular beer. As predicted, comprehension time for sentence (3d) in this sequence exceeded that in sequence (3a)–(3d). This was in spite of the repetition of *beer* in (3c)–(3d).

b. Inference Verification Time. If a particular inference is drawn during the course of comprehension, then it should take no longer to later verify a sentence expressing that inference than a corresponding sentence that expresses an explicit idea of the message. Singer (1980; Singer & Ferreira, 1983) argued that backward inferences are likely to accompany comprehension because they preserve the coherence of a message. In contrast, corresponding forward inferences do not fulfill this function. To test these hypotheses, Singer (1980) asked subjects to read brief texts, such as (4a), (4b), and (4c). Sequence (4a) states that the tooth was pulled by a dentist. To understand the second sentence of (4b), one needs to draw the backward inference that the dentist pulled the tooth. Finally, sequence (4c) permits a forward inference about a dentist, but this inference does not contribute to the coherence of the message.

(4a) The dentist pulled the tooth painlessly. The patient liked the new method.

(4b) The tooth was pulled painlessly. The dentist used a new method.

(4c) The tooth was pulled painlessly. The patient liked the new method.

(4d) The dentist pulled the tooth painlessly.

After reading sequence (4a), (4b), or (4c), the subject had to verify statement (4d). Mean correct verification times of 1884, 1897, and 2136 msec were measured in the explicit, backward inference, and forward inference conditions, respectively. The approximately equal verification times in the explicit and backward inference conditions supported the hypothesis that the backward inferences under inspection had accompanied comprehension. In contrast, the forward inferences were apparently drawn at retrieval time. Singer and Ferreira (1983) obtained a similar result in the study of inferences about the consequences of events and actions.

c. Incorrect Recognition of Backward Inferences. Thorndyke (1976) examined his subjects' recognition of complex backward inferences. The subjects read stories that included sentences such as (5a). According to Thorndyke, the understanding of (5a) might lead to inferences such as those expressed by (5b) and (5c).

(5a) The hamburger chain owner was afraid that his love for french fries would ruin his marriage.

(5b) The hamburger chain owner's wife didn't like french fries.

(5c) The hamburger chain owner was very fat.

(5d) The hamburger chain owner decided to join weight-watchers in order to save his marriage.

At a later point in the story, sentence (5d) was encountered. This sentence is consistent with inference (5c), but not with (5b). Thorndyke argued that understanding (5d) should have the impact of consolidating earlier inferences with which it is consistent and eliminating inconsistent ones. In a subsequent recognition test, the subjects (incorrectly) reported recognizing consistent inferences, such as (5c), 58% of the time, whereas inconsistent ones such as (5b) were recognized only 6% of the time. This outcome supported the proposal that readers work backward from sentences such as (5d) to evaluate competing inferences. Singer (1980, Experiments 1 and 2) also provided evidence for the incorrect recognition of test sentences that express backward inferences.

d. Cued Recall. In many circumstances, the complex relation between a target sentence and its antecedent must be inferred. For example, a complete appreciation of sentence (6c) in the context of (6a) requires the backward inference that the cat leaping on the table *caused* Linda to put it outside (Schank & Abelson, 1977; Trabasso *et al.,* 1984).

Black and Bern (1981) proposed that if the ideas underlying (6a) and (6c) are integrated by a causal inference, then sentence (6a) should later function as an effective cue for the recall of (6c). They contrasted sequence (6a)–(6c) with sequence (6b)–(6c). Black and Bern considered the temporal relationship that exists between (6b) and (6c) to be less crucial to text coherence than a causal relationship. Therefore, (6b) and (6c) are less likely to be linked by backward inference.

(6a) The cat leapt up on the kitchen table.
(6b) The cat rubbed against the kitchen table.
(6c) Linda picked up the cat and put it outside.

Black and Bern's (1981) subjects read four stories that included causal and temporal sequences of sentences. After a 15-min intervening task, the subjects received causal and temporal recall prompts such as (6a) and (6b), respectively. Causal antecedents prompted recall of their targets 58% of the time vs 43% for temporal antecedents, a significant difference. This outcome supported the hypothesis that readers frequently draw backward causal inferences.

In contrast to backward inferences, the reader's ability to draw forward inferences during comprehension appears subject to the restrictions of processing demands. There simply is inadequate time to draw all reasonable inferences during comprehension. In this vein, evidence that forward inferences do not accompany reading has been provided by Belmore, Yates, Bellack, Jones, and Rosenquist (1982), Corbett & Dosher (1978), Downey (1979), Just and Carpenter (1978), Singer (1979a,b, 1980), and Singer and Ferreira (1983).

Let us next consider the dimension of implicational probability. It might seem reasonable to hypothesize that probable inferences will accompany comprehension and less probable ones will not. As discussed earlier, however, there is evidence that people do not reliably draw forward inferences during comprehension about even strongly implied ideas (Corbett & Dosher, 1978; Singer, 1976, 1979a,b; Singer & Ferreira, 1983). Conversely, Clark (1977) argued that backward inferences (implicatures) *will* accompany the encoding of a message, regardless of implicational probability. For example, the probability of a room having a chandelier may be low. However, upon reading, *Sue walked into the room, the chandeliers sparkled brightly,* one readily infers that the room had chandeliers. Thus, it does not seem that the dimension of implicational probability itself determines whether or not a particular inference will accompany comprehension.

With regard to the dimension of "type of relation," many investigators have proposed that the ideas that contribute to the causal structure of a text are particularly crucial to meaning (e.g., Schank & Abelson, 1977). Accordingly, it might be proposed that people will reliably infer causes, motives, and reasons during reading, but not roles or parts. Once again, however, existing evidence does not support this conjecture. Singer has reported that people do not draw forward inferences about probable roles, such as agent, patient, and instrument (Singer, 1979a,b), nor about at least one type of idea that contributes to causal structure, namely, consequences (Singer & Ferreira, 1983). In another study, Downey (1979) similarly reported that readers did not draw forward inferences about a character's motives. Thus, it does not appear that the type of relation linking an idea with its implication determines whether a corresponding inference will result. It should be acknowledged, however, that research concerning this point is far from complete.

Consider, finally, the logical–pragmatic dichotomy. Because logical implications are certain, it might be hypothesized that they result in inferences more reliably than pragmatic implications. However, there are many reasons that this cannot be true. First, the computation of all logical inferences would result in a "combinatorial" explosion of inferences (Charniak, 1975; Schank, 1978; Singer, 1980). For example, if one reads that *Cindy ate a carrot,* it is unlikely that the resulting message representation would include the proposition that "Cindy ate a vegetable." The number of such logical inferences is unlimited, and readers do not have adequate cognitive resources to pursue the logical implications of every facet of a message.

Second, many logical inferences may be beyond the skill of a particular reader or be too time-consuming to permit an inference during encoding. If one reads, *Fred told the teacher the derivative of* x^2, the inference that the answer "$2x$" was provided depends on one's knowledge of calculus.

There is one interesting domain of logical implication that, with at least moderate reliability, does result in inference processing during encoding. It concerns situations in which a text orders objects or concepts along one or more dimensions. In one study, Potts (1972) asked subjects to read passages that included sequences such as, *the bear was smarter than the hawk, the hawk was smarter than the wolf, and the wolf was smarter than the deer.* Later, it took subjects less time to verify an implied statement such as, *the bear was smarter than the deer,* than to verify explicit statements such as, *the wolf was smarter than the deer.* Certainly, such a result can only be understood with reference to some sort of inference processing that accompanies the initial encoding (see also Mayer, 1979; Shoben, 1976).

This phenomenon has been explained with reference to a "constructive" analysis (e.g., Trabasso & Nicholas, 1980). This states that the reader constructs an internal model of the dimensions under consideration, locating each object on each dimension. Comparisons between objects far apart on a dimension will be less time-consuming than comparisons between adjacent ones because the distal objects differ more from one another than do adjacent objects. A similar effect has been detected with reference to people's knowledge of the world. It takes less time to agree that *an elephant is bigger than a mouse* than *a squirrel is bigger than a mouse* (Rips, Shoben, & Smith, 1973; Schaeffer & Wallace, 1970).

Readers appear to construct similar sorts of representations when they are informed about the relative spatial location of objects. Told, for example, that "three turtles were on a log and a fish swam beneath *them,*" listeners later incorrectly recognized a test sentence that stated that the fish swam beneath *it* (i.e., the log) (Bransford, Barclay, & Franks, 1972). The authors concluded that the listeners constructed an internal representation of the relative positions of the objects described.

In general, however, the logical–pragmatic distinction does not seem to identify which inferences will accompany comprehension. Logically implied categories or problem solutions often do not accompany comprehension. Conversely, pragmatic inferences *may* occur during encoding, especially when they contribute to coherence.

D. Conclusions

Existing evidence would thus suggest that of the four dimensions of inference examined here, only the forward–backward dichotomy can be judged to have psychological validity with reference to the locus-of-inference problem. However, this conclusion would be different if the criteria of psychological validity included the reader's ability to draw an inference *after* the original message was encoded. Using this framework, the probability dimension would now be quite pertinent. If a message has discussed a room, the reader can later confidently conclude that it had walls even though no such inference had accompanied comprehension. Of course, less probable relations would result in the reader's uncertainty.

In the inspection of inferences after comprehension, Harris (1974) has provided evidence supporting the psychological validity of the logical–pragmatic distinction. He reported that immediately after reading sentences, subjects were highly confident of the truth of their logical implications, but recognized the uncertainty of the truth of pragmatic implications. When the test was delayed by several minutes, however, both logical and pragmatic implications were confidently judged to be true. These results revealed differences in the psychological impact of logical and pragmatic implications (cf. Sulin & Dooling, 1974).

In this section, it has been proposed that at least four dimensions underlie the many types of inference that have been identified by theorists. These four dimensions are logical vs pragmatic inference, forward vs backward inference, type of implied relation, and probability of implication. The four dimensions are not completely orthogonal to one another. For example, the logical–pragmatic distinction is partly confounded with implicational probability.

Of the four dimensions, only the forward–backward distinction appears to indicate which inferences will accompany comprehension. The logical–pragmatic dichotomy and implicational probability dimension are useful in the consideration of which inferences may be drawn after a message has been encoded. However, the dimensions have clear taxonomic value because they help to organize many of the types of inference that have been identified in the literature (Clark, 1977; Harris & Monaco, 1978; Rieger, 1975; Trabasso, 1981). Thus, these dimensions may be useful in formulating incisive questions about inference processing.

IV. FACTORS GUIDING THE DRAWING OF INFERENCES

The present section changes the focus of the investigation from kinds of inference to factors that influence the computation of inferences during comprehension. In Section III, it was suggested that neither the logic nor probability of an inference, nor the type of inferred relation, seems to be paramount in determining whether the inference will be drawn during reading. In contrast, researchers have, by now, examined numerous variables that appear to have considerable impact on inference processing. This section will review some of the pertinent research, distinguishing between those variables which refer to characteristics of texts and those which refer to characteristics of the reader.

A. Text Characteristics

1. Coherence Requirements

One of the dimensions of inference identified in Section III was that of forward vs backward inferences. To review, if one reads, *The patient was examined at the hospital,* one might draw the forward inference that the patient was examined by a doctor. In contrast, consider the sequence, *the patient was examined at the hospital, the doctor prescribed some medicine.* In the latter case, the backward inference that the doctor examined the patient is necessary to preserve the coherence of the sequence.

The forward–backward continuum was considered as a dimension of inference in Section III because it had been so identified by inference researchers. However, in contrast with the other three dimensions, the forward–backward dichotomy refers more to a characteristic of texts than to distinct kinds of inferences. The characteristic in question concerns the role of an inference in contributing to text coherence.

The psychological validity of the forward–backward distinction has already been considered in Section III and will not be reexamined in detail here. There is considerable evidence that backward inferences about a wide variety of relations do accompany comprehension while comparable forward inferences are not drawn on line. In fact, many recent studies of inference processes have examined only backward inferences, explicitly or implicitly pointing out that backward inferences play the greater role in comprehension (e.g., Black & Bern, 1981; Hayes-Roth & Thorndyke, 1979; Hayes-Roth & Walker, 1979; Walker & Meyer, 1980). While focusing on backward inferences, these investigators have examined several other variables that may influence inference processing, including theme, distance, and the reader's task.

2. Theme and Importance

It was argued earlier that processing limitations prohibit the reader from drawing all of the reasonable inferences that are suggested by a text. One hypothesis that has been proposed by several investigators is that the inferences accompanying comprehension may predominantly concern the theme of a text rather than its peripheral ideas. In these studies, theme has primarily been defined by invoking certain theories of text representation, such as those of Kintsch (1974) and Meyer (1975) (but see Omanson, 1982). In Kintsch's (1974) system, for example, the propositions underlying a text are assigned to a hierarchical tree or network that represents the meaning of the text. Those propositions at the "higher" levels of the tree are considered to be more theme related. In support of this proposal, Kintsch *et al.* (1975) reported that in free recall of text, high-level propositions are recalled more reliably than low-level propositions. Kintsch *et al.* (1975) referred to this result as the *levels effect*.

To study this "inference-theme" hypothesis, several investigators have inspected Clark's (1977) inference category, "direct reference" (Cirilo, 1981; Cirilo & Foss, 1980; Hayes-Roth & Thorndyke, 1979; Walker & Meyer, 1980). Walker and Meyer (1980) studied the inferences that may result when direct reference is accomplished. Their subjects read a text that included the sentences, *The Spring Episode was the first revolution in Morinthia,* and *All Morinthian revolutions were failures.* Across different text versions, these ideas were either at high or low levels of the text representation, that is, either thematic or peripheral. The subjects were ultimately timed while they judged the truth of implied facts, such as *the Spring Episode was a failure.* As predicted, the subjects were more accurate in their judgments of implications derived from thematic facts than peripheral facts. Furthermore, the subjects needed almost 1 sec more to verify peripheral facts than thematic facts, although this difference was not significant.

In a similar study, Eamon (1978–1979) timed subjects when they judged logical inferences extracted from transitive relations. For example, the subjects read a passage including the sentences, *Corntown is in Lake County,* and, *Lake County is in Montana.* Later, they were timed when they verified true or false implications, such as, *Corntown is in Montana,* or *Corntown is in Idaho.* In different experimental conditions, *Corntown* was either thematized, by frequent reference, or not thematized. Eamon found that verification was faster for implications related to the theme than for those not related to the theme. This result was observed only for true sentences. Eamon also reported that theme-related inferences were verified faster than some sentences that appeared explicitly in the text.

Cirilo (1981) studied the impact of the height of ideas in text structure upon readers' ability to identify their referents. Text components were classified as high or low with reference to the story grammar analysis of Thorndyke (1977). One group of readers was instructed to read the text casually while a second group was instructed to anticipate a recall test. Cirilo predicted that it would be easier to identify the referents of the ideas high in the text structure. In agreement with this expectation, reading times were faster for sentences presenting high instead of low ideas for both subject groups.

Goetz (1977) varied the importance of a text idea by coupling it with different consequences. For example, missing a plane could result in either being late for a business meeting or avoiding death in a plane crash. Goetz' subjects made more accurate judgments about implications concerning the ideas in the important condition than in the unimportant condition.

While thematic variables thus influence a reader's judgments of implied ideas, is it correct to also conclude that these inferences accompany comprehension? There is some evidence to support such a proposal, but it is necessary to be cautious. For example, Walker and Meyer (1980, p. 273) reported that true thematic inferences were verified as quickly as comparable explicit statements. However, this was the case only when the two statements yielding the inference were adjacent to one another in the text. Similarly, Eamon's (1978–1979) subjects verified thematic implications faster than some explicit statements, but the implicit and explicit statements concerned systematically different concepts in a transitive series. Goetz suggested that the best approach "might be to assume that inference can occur at either time (encoding or retrieval), and to study variables which control whether or not inferences will be made at comprehension" (Goetz, 1977, p. 22). Adopting this approach, it is concluded from the evidence reviewed here that theme is such a variable.

The studies that have addressed the inference-theme hypothesis have raised the question of the mechanisms that mediate the influence of theme on inference processing. Cirilo (1981) presented a reasonably detailed proposal concerning this problem. This issue will be taken up in Section V.

3. Distance

One factor that should have a considerable impact on backward inferences in particular is that of distance. That is, it should be easier to identify a word with its referent when the referent has appeared recently (near) in the text, than when it has appeared much earlier (far). The variable of distance has been inspected in several investigations, some of which addressed the theme variable as well.

Hayes-Roth and Thorndyke (1979) manipulated distance by having two related facts appear in the same text or in different texts. The integration of the two facts resulted in logical inferences like those studied by Walker and Meyer (1980) (discussed earlier). Hayes-Roth and Thorndyke's subjects combined the two related facts more accurately in the near condition than far condition. Similarly, Walker and Meyer (1980) used the dependent measures of accuracy and response time to inspect logical inferences resulting from fact integration. Crucial pairs of facts appeared near or far apart in the same text. The subjects were more accurate and faster in judging the implications of near than far facts.

Cirilo (1981) also inspected the influence of distance upon inferences resulting from the identification of a referent. As he predicted, his subjects read target sentences with near referents faster than those with far referents. However, this result was observed only for readers who anticipated a test and not for "casual" readers. Cirilo (1981, pp. 364–365) explained the latter outcome by suggesting that casual readers may be able to extract the general meaning of a text while disregarding some of the fine detail. He argued that attention to this detail is a necessary condition for the appearance of the distance effect.

Erlich and Johnson-Laird's (1982) subjects read descriptions of the relative spatial positions of several objects. The texts were either continuous (such as, *The knife is in front of the pot, the pot is on the left of the glass, the glass is behind the dish*) or discontinuous (such as, *The knife is in front of the pot, the glass is behind the dish, the pot is on the left of the glass*). One feature of the discontinuous sequences was that the second sentence intervened between the third sentence and its referent in the first sentence. Across three experiments, subjects produced more accurate descriptions of the objects described by continuous sequences than discontinuous sequences. In Experiment 3, subjects needed about 4.0 sec more to read the third sentence of discontinuous sequences. While distance was not independent of continuity in this procedure, the results again suggest that distance interferes with integrative inference processes.

4. Interestingness

Consideration of the motivations of readers suggests that the interestingness of a text may guide inference processing. While this hypothesis has not received extensive examination, both Kintsch (1980) and Schank (1978) presented detailed arguments in support of this view. Schank proposed that certain topics and concepts are inherently interesting, such as an invasion, death, danger, or events of personal relevance to the reader. Also interesting are unexpected events. In this vein, most of what usually happens in a restaurant is not interesting. However, if the waiter spills the soup or the diner has forgotten his wallet, there is greater interest by virtue of the fact that these events are unusual in the restaurant context.

Kintsch (1980) placed particular emphasis on the relation between an event and the reader's own knowledge. To be most interesting, a text would have to present ideas that are somewhat, but not overly, familiar to the reader. Kintsch also argued that, to be interesting, a text must present a certain degree of uncertainty.

Both Kintsch and Schank proposed that interestingness should influence both forward and backward inferences. This would result from the fact that the reader is assumed to attend more carefully to that which is interesting. In one study that indirectly bears on this issue, Nezworski, Stein, and Trabasso (1982) varied the role of a specific statement across different versions of a story. In one story, for example, Mary lies to Peter about why she can't play with him. The critical information in the story is that Mary is making a secret trip to buy Peter a birthday present. In different versions of the story, this fact occurred in different information categories, such as "setting," "consequence," or "reaction." Memory for the crucial facts did not differ as a function of the category in which the fact appeared. This contrasted with Mandler and Johnson's (1977) finding that story recall in adults and children varies systematically among story information categories (see also Stein & Glenn, 1979). The result of Nezworski *et al.* (1982) indicates that the interestingness of the content of an idea in a text can have a considerable impact upon its memorability. It is reasonable to propose, in turn, that interestingness will likewise influence inference processing.

B. Reader Characteristics

Readers vary along many dimensions. Because inference processing requires the retrieval of one's knowledge of the world, it follows that inference processing depends on the particular knowledge available to the reader and his or her ability to retrieve it. For example, readers may differ in verbal ability (Hunt, 1978), age (Cohen, 1979; Till & Walsh, 1980) and available cognitive resources (Britton, Holdredge, Curry, & Westbrook, 1979). The present subsection will briefly review the impact of two reader dimensions on inference processing: the task performed by the reader and the knowledge of the reader concerning the topic of a text.

1. Orienting Tasks in Reading

Many investigators have proposed that reading does not refer to a single activity, but rather that one may read with the intention of learning, solving a problem, summarizing, or simply enjoying. Kieras (1981), for example, proposed alternate process models for reading to determine the topic of a text, reading in anticipation of a recall task, and free reading. He provided evidence that reading task has a qualitative impact on the time people take to read different parts of a passage.

Several investigators have specifically examined the effect of the reader's task on inference processing. These studies have invoked the principles of depth of processing (Craik & Lockhart, 1972), transfer-appropriate training (Morris, Bransford, & Franks, 1977), and the more general notion of "orienting tasks."

In a landmark paper, Craik and Lockhart (1972) argued that a stimulus may be processed at deep or shallow levels. In general, deep processing involves the extraction of meaning, while shallow processing entails the examination of the superficial features of a stimulus. In reading, counting the number of nouns in a text would constitute shallow processing, while judging the degree of pleasantness conveyed by a text would exemplify deep processing.

Craik and Lockhart's thesis suggested to investigators of language comprehension that inference processing might be curtailed in shallow tasks. In one study, Schallert (1976) presented completely ambiguous passages to her subjects. For example, one passage could be interpreted as referring either to a baseball game or to work in a glass factory. The subjects were provided with one theme, the other theme, or no theme at all. Furthermore, the subjects were instructed either to judge the degree of ambiguity of the passage (deep task) or to count the number of pronouns (shallow task). In one of the tests that followed, the subjects received test sentences that were related either to the theme they had been told about or to the other theme. As predicted, subjects incorrectly recognized implicational sentences related to the given theme more often than the other theme, but only when they performed the deep task.

Similarly, Till and Walsh's (1980) deep processors rated the pleasantness of sentences that they read, while their shallow processors counted the words in the sentences. Later, the subjects were given, as recall cues, words from the sentences or words implied by the sentences. The deep processors used the implicit cues as effectively as the explicit ones, whereas the shallow processors showed a deficit with the implicit cues. At the very least, it is reasonable to conclude that the shallow processors encoded the meaning of the sentences less effectively than the deep processors.

Morris *et al.* (1977) proposed that shallow processing does not yield inherently weaker memory traces than deep processing, but rather memories that are pertinent to different types of "transfer" tasks. Pursuing this notion of "transfer-appropriate training," Mayer and Cook (1981) asked some subject to repeat (shadow) the words of a passage (about radar) which they heard, while others were simply asked to listen normally (nonshadowers). Afterwards, the subjects were tested on their memory for the wording, syntax, and meaning of the passages as well as on their ability to apply the information of the passage in a new context. The nonshadowers scored better only on the application of the information. The application test required the subject to generalize the information from the passage, which can be viewed as an inferential activity. Conversely, the shadowers were marginally better than the nonshadowers in their memory for the precise wording of the passage. This outcome supported the principle of transfer-appropriate training, and it also elaborated the role of the reader's task on inference processing.

One shortcoming of the depth-of-processing notion is that it seems inevitable that if one prevents a reader from attending to text meaning, inferential elaboration will be curtailed. Some of those who have studied the impact of reading tasks have, therefore, not invoked "depth of processing." Instead, they have attempted to identify specific sets of goals that characterize different reading "orienting tasks" (e.g., Walker & Meyer, 1980; Cirilo, 1981). They have suggested that these goals may guide the construction of quite different internal representations of text meaning. These investigators have offered predictions of qualitatively different patterns of inference processing for different orienting tasks.

Walker and Meyer (1980) (who also examined the factors of theme and distance) instructed one group of subjects simply to read passages at a normal pace. A second group of subjects was instructed to reread the text, if necessary, so that they might learn the details of the passage. "Learners" were more accurate than "readers" in verifying facts implied by the integration of two sentences. The learners also produced these implications more often than the readers in a free-recall task. Finally, the measure of verification time revealed an interesting task × distance interaction. While readers needed about 0.4 sec more to reconcile far than near facts (7.2 sec vs 6.8 sec), learners needed about 4.0 sec more (9.6 sec vs 5.6 sec). Walker and Meyer (1980) concluded that the intention of the learners to acquire the detail of a passage hindered their integration of distant fact pairs. However, the fact that the learners presumably stored the explicit ideas of the text in an effective manner gave them an advantage in integrating these facts at test time, as evidenced by the accuracy data.

Cirilo (1981) considered the impact of interfact distance and height (thematic relatedness) on inference processing in different reading tasks. He argued that distance should have its greatest impact upon tasks demanding attention to detail. Conversely, height was argued to primarily affect tasks demanding attention to the gist of a text. Cirilo's subjects (1) read text fragments, anticipating a test of verbatim recall (detail), (2) read entire texts, anticipating a comprehension test (detail and gist), or (3) read entire texts as a filler activity in a mock experiment (gist only).

Cirilo (1981) measured the time that subjects took to read certain crucial sentences. As predicted, the task that demanded attention to both detail and gist yielded significant effects of both distance and height, and the gist-only task yielded only an effect of height. These results were somewhat undercut by the fact that the distance effect was not significant for the detail-only task. In spite of this, Cirilo's study provides a good example of the way that reading-task differences may be pursued in the study of inference processing.

2. Knowledge

Inferences result when the reader extrapolates beyond an explicit message by drawing upon his or her knowledge of the world. It is a direct corollary, therefore, that different readers' knowledge will inevitably result in different patterns of inference. Anderson, Reynolds, Schallert, and Goetz (1976b) illustrated the impact of reader knowledge on inference processing. Like Schallert (1976), they created passages that could be interpreted in two distinct ways. One passage, for example, could be interpreted as referring to a prison setting or a wrestling match. It discussed concepts like *lock,* which could refer to a cell door or to a wrestling hold. Anderson *et al.* presented the passages to special samples of subjects, who were expected to see one interpretation but not the other. For example, the members of a weight-lifting class were expected to detect the wrestling interpretation. It was found that, in a multiple-choice task, subjects predominantly reported recognizing implicational test sentences related to their special background. Thus, the reader's knowledge may influence the interpretation of a text, which may in turn affect the reader's inferential processing at the time of retrieval.

Spilich, Vesonder, Chiesi, and Voss (1979) conducted a highly detailed study of the representation of a passage describing a baseball game by listeners either high or low in their knowledge of baseball. Spilich *et al.* identified the statements in their text as being either "game irrelevant" or as pertaining to game setting, to the goal structure of a baseball game, or to game actions. The authors reported that high-knowledge subjects showed better memory for all categories of game-relevant information, whereas there was no difference between high- and low-knowledge subjects on game-irrelevant statements. Thus, these results revealed an important qualitative difference in the representation of text by readers with different degrees of knowledge.

Post, Greene, and Bruder (1982) extended these findings to the study of inference processing by high- and low-knowledge individuals. In this study, the subjects read, rather than heard, descriptions of baseball games. The authors constructed test sentences that, with reference to a baseball game, represented seven different types of inference. For example, test sentences could express the implications of the text about (1) nongame information, like the weather, (2) various types of information pertinent to the game, like whether the shortstop threw the ball to first base, or (3) the "high-order integration" of game information, like how many hits a player had.

The measures of verification accuracy and latency revealed similar patterns of results. High-knowledge readers had large advantages over low-knowledge readers on several categories of game information. However, the two groups did not differ for nongame information or high-order integrations. Because the authors did not test the subjects on explicit text statements as well, it is impossible to determine which inferences of the high-knowledge readers accompanied comprehension. Nevertheless, the results indicate that the pertinent knowledge of the reader plays a large role in the computation of inferences either during or after reading.

C. Interactions among Inference Variables

This section has discussed several text and reader variables that have been shown or argued to guide inference processing. It is hard to imagine that these variables function in a simple fashion. Instead, it is more likely that they interact in a myriad of ways.

Since n variables can exert $2^n - 1$ simple effects and interactions, it is prohibitive to try to address very many of the possible interactions among the variables considered in this section. Instead, brief descriptions will be provided of a few of these interactions, ones for which empirical evidence has been provided.

It was mentioned earlier that Walker and Meyer (1980) found a distance × task interaction in integrative inference processing. "Readers" needed 0.4 sec more to reconcile distant facts than close facts, whereas "learners" needed 4.0 sec more. Similarly, Cirilo (1981) found a significant distance effect for readers anticipating a comprehension test, but not for casual readers. These two studies are consistent in their demonstration that the distance between related facts has a greater impact on inference processing when readers attend to detail than when they focus on the gist of a passage.

Post *et al.* (1982) provided evidence that theme and knowledge interact in their impact on inference processing. Their high-knowledge readers greatly outperformed low-knowledge readers in their judgments of theme-related (baseball) statements, but not for non-theme-related statements.

One might expect the text variables of theme and distance to interact in their influence on the inferences that accompany encoding. That is, it is conceivable that great distance between related facts might make it difficult to integrate them if they are peripheral to the text theme, but not if they are highly thematic. The rationale of this proposal is that theme-related ideas may remain longer in working memory than peripheral ideas or may be more easily retrieved from long-term memory when necessary. Walker and Meyer's (1980) data are suggestive of this proposed interaction, but it did not reach statistical significance. Cirilo (1981), however, detected no sign of this interaction.

In summary, it seems inevitable that the many variables guiding inference processing will interact in complex ways. In spite of this, it is unlikely that the problem of inference can be completely characterized in terms of a list of main effects and interactions of variables influencing inference. Rather, inference processing will only be captured with reference to relatively comprehensive theories of language comprehension. While such theory development is in its early phases, some investigators have, by now, advanced some major proposals which clearly bear on the problem of inference in language comprehension. Some examples will be considered in Section V.

V. THEORETICAL FORMULATIONS OF INFERENCE—AND COMPREHENSION

The goal of this section is to demonstrate how existing theory may be brought to bear on the problem of inference. The focus will be on the coherence graph model (CGM) of Kintsch and van Dijk (1978), particularly because several of the investigators whose work was considered earlier have made extensive use of this model (Cirilo, 1981; Mayer & Cook, 1981; Spilich *et al.,* 1979). Then, a brief account will be provided of the pertinence to inference processing of script and schema theory (e.g., Anderson *et al.,* 1976b; Rumelhart & Ortony, 1976).

A. The Coherence Graph Model

1. The Model

Kintsch and van Dijk (1978) presented a theoretical account of language comprehension and production. One distinct feature of this proposal was that it provided considerable detail concerning both the internal representation of text and the cognitive processes that contribute to the storage and retrieval of the representation.

The CGM is complex and can only be outlined here. According to Kintsch and van Dijk (1978), text comprehension results in the construction of two ordered, hierarchical graphs, called the *microstructure* and the *macrostructure*. Consider first the construction of the microstructure. The reader begins by examining a "chunk" of text and identifying its underlying propositions. An important proposition from the first chunk is designated as the *superordinate proposition*. The remaining propositions are connected to the superordinate or to one another on the basis of argument overlap. This results in each proposition being assigned to a specific level in the hierarchy, with the superordinate being the only level 1 proposition.

When all of the propositions in the first chunk of text are connected, a small number of these, typically between two and four, are held over in working memory, with higher level and more recent propositions having a greater chance of being retained. Processing then proceeds to the next "cycle," and the reader strives to connect the propositions of the next chunk of text with those retained in working memory. This results in a growing network of interrelated propositions.

Sometimes, a proposition cannot be linked to any of those in the working memory. In this event, the reader first strives to reactivate, from long-term memory, a proposition from an earlier chunk that has not been held over in working memory. If this fails to produce an appropriate proposition, then the model posits that an *inference* is drawn to link the current proposition to the existing network. However, the model does not specify which inference results.

The macrostructure of a text refers to a second internal representation, one that particularly captures the gist of the text. Like the microstructure, the macrostructure consists of a set of hierarchically organized connected propositions. However, these "macropropositions" are obtained by the application of special operators, called macrorules, to the microstructure. Macrorules "adopt" important micropropositions, delete unimportant ones, and extract generalizations from related sets of micropropositions. The resulting macropropositions are much smaller in number than the micropropositions.

The macrorules are applied to the microstructure under the control of a "schema." A schema is a knowledge structure of the reader that specifies the usual form of the type of text under consideration. For example, a story schema would make reference to categories of story statements like settings, reactions, and consequences (Stein & Glenn, 1979). According to Kintsch and van Dijk (1978), the application of macrorules to the microstructure of a story produces macropropositions that are closely identified with these story categories.

Spilich *et al.* (1979) and Vipond (1980) have provided evidence that the construction of the micro- and macrostructures may access separate working memory buffers. Furthermore, the coherence graph model has been extended and applied by many investigators (e.g., Mayer & Cook, 1981; Miller & Kintsch, 1980; Singer, 1982; Vipond, 1980). Even without considering these extensions, the present outline is adequate to demonstrate the relevance of the model to problems of inference.

2. Inference according to the CGM

The CGM posits that an inference occurs when the reader encounters a proposition that can be connected neither to a proposition in working memory nor to a proposition reactivated from long-term memory. These inferences are, in fact, backward or bridging inferences. That is, Kintsch and van Dijk (1978) state that an inference is drawn which links the current proposition to one already included in the micro- or macrostructure.

It is considered a shortcoming of the CGM that it does not specify *which* bridging inference occurs. It does not because it is not equipped with the knowledge of word meaning and of familiar situations that would be necessary to permit such inferences.

The CGM also accounts for the category of backward inference called direct reference (Clark, 1977). That is, each time two propositions are linked on the basis of argument overlap, a referent for the proposition under current consideration has been inferred. Kintsch and van Dijk do not explicitly discuss this activity as an example of inference processing.

The operation of some of the CGM macrorules is clearly inferential in nature. For example, from the sentence, *Sue hid the chalk and glued the pages together,* the macrorule of generalization might abstract the idea "Sue played some pranks." Inferences of this sort have been studied by Masson and Alexander (1981) and Till and Walsh (1980).

In contrast, the CGM does not posit the computation of forward inferences. Even highly probable implied arguments and propositions are not shown to be added to the microstructure of a text. In view of the fact that many forward inferences are delayed until retrieval time (e.g., Singer, 1979b, 1980), this feature should not be viewed as a weakness of the CGM.

3. Inference Variables and the CGM

The CGM provides tentative explanations of the impact of many of the variables of inference discussed in Section IV. In fact, the CGM has been invoked by the investigators of several of the studies which documented the impact of these variables.

   a. Theme. Readers are more accurate and faster in their judgments of the theme-related implications of a text than of non-theme-related ones

(Cirilo, 1981; Eamon, 1978–1979; Goetz, 1977; Walker and Meyer, 1980). Because thematic ideas appear at high levels of the text microstructure, they are more likely to be retained in working memory when processing advances to a new cycle. This makes thematic propositions more readily available to be linked or integrated with incoming propositions, resulting in backward inferences.

Cirilo (1981) pointed out that theme-related propositions are relatively likely to be adopted to the macrostructure of a text. Macropropositions are likely to remain in working memory for several processing cycles because of the relatively small number of macropropositions and the large size of the macroprocessing memory buffer (Vipond, 1980). Therefore, theme-related ideas are more likely to reside in working memory and, hence, to contribute to backward and possibly forward inferences.

b. Distance. Several studies have provided evidence that the distance between two facts in a text influences the likelihood that these facts will be inferentially linked (Cirilo, 1981; Erlich & Johnson-Laird, 1982; Hayes-Roth & Thorndyke, 1979; Walker & Meyer, 1980). This effect can be easily understood in the framework of the CGM, even though the power of such a model is not needed to account for this outcome. Briefly, Cirilo (1981) has noted that most propositions tend to be excluded from working memory after a few processing cycles beyond the chunk in which they appeared. Therefore, the greater the distance separating two facts in a text, the less likely that the antecedent will be readily available (i.e., in working memory) to participate in backward, integrative inferences. Although a proposition may be retrieved or reactivated from long-term memory, it is not certain that this will reliably occur.

c. Knowledge. Spilich *et al.* (1979) applied the CGM to the free-recall protocols of their high- and low-baseball-knowledge subjects. They proposed that memory differences between high- and low-knowledge subjects could be related to differences between the schema guiding their macroprocessing. Whereas Kintsch and van Dijk (1978) proposed that macroprocessing is controlled by text schemas, Spilich *et al.* (1979) invoked schemas of knowledge about baseball. Spilich *et al.* argued that the baseball schemas of high-baseball-knowledge individuals are more refined in their representation of the goals and actions of a baseball game as well as the interrelation of these goals and actions. Differences between the schemas of high- and low- knowledge individuals would result in the adoption of different propositions to the macrostructure. High-knowledge comprehenders would construct a text representation with better organization, which would facilitate the recall of the text.

The analysis of Spilich *et al.* has direct implications for the inference study of Post *et al.* (1982). Post *et al.* found that high-knowledge readers judged the game-related implications of a baseball text more accurately and faster than low-knowledge readers. Several of the categories examined by Post *et al.* can be directly related to a hypothetical baseball schema. The schema would include reference to the batter's goal of avoiding strikes and obtaining balls. This goal would encourage the knowledgeable reader to update strike and ball information. Post *et al.* provided evidence supporting this prediction. Post *et al.*'s other game-related inference categories can likewise be linked to the baseball schema.

d. Task. Cirilo (1981) examined the sentence reading times of subjects who either read text fragments, read whole texts expecting a comprehension test, or read whole texts casually. In terms of the CGM, Cirilo proposed that these three tasks require primarily microprocessing, micro- and macroprocessing, and primarily macroprocessing, respectively. According to Cirilo, interproposition distance should have a considerable impact on microprocessing because no macrostructure is available to guide fact integration if a proposition has not been retained in working memory. Conversely, the height or thematicity of a proposition should have its greatest influence on macroprocessing.

As discussed in Section IV, Cirilo's (1981) data only partly supported his analysis: no distance effect was detected in the reading of the fragments. Nevertheless, his analysis gives a good indication of how the CGM can be brought to bear upon different reading tasks.

It was described earlier that Mayer and Cook (1981) found that subjects who shadowed a text about radar were less able to apply the text knowledge in new contexts, but showed better lexical memory than people who listened normally. Mayer and Cook (1981) applied an innovative CGM analysis to these findings. First, they identified 69 "idea units" conveyed by the text. These idea units encompassed more information than is typical of Kintsch and van Dijk's propositions. Second, they created a macrostructure based not on a text schema but on a schema of knowledge about radar. This resembled Spilich *et al.*'s (1979) use of a baseball schema. Furthermore, Mayer and Cook's (1981) macrostructure included all 69 idea units, whereas according to the CGM, the macrostructure includes many fewer propositions than the microstructure. Third, Mayer and Cook created a microstructure based on idea familiarity rather than on Kintsch and van Dijk's principles of microprocessing.

Mayer and Cook classified each idea unit as belonging to level 1, 2, or 3 in each of the macro- and microstructures. They predicted that macro-level would predict text recall better for nonshadowers than shadowers, and vice versa for microlevel. These predictions were based on the proposal that the shadowing task reduces available cognitive capacity, which in turn limits macroprocessing.

Regression analysis revealed that, as predicted, microlevel predicted the recall of the shadowers better than the nonshadowers, and that the slope of the recall curve was greater for shadowers. Macrolevel, in contrast, predicted the recall of the two groups equally well. However, the slope of recall as a function of macrolevel was greater for nonshadowers than shadowers. These analyses supported most aspects of Mayer and Cook's predictions.

With respect to the CGM, reading tasks might also influence processing by causing the activation of different text schemas. For example, Hooke (1979) instructed different groups of subjects to read a text in order either to understand a story it conveyed or to solve an underlying logical problem. Hooke detected different patterns of reading and rereading times between her groups. According to the CGM, one's story and problem-solving schemas should result in very different sets of propositions being assigned to the text macrostructure. This should lead to the observations of qualitative differences in reading times and memory performance between the two groups.

4. Summary

The goal of this subsection has been to illustrate how a relatively comprehensive model of language understanding may address a wide variety of aspects of the problem of inference. The CGM of Kintsch and van Dijk (1978) was selected as an example of a theory that strives to address many facets of comprehension. While the CGM does not indicate how one makes reference to long-term world knowledge during comprehension, it nevertheless suggests tentative explanations of the impact of several variables that guide inference processing.

B. Script and Schema Theory

Many investigators have discussed the nature of detailed knowledge structures that can be invoked to mediate text comprehension. The role of text schemas in understanding was considered earlier (Kintsch & van Dijk, 1978; Stein & Glenn, 1979). Another type of knowledge structure, the "script" (alternately, "frame" or "schema"), includes information pertinent to familiar complex contexts, such as grocery shopping.

The concept of a schema was introduced to modern psychology by Bartlett (1932). More recently, the role of schemas in language comprehension has been considered by numerous investigators (e.g., Anderson & Pichert, 1978; Charniak, 1975; Rumelhart & Ortony, 1976; Schank & Abelson, 1977). Very briefly, these theorists argue that the presentation of a text about a complex but familiar context, such as grocery shopping, results in the activation of a corresponding knowledge structure in the mind of the reader. The grocery shopping script would include reference to the usual participants in this context (like the cashier), usual objects (like a shopping cart), enabling conditions (like having some money), and a "causal chain" of events (Schank & Abelson, 1977).

Most theoretical treatments of scripts indicate that the statements of a text are integrated with the pertinent script or, at least, a copy of the script (Charniak, 1975). This analysis suggests many ways for scripts to guide inference processing. First, the identification of text statements with parts of the pertinent script provides an organization for the story statements that may be considered to be inferential in nature. Second, scripts contribute to backward inferences. To understand the sequence, *Bob went grocery shopping, the cart had a broken wheel,* one needs to determine the relation between the word "cart" and the antecedent sentence. By referring to the grocery shopping script, the reader may draw the backward inferences that Bob used a cart and that this cart was a shopping cart (cf. Anderson, Pichert, Goetz, Schallert, Stevens, & Trollip, 1976a).

Third, scripts also provide a basis, if not a process, for forward inference. If a passage about grocery shopping makes no reference to a cashier, the activation of the grocery shopping script might result in a forward inference about a cashier's participation. Rumelhart and Ortony (1976) have discussed this possibility with reference to the notion of "filling unassigned variables." While the availability of a script would permit such forward inferences, it is nevertheless reemphasized that forward inference processing may be quite limited in ordinary comprehension due to cognitive resource limitations.

The impact of scripts upon inference processing has been documented experimentally, especially by Anderson and colleagues (e.g., Anderson & Pichert, 1978; Anderson *et al.,* 1976a,b; Schallert, 1976). As discussed in Section IV, Anderson *et al.* (1976b) invoked the concept of schema in their examination of the role of readers' knowledge in comprehension and the drawing of inferences. However, some empirical qualifications of the role of script theory have also been offered. For example, in one experiment, Bower, Black, and Turner (1979) asked subjects to read one story about a visit to a doctor's office and another story that dealt with a trip to the dentist. In a recognition test, subjects sometimes confused the sentences from the two stories. This should not have occurred if the representation of each story was stored in the framework of a distinct script. Bower *et al.* (1979) and Schank (1980) have explored the theoretical implications of this result.

In spite of such difficulties, it seems inevitable that a complete treatment of inference will need to refer extensively to scripts and schemas. The centrality of these concepts in the study of language comprehension is illustrated by the position of Auble and Franks (1983), who suggest that the comprehension of a sentence is achieved when the reader has activated the pertinent schema.

VI. SUMMARY AND CONCLUSIONS

Inference so pervades language comprehension that the two are, in some ways, synonymous. For the purposes of this discussion, "inference" was defined with reference to the propositional encoding of complex messages. From this perspective, an "inference" corresponds to either the addition of an entire proposition to the representation of a message or the addition of an argument to an existing proposition. Conversely, the transient activation of concepts in memory was not considered to guarantee that an inference has resulted. Furthermore, there was no particular focus on reconstructive memory for text.

During the 1970s, several investigators asked whether highly probable instruments and consequences are inferred during the encoding of a message. Evidence based on the false recognition of implicational test sentences and on the effectiveness of implicit recall cues seemed to suggest that these inferences do accompany comprehension. Later empirical studies, however, presented contradictory evidence and also identified some shortcomings of the recognition and cued-recall methods for studying inference. All of these studies helped to refine the formulation of questions about inference and the methods available to study inference.

Several investigators have presented taxonomies of inference which have referred to dozens of inference categories that merit inspection. Four dimensions which help to organize these inference categories were discussed. (1) Logical implications are 100% certain and are based on identifiable rules, whereas pragmatic implications are less than certain and are derived from world knowledge. (2) Forward inferences extrapolate from a text, whereas backward inferences are necessary to preserve the coherence of a text. (3) Inferences may pertain to many semantic relations, such as agents, instruments, causes, consequences, and motives. (4) Implications may be of high or low probability.

These four dimensions impose some degree of organization upon previous taxonomies of inference. Although several of the dimensions help to specify which inferences are drawn *after* a message is encoded, only the forward–backward dichotomy appears to distinguish between inferences that accompany comprehension and those that do not.

A fruitful approach of recent inference studies has been to inspect text and reader variables that may have an impact on inference processing. Empirical evidence and/or intuition indicate that the coherence requirements, theme, and interestingness of a text all guide the inferences that accompany comprehension. The distance between related facts in text influences the likelihood that they will be inferentially linked. Both the knowledge and the orienting task of readers have also been shown to affect the inferences that one draws.

The problem of inference can be thoroughly understood only with reference to comprehensive models of language understanding. The coherence graph model of Kintsch and van Dijk (1978) suggests explanations for the effects of the text and reader variables mentioned earlier. Modern script and schema theory describes the complex knowledge structures that must underlie the drawing of inferences. An understanding of the processing and representation of inferences will advance with the refinement of such theories.

REFERENCES

Anderson, J. R. (1976). *Language, memory, and thought.* Hillsdale, NJ: Erlbaum.

Anderson, J. R., & Hastie, R. (1974). Individuation and reference in memory: Proper names and definite descriptions. *Cognitive Psychology, 6,* 495–514.

Anderson, R. C., & Pichert, J. W. (1978). Recall of previously unrecallable information following a shift in perspective. *Journal of Verbal Learning and Verbal Behavior, 17,* 1–12.

Anderson, R. C., Pichert, J. W., Goetz, E. T., Schallert, D. L., Stevens, K. V., & Trollip, S. R. (1976a). Instantiation of general terms. *Journal of Verbal Learning and Verbal Behavior, 15,* 667–679.

Anderson, R. C., Reynolds, R. E., Schallert, D. L., & Goetz, E. T. (1976b). *Frameworks for comprehending discourse.* Laboratory for Cognitive Studies in Education, Technical Report No. 12. Urbana, IL: University of Illinois.

Auble, P., & Franks, J. J. (1983). Sentence comprehension processes. *Journal of Verbal Learning and Verbal Behavior, 22,* 395–405.

Bartlett, F. C. (1932). *Remembering.* London: Cambridge University Press.

Belmore, S. M., Yates, J. M., Bellack, D. R., Jones, S. N., & Rosenquist, S. E. (1982). Drawing inferences from concrete and abstract sentences. *Journal of Verbal Learning and Verbal Behavior, 21,* 338–351.

Black, J. B., & Bern, H. (1981). Causal inference and memory for events in narratives. *Journal of Verbal Learning and Verbal Behavior, 20,* 267–275.

Bower, G. H., Black, J. B., & Turner, T. J. (1979). Scripts in memory for text. *Cognitive Psychology, 11,* 177–220.

Braine, M. D. S., & Wells, R. S. (1978). Case-like categories in children: The actor and some related categories. *Cognitive Psychology, 10,* 100–122.

Bransford, J. D., Barclay, J. R., & Franks, J. J. (1972). Semantic memory: A constructive versus interpretive approach. *Cognitive Psychology, 3,* 193–209.

Bransford, J. D., & Franks, J. J. (1971). The abstraction of linguistic ideas. *Cognitive Psychology*, **2**, 331–350.

Britton, B. K., Holdredge, T. S., Curry, C., & Westbrook, R. D. (1979). Use of cognitive capacity in reading identical texts with different amounts of discourse level meaning. *Journal of Experimental Psychology: Human Learning and Memory*, **5**, 262–270.

Chafe, W. L. (1972). Discourse structure and human knowledge. In J. Carroll & R. Freedle (Eds.), *Language comprehension and the acquisition of knowledge*. New York: Winston.

Charniak, E. (1975). Organization and inference in a frame-like system of common knowledge. In R. Schank & B. Nash-Webber (Eds.), *Theoretical issues in natural language processing*. Cambridge, MA: MIT.

Cirilo, R. K. (1981). Referential coherence and text structure in story comprehension. *Journal of Verbal Learning and Verbal Behavior*, **20**, 358–367.

Cirilo, R. K., & Foss, D. J. (1980). Text structure and reading time for sentences. *Journal of Verbal Learning and Verbal Behavior*, **19**, 96–109.

Clark, H. H. (1977). Inferences in comprehension. In D. LaBerge & S. J. Samuels (Eds.), *Perception and comprehension*. Hillsdale, NJ: Erlbaum.

Clark, H. H., & Clark, E. V. (1977). *Psychology and language*. New York: Harcourt.

Clark, H. H., & Lucy, P. (1975). Understanding what is meant from what is said: A study in conversationally conveyed requests. *Journal of Verbal Learning and Verbal Behavior*, **14**, 56–72.

Cohen, G. (1979). Language comprehension in old age. *Cognitive Psychology*, **11**, 412–429.

Corbett, A. T., & Chang, F. R. (1983). Pronoun disambiguation: Accessing potential antecedents. *Memory & Cognition*, **11**, 283–294.

Corbett, A. T., & Dosher, B. A. (1978). Instrument inferences in sentence encoding. *Journal of Verbal Learning and Verbal Behavior*, **17**, 479–492.

Craik, F. I. M., & Lockhart, R. S. (1972). Levels of processing: A framework for memory research. *Journal of Verbal Learning and Verbal Behavior*, **11**, 671–684.

Dooling, D. J., & Christaansen, R. E. (1977). Episodic and semantic aspects of memory for prose. *Journal of Experimental Psychology: Human Learning and Memory*, **4**, 428–436.

Downey, D. M. (1979). *The role of motivational inferences in story comprehension*. Unpublished manuscript, Department of Communication Disorders and Speech Science, University of Colorado, Boulder.

Eamon, D. B. (1978–1979). Selection and recall of topical information in prose by better and poorer readers. *Reading Research Quarterly*, **14**, 244–257.

Erlich, K., & Johnson-Laird, P. N. (1982). Spatial descriptions and referential continuity. *Journal of Verbal Learning and Verbal Behavior*, **21**, 296–306.

Fillmore, C. J. (1968). The case for case. In E. Bach & R. Harms (Eds.), *Universals in linguistic theory*. New York: Holt.

Frederiksen, C. H. (1975). Acquisition of semantic information from discourse: Effects of repeated exposures. *Journal of Verbal Learning and Verbal Behavior*, **14**, 158–169.

Garrod, S., & Sanford, A. (1977). Interpreting anaphoric relations: The integration of semantic information while reading. *Journal of Verbal Learning and Verbal Behavior*, **16**, 77–90.

Goetz, E. T. (1977). *Inferences in the comprehension of and memory for text*. Technical Report No. 49, Center for the Study of Reading. Urbana, Illinois: University of Illinois.

Harris, R. J. (1974). Memory and comprehension of implications and inferences of complex sentences. *Journal of Verbal Learning and Verbal Behavior*, **13**, 626–637.

Harris, R. J., & Monaco, G. E. (1978). The psychology of pragmatic implication: Information processing between the lines. *Journal of Experimental Psychology: General*, **107**, 1–22.

Haviland, S. E., & Clark, H. H. (1974). What's new? Acquiring new information as a process in comprehension. *Journal of Verbal Learning and Verbal Behavior*, **13**, 512–521.

Hayes-Roth, B., & Thorndyke, P. W. (1979). Integration of knowledge from text. *Journal of Verbal Learning and Verbal Behavior*, **18**, 91–108.

Hayes-Roth, B., and Walker, C. (1979). Configural effects in human memory: The superiority of memory over external information as a basis for inference verification. *Cognitive Science*, **3**, 119–140.

Hooke, L. R. (1979). *The uses of knowledge*. Unpublished doctoral dissertation, University of Colorado, Boulder.

Hunt, E. (1978). Mechanics of verbal ability. *Psychological Review*, **85**, 109–130.

Johnson, M. K., Bransford, J. D., & Solomon, S. K. (1973). Memory for tacit implications of sentences. *Journal of Experimental Psychology*, **98**, 203–205.

Just, M. A., & Carpenter, P. A. (1978). Inference processes during reading: Reflections from eye fixations. In J. W. Senders & R. A. Monty (Eds.), *Eye movements and the higher psychological functions*. Hillsdale, NJ: Erlbaum.

Kieras, D. E. (1981). Component processes in the comprehension of simple prose. *Journal of Verbal Learning and Verbal Behavior*, **20**, 1–23.

Kintsch, W. (1974). *The representation of meaning in memory*. Hillsdale, NJ: Erlbaum.

Kintsch, W. (1980). Learning from text, levels of comprehension, or: Why would anyone read a story, anyway. *Poetics*, **9**, 87–98.

Kintsch, W., Kozminsky, E., Streby, W. J., McKoon, G., & Keenan, J. M. (1975). Comprehension and recall of text as a function of content variable. *Journal of Verbal Learning and Verbal Behavior*, **14**, 158–169.

Kintsch, W., and van Dijk, T. A. (1978). Toward a model of text comprehension and production. *Psychological Review*, **85**, 363–394.

Mandler, J. M., & Johnson, N. S. (1977). Remembrance of things parsed: Story structure and recall. *Cognitive Psychology*, **9**, 111–151.

Masson, M. E. J., & Alexander, J. H. (1981). Inferential processes in sentence encoding and recall. *American Journal of Psychology*, **94**, 399–416.

Mayer, R. E. (1979). Qualitatively different encoding strategies for linear reasoning premises: Evidence for single association and distance theories. *Journal of Experimental Psychology: Human Learning and Memory*, **5**, 1–10.

Mayer, R. E., & Cook, L. (1981). Effects of shadowing on prose comprehension and problem solving. *Memory & Cognition*, **9**, 101–109.

McKoon, G., & Ratcliff, R. (1980). Priming in item recognition: The organization of propositions in memory for text. *Journal of Verbal Learning and Verbal Behavior*, **19**, 369–386.

Meyer, B. J. F. (1975). *The organization of prose and its effects on memory*. Amsterdam: North-Holland Publ.

Meyer, D. E., & Schvaneveldt, R. W. (1971). Facilitation in recognizing pairs of words: Evidence of a dependence between retrieval operations. *Journal of Experimental Psychology*, **90**, 227–234.

Miller, J. R., & Kintsch, W. (1980). Readability and recall of short prose passages: A theoretical analysis. *Journal of Experimental Psychology: Human Learning and Memory*, **6**, 335–354.

Morris, C. D., Bransford, J. D., & Franks, J. J. (1977). Levels of processing versus transfer appropriate training. *Journal of Verbal Learning and Verbal Behavior*, **16**, 519–534.

Nezworski, T., Stein, N. L., & Trabasso, T. (1982). Story structure versus content in children's recall. *Journal of Verbal Learning and Verbal Behavior*, **21**, 196–206.

Norman, D. A., & Rumelhart, D. E. (1975). *Explorations in cognition*. San Francisco: Freeman.

Omanson, R. C. (1982). The relation between centrality and story category variation. *Journal of Verbal Learning and Verbal Behavior*, **21**, 326–337.

Paris, S., & Lindauer, B. K. (1976). The role of inference in children's comprehension and memory for sentences. *Cognitive Psychology*, **8**, 217–227.

Post, T. A., Greene, T., & Bruder, G. (1982). *"On-line" text processing in high- and low-knowledge individuals*. Presented at the annual meeting of the Psychonomic Society, Minneapolis, MN.

Potts, G. R. (1972). Information processing strategies used in the encoding of linear orderings. *Journal of Verbal Learning and Verbal Behavior*, **11**, 727–740.

Quillian, M. R. (1968). Semantic memory. In M. Minsky (Ed.), *Semantic information processing*. Cambridge, MA: MIT Press.

Rieger, C. (1975). The common-sense algorithm as a basis for computer models of human memory, inference, belief, and contextual language comprehension. In R. Schank & B. Nash-Webber (Eds.), *Theoretical issues in natural language processing*. Cambridge, MA: MIT, An interdisciplinary workshop.

Rips, L. J., Shoben, E. J., & Smith, E. E. (1973). Semantic distance and the verification of semantic relations. *Journal of Verbal Learning and Verbal Behavior*, **12**, 1–20.

Rumelhart, D. E., & Ortony, A. (1976). The representation of knowledge in memory. In R. Anderson, R. Spiro, & W. Montague (Eds.), *Schooling and the acquisition of knowledge*. Hillsdale, NJ: Erlbaum.

Schaeffer, B., & Wallace, R. (1970). The comparison of word meanings. *Journal of Experimental Psychology*, **86**, 144–152.

Schallert, D. L. (1976). Improving memory for prose: The relationship between depth of processing and context. *Journal of Verbal Learning and Verbal Behavior*, **15**, 621–632.

Schank, R. C. (1976). The role of memory in language processing. In C. Cofer (Ed.), *The nature of human memory*. San Francisco: Freeman.

Schank, R. C. (1978). *Interestingness: Controlling inferences*. Research Report No. 145. New Haven, CT: Yale University, Department of Computer Science.

Schank, R. C. (1980). Language and memory. *Cognitive Science*, **4**, 243–284.

Schank, R. C., & Abelson, R. (1977). *Scripts, plans, goals, and understanding*. Hillsdale, NJ: Erlbaum.

Shoben, E. J. (1976). The verification of semantic relations in a same–different paradigm: An asymmetry in semantic memory. *Journal of Verbal Learning and Verbal Behavior*, **15**, 365–379.

Singer, M. (1976). Context inferences in the comprehension of sentences. *Canadian Journal of Psychology*, **30**, 39–46.

Singer, M. (1977). A constitutent comparison model of a picture-first verification task. *Memory & Cognition*, **5**, 269–272.

Singer, M. (1979a). Temporal locus of inference in the comprehension of brief passages: Recognizing and verifying implications about instruments. *Perceptual and Motor Skills*, **49**, 539–550.

Singer, M. (1979b). Processes of inference in sentence encoding. *Memory & Cognition*, **7**, 192–200.

Singer, M. (1980). The role of case-filling inferences in the coherence of brief passages. *Discourse Processes, 3*, 185–201.

Singer, M. (1982). Comparing memory for natural and laboratory reading. *Journal of Experimental Psychology: General, 111*, 331–347.

Singer, M., & Ferreira, F. (1983). Inferring consequences in story comprehension. *Journal of Verbal Learning and Verbal Behavior, 22*, 437–448.

Spilich, G. J., Vesonder, G. T., Chiesi, H. L., & Voss, J. F. (1979). Text processing of domain-related information for individuals with high and low domain knowledge. *Journal of Verbal Learning and Verbal Behavior, 18*, 275–290.

Stein, N. L., & Glenn, C. G. (1979). An analysis of story comprehension in elementary school children. In R. O. Freedle (Ed.), *New directions in discourse processing.* Hillsdale, NJ: Erlbaum.

Sulin, R. A., & Dooling, D. J. (1974). Instrusion of a thematic idea in retention of prose. *Journal of Experimental Psychology, 103*, 255–262.

Thorndyke, P. W. (1976). The role of inferences in discourse comprehension. *Journal of Verbal Learning and Verbal Behavior, 15*, 437–446.

Thorndyke, P. W. (1977). Cognitive structures in comprehension and memory of narrative discourse. *Cognitive Psychology, 9*, 77–110.

Till, R. E., & Walsh, D. A. (1980). Encoding and retrieval factors in adult memory for implicational sentences. *Journal of Verbal Learning and Verbal Behavior, 19*, 1–16.

Trabasso, T. (1981). On the making of inferences during reading and their assessment. In J. T. Guthrie (Ed.), *Comprehension and teaching: Research reviews.* Newark, DE: International Reading Association.

Trabasso, T., & Nicholas, D. W. (1980). Memory and inferences in the comprehension of narratives. In F. Wilkening, J. Becker, & T. Trabasso (Eds.), *Information integration by children.* Hillsdale, NJ: Erlbaum.

Trabasso, T., Secco, T., & van den Broek, P. (1984). Causal cohesion and story coherence. In H. Mandl, N. Stein, & T. Trabasso (Eds.), *Learning and comprehension of text.* Hillsdale, NJ: Erlbaum.

Turner, A., & Greene, E. (1978). Construction and use of a propositional text base. *JSAS Catalog of Selected Documents in Psychology, 8*, 58 (Manuscript No. 1713).

Vipond, D. (1980). Micro- and macroprocesses in text comprehension. *Journal of Verbal Learning and Verbal Behavior, 19*, 276–296.

Walker, C. H. & Meyer, B. J. F. (1980). Integrating different types of information in text. *Journal of Verbal Learning and Verbal Behavior, 19*, 263–275.

Warren, W. H., Nicholas, D. W., & Trabasso, T. (1979). Event chains and inferences in understanding narratives. In R. O. Freedle (Ed.), *New directions in discourse processing.* Hillsdale, NJ: Erlbaum.

INDEX

CONTENTS OF PREVIOUS VOLUMES

VOLUME 4

VOLUME 5